EARLY PRAISE FOR BREAD BAGS & BULLIES

"If you loved the ever popular *A Christmas Story*, be prepared for another classic. *Bread Bags & Bullies* is a must read! Funny, poignant, and heart-warming—Steven Manchester is a master storyteller."

– Jamie Farr, Actor, *M.A.S.H.*

"*Bread Bags & Bullies* is a detailed eye-opening experience of the Big Hair decade. Enjoyable whether you were there or not—or just can't quite remember it."

– Barry Williams, Actor, *The Brady Bunch*

"Steven Manchester's *Bread Bags & Bullies* captures a simpler time, just before technology began dominating America's time and attention. This nostalgic story is hilarious, told by a family of characters you won't soon forget. A must read!"

– Ed Asner, Actor, *Lou Grant*

"Steve Manchester's *Bread Bags & Bullies* is a fantastic blast from the past, evoking all the fun and nostalgia of the '80s—even my big hair!"

– Audrey Landers, Actress, *Dallas*

"An extraordinary recall of 1980s pop culture, *Bread Bags & Bullies* will make you laugh out loud as you revisit the pains and pleasures of growing up. The book made me want to pick up the phone, call my brother in Nebraska and reminisce about our own snow day adventures."

– Douglas Barr, Actor, *The Fall Guy*

"Steve Manchester's newest novel, *Bread Bags & Bullies*, is a well-written love letter to the '80s—bringing me home with every page turned."

     – Bertie Higgins, '80s Recording Artist, *Key Largo*

"*Bread Bags & Bullies* is so—like, totally—'84, it makes me want to get out my leg warmers and glow sticks, backcomb my hair, and romp around the room to *Footloose*. And then I remember, I don't *have* any hair."

     – Thomas Dolby, '80s Recording Artist,
     She Blinded Me with Science

"Manchester's book, *Bread Bags & Bullies*, brings to mind many of our techno ditties. 'How you gonna keep 'em down on Maggie's Farm once they've seen Devo?'"

     – Gerald V. Casale of DEVO, *Whip It*

"In *Bread Bags & Bullies*, Steven Manchester expertly captures domestic life for a US family growing up in the '80s. From MTV to video games, the new age is upon us. *Bread Bags & Bullies* is a perfect observation of the times."

     – Geoff Downes of The Buggles, *Video Killed the Radio
     Star (1st video on MTV)*

"You had to be there, but if you weren't there . . . read *Bread Bags & Bullies*. It's a great story for everyone!"

     – Stacey Q, '80s Pop Star, *Two of Hearts*

"I loved *Bread Bags & Bullies*. Steve Manchester hit on a lot of cool stuff from the '80s. I could totally relate."

     – Paul Stroessner, Editor, *Return to the 80s*

"In *Bread Bags & Bullies,* Steve Manchester took me back in time. Do yourself a favor and relive some of your wonderful—and not so wonderful—memories of a more innocent time in your life, when your biggest concerns were pop quizzes and that bright-red zit growing on the side of your nose."

– Paul D'Angelo, Comedian, *Comedy Central*

"*Bread Bags & Bullies* is a much-appreciated time capsule back to a simpler and thankfully innocent time. Author Steven Manchester repaints the decade's pop culture with the most pleasing of palettes, showing us why the 1980s are ingrained in our generation's DNA."

– Steve Spears, Podcast Editor, *Stuck in the 80s;*
Columnist, *Tampa Bay Times*

"Nobody appreciates '80s nostalgia more than me, so believe it when I tell you that Steve Manchester spins a deeply satisfying tale with *Bread Bags & Bullies.* Took me right back to the greatest decade to be a kid."

– Old School Tim, '80s writer, contributor and
aficionado from Twitter's *@OldSchool80s*

"From the moment I started reading *Bread Bags & Bullies,* I found myself being transported right back to the world which I grew up in, when wearing stone-washed jeans and Swatch watches was the norm. A very engaging and satisfying nostalgia-fest."

– Mark Nobes, Editor, *Simplyeighties.com*

"Steven Manchester's *Bread Bags & Bullies* recalls those halcyon summer days where children roamed free—and definitely never wore helmets!"

– Tripp and Andrew Laino, Podcast Hosts,
Dissecting the '80s

"If you grew up in the '80s like I did, you'll absolutely love this novel! Steven Manchester's expertly-crafted story will instantly transport you to another time and place—where the heart and spirit of the story and its characters are truly timeless."

— Janet Hadden, Editor, *Eighties Grooves*

"*Bread Bags & Bullies* was a nostalgic sled ride back to my childhood era. I've read several books set in the '80s over the past several years and *Bread Bags & Bullies* is definitely one I'll be keeping in my virtual library."

— Jason Gross, Editor, *Rediscover the 80s*

"*Bread Bags & Bullies* gave us the opportunity to see the '80s through the eyes of an American teenager of the time. It is a story that will touch your heart."

— Christian Cavaciuti, Editor, *Gli Anni 80*

"As we used to say in the '80s, this book is 'awesome!' From English muffin pizzas and building snow forts to the Big Hair Bands and the one-penny deal offered by the Columbia House Record & Tape Club, I was brought right back to where it all happened."

— George Austin, Editor, *Somerset Spectator*

"Reading *Bread Bags & Bullies* was like reminiscing my early teens in technicolor. Steve Manchester has a way of painting a picture with his words that not only comes to life but, if you're lucky, takes you home to your memories of a much simpler time."

— Sue Nedar, Founder & President, *Footlights Repertory Co.*

BREAD BAGS & BULLIES

Surviving the '80s

by

Steven Manchester

To Donna –
Enjoy memory Lane!

[signature] '19

Luna Bella Press
Copyright © 2019 by Steven Manchester

Cover art by Brian Fox and Keith Conforti
Book design by Barbara Aronica-Buck

Print ISBN-13: 978-0-9841842-8-6
E-book ISBN-13: 978-0-9841842-7-9

Visit our website at www.LunaBellaPress.com

First Luna Bella Press Printing: November 2019

Printed in The United States of America

For Pop, my foundation

"Have a nice weekend."

ACKNOWLEDGMENTS

First and forever, Jesus Christ—my Lord and Savior. With Him, all things are possible.

Paula, my beautiful wife, for loving me and being the amazing woman she is.

My children—Evan, Jacob, Isabella and Carissa—for inspiring me.

Mom, Billy, Julie, Caroline, Caleb, Randy, Kathy, Philip, the Baker girls, Darlene, Jeremy, Baker, Aurora, Jen, Jason, Jack, Lucas, Laura, the DeSousa's—my beloved family.

My talented and generous BETA Team: Dan & Sue Aguiar, George Austin, Darlene Ballard, Stephanie Borden Brown, Jason & Jen Fazzina, Binnie Fogg, Brian Fox, Bella Manchester, Evan Manchester, Jacob Manchester, Paula Manchester, Russ McCarthy, Sue Nedar, Jeff & Julia Schoonover, Claude Tetreault, Hen Zannini.

Westport High School's Class of 1986.

Lou Aronica, my mentor and friend.

My life has been richly blessed for having known each one of you.

Dear Reader,

On September 5, 1945, my father, William Manchester, entered this crazy world with the same promise we each get—life is what you make it. He grew into a good man, the salt-of-the-earth, always willing to help anyone in need. Dedicated to his family, he exercised a backbone forged from steel—usually working two jobs—to feed and clothe his five children. He was funny. He was kind. He was my greatest hero.

On September 5, 2018, my father, William Manchester, left this crazy world with all that he'd earned—the eternal love and undying respect of a grateful family.

This book is both a love letter to my father and a well-deserved thank you note. Without my dad, I could have never been me.

Within each comical passage and every heartfelt scene, *Bread Bags & Bullies* is a tribute to my greatest hero—my dad—who remains present in every fiber of my being.

– Steve Manchester

"I hate to break it to you boys, but your family has nothing . . ." He smiled. ". . . which is a great place to start because when you think about it, you have nothing to lose." He added a wink. "So, go out into the world and chase it down!"

– Uncle Skinny

CHAPTER 1

PRESENT DAY

So many channels and not a thing to watch, I thought, my thumb clicking away on the sleek remote control. *Back in my day, we only had three TV stations and those were always . . .* I chuckled. *Wow, when did I actually become my father?* Without permission or protest, my vivid imagination flashed back to a simpler time in my life—the 1980s. *When my brothers and I weren't playing Tin Can Alley—crooked rifle barrel and all—we were hypnotized by The Dukes of Hazzard, The Fall Guy, The A-Team and . . .*

"Stop it, you're hurting me!" someone screamed; the piercing sound could have easily been confused for a shrieking teakettle.

What the hell? I thought, startled from my daydream. My hands instinctively clutched the armrests on my leather recliner. As I reached for the handle on the side of the chair, I heard another loud sound; it was either a healthy slap, skin-on-skin, or a watermelon being dropped from a bridge and splattering on concrete.

My heart dropped at the same time as the chair's footrest. *Here we go again,* I thought. Launching from my chair, I planted my first step only to discover that my legs were sleeping on pins and needles, causing me to hobble on dead stumps out of the darkened living room.

My two boys—Dylan and Alex—had just started their winter break from school and were already at each other's throats. *This is gonna be one long week*, I confirmed in my head, looking forward to my wife's return from her mom's.

'Ouuuu!" came another squeal, inspiring me to pick up the pace—while trying not to take a swan dive.

"Get off me, you big bully," I heard, as I reached my sons' bedroom.

I threw open the door to see my oldest, Dylan, pinning his brother Alex's shoulders to the carpeted floor, a dangling string of spit inches from the convulsing kid's forehead.

"Dylan!" I yelled, grabbing his t-shirt collar and giving it a firm yank, catapulting him off his squirming brother.

Dylan scrambled to his feet. When he faced me, it took a moment for his wild eyes to register reality.

"Enough," I hissed, maintaining my hard gaze and ensuring that he knew exactly what I was thinking.

"He's an animal, Dad," Alex whined, still lying on the floor like a helpless turtle that couldn't right itself.

My mind swam in disappointment. I couldn't decide which one I was more upset with—the thoughtless brute, or his willing victim. "Get up, Alex," I yelled, starting on the path of least resistance.

While Dylan continued to huff and puff, Alex slowly stood upright.

"Now can someone please tell me what's going on in here?" I asked.

"He's a bully . . ." Alex yelled.

"He's a wuss . . ." Dylan yelled at the same time.

"Dylan first," I told them.

"But Dad!" Alex squealed, folding his arms across his chest.

"You'll have your turn," I told him, "go ahead, Dylan."

My eleven-year-old took a deep breath and steadied himself before kicking off his explanation. "I'm so sick of him acting like some punk ass at school."

"I'm not a . . ." Alex started.

"First of all, watch your mouth," I told him, interrupting them both, "and what does that mean, anyway?"

"It means that my brother, the cupcake, refuses to stand up for himself and that all the kids at school are laughing at him," Dylan said, shaking his disgusted head.

I looked at Alex. He shrugged.

Ugh . . .

"It's embarrassing," Dylan continued. "Someone needs to toughen him up, so I decided that I'd . . ."

"So, you decided you'd be a good brother and beat on him?" I asked, sarcastically cutting him off again. "Just you being kind . . . is that right?"

He nodded, sincerely. "Just doing my job, Dad."

"You can't be serious, Dyl." I pointed toward the door. "Leave us for now."

"But Dad . . ."

"Now! And I'll deal with your idea of kindness later."

"But I was only trying to help him," Dylan vowed.

"Of course you were, and I plan on helping you the same way later. You see, it's my job to cultivate good men and, from what I just witnessed, I have a lot of work ahead of me." I pointed toward the door again. "Goodbye, Dyl."

After Dylan slammed the door shut, I took a seat on Alex's bed.

"Okay, let's hear it." I patted the seat next to me. "What's going on with you at school?"

My nine-year-old took a seat beside me; his eyes filled and his bottom lip began to quiver. "Dad, it's just . . ." He stopped, struggling not to cry.

"Listen, I'm here to help you figure this out, Alex," I told him, "but I can't help you if I don't know what's going on." I put my arm around his trembling shoulder. "Don't be upset. Just tell me what's happening at school."

He took a few deep breaths, trying to calm himself. "There's this kid that picks on me all the time."

"Okay, let's start with this kid's name."

"Matt," he reluctantly said, "his name's Matt."

I nodded. "And Matt picks on you, how?"

"It started by him calling me names and then he began hitting me. Matt's mean to everyone, but he really . . ."

"What?" I blurted, halting him—my blood pressure on the rise. "He's actually put his hands on you?"

He nodded, his shameful eyes now focused on the floor.

"Have you done anything to stop him, Alex?" I asked.

He shook his head.

I hated to ask the next question, but I had to. "Have you even tried to stand up to him?"

He shook his head again.

"Why not?" I asked, placing my finger under his chin and lifting his face until he was making eye contact again.

"Because I'm . . . I'm scared of him," he stuttered.

Ugh, some things never change, I thought. *You'd think we would have all evolved by now.*

"I'm sorry, Dad, but I can't help it," he said, waiting for me to speak.

"We've talked about this, Alex. Fear or no fear, sometimes we need to stand up, right?" As soon as I said it, the hairs on my forearms snapped to attention. It was the very same message my father had repeated throughout my twisted childhood.

In the blink of an eye, I was back at 602 State Road, learning harsh lessons mandated by a hard man.

• • •

"Even when you're afraid, really scared, and it's hard to stand up," Pop told me and my two brothers, "that's exactly when you have to stand up and be a man. You'll regret it, if you don't. Trust me, it'll haunt you your whole life. Do you understand me, boys?"

"Yeah, Pop, we do," we sang in chorus.

With tattooed biceps and dark muttonchops, our father was handsome in a James Dean-grown-older kind of way. "You make sure of it," he added, his brown eyes now distant and sad. "Fear or no fear, just make sure you stand up."

"We will, Pop."

"Okay then."

• • •

I returned to my blonde son's sorrowful face. "You have to stand up to Matt," I told him, "you know that, right?"

"But I've never fought . . ."

"I'm not saying you need to fight him, Alex, but you do need to stand up for yourself and let him know that you're not going to be anyone's punching bag." I shook my head.

"But he's a lot bigger than me."

I remember the terror well, son, I thought, nodding.

"And he picks on everyone, Dad, not just me."

I nodded again. "But this isn't about him or anyone else, is it? I mean, who cares about some knucklehead named Matt, right?"

A grin threatened to break through his pitiful scowl.

"This is about you, Alex, and how you feel about yourself." I peered hard into his eyes. "Maybe even how you feel about yourself for the rest of your life." I chose my next words carefully. "Fear is a monster and, if you don't shine a light on it . . . if you allow it to stay in the shadows . . . then that monster will only continue to grow and gain more power over you." I paused. "Does that make sense?"

He nodded. "I get it, Dad, but it's not that easy."

"Oh, I know, trust me. But easy has nothing to do with any of this," I explained.

"But what if I get into trouble at school with Principal DeSousa? She won't . . ."

"Let me worry about Principal DeSousa." I gave his shoulder a squeeze. "Let's spend some time this week coming up with a game plan that you can feel good about, okay?"

As he nodded, I could see the first hint of relief creeping into his eyes.

"Now go to bed and get some sleep," I told him, adding a wink. "And stop worrying. I've got your back on this."

A full-blown smile finally arrived. "You probably weren't afraid of anything when you were a kid, huh, Dad?" he said, jumping into bed and pulling the covers up under his chin.

"Oh, you'd be surprised," I said, snickering. "When we were kids, your uncles and I were afraid of a lot of things."

"Really?"

"Really," I said, kissing his spit-free forehead. "Now get some sleep. I need to go deal with your brother."

"I hope you make that animal cry," he muttered.

"No, you don't," I told him. "He's your brother and you guys have no idea how much you mean to each other." I smiled. "Not yet, anyway."

Dylan was sitting in the dark living room, awaiting his unknown fate.

I turned on the light. "Alex is your little brother," I began, taking a seat beside him on the couch. "You should be . . ."

"But he's such a wuss, Dad."

"Enough with the name-calling," I told him. "It's not okay."

"Yeah, like you didn't call your brothers names when you were growing up?"

Oh, if you only knew, I thought. "That was a different time, Dyl, which still doesn't make it right." I thought for a moment. "Words have power and when they make people feel bad, they're not okay to use, right?"

The boy conceded with a nod.

I gave it some thought. *When I was a kid, we had to survive a lot worse than name-calling.* I shook my head. *Bullying was pretty much a top-ranked sport.*

Dylan looked at me, still awaiting his punishment.

"As I was saying, you should be trying to help Alex, not hurt him."

"Dad, it's absolutely ridiculous how he lets that monkey abuse him."

"And it didn't dawn on you that maybe you should step in and help your brother with the situation?"

"You want me to fight Matt?" he asked.

Ummmm . . . I thought, pausing for too long. "I didn't say that. But if it were my little brother getting bullied, I know I'd be having a talk with that monkey."

He looked at me for a long while before nodding that he understood.

"Listen, I need to work with Alex on overcoming some of his fears and I could really use your help with that," I told him, "but you beating on him and chipping away at whatever confidence he does have isn't going to help anyone, is it?"

He nodded again, before sighing heavily from frustration.

"What?" I asked. "Tell me."

"It's just . . . you don't know what it's like to have a brother that's such a pain in the . . ." He stopped himself from cussing.

I chuckled. I couldn't help it.

". . . or having to grow up in such a messed-up family."

Messed up family? I thought, snickering. *Not getting new sneakers every two weeks or having to eat leftovers once in a while hardly defines being raised in a messed-up family.* "Oh, I don't, huh?" I said.

He looked at me, clearly surprised that I wasn't angry at the insult.

"Go to bed, Dyl," I told him, "and keep your hands off your brother from now on. If you don't . . ."

"I will," he said, "I will." He looked at me, confused. "What about this thing with Matt?"

"We'll figure it out," I told him.

With a single nod, he left the room.

Growing up in a messed-up family, I repeated in my mind, chuckling more. *Is there a greater blessing?*

It was late when I discovered that my son had prompted an unexpected stroll down memory lane. Sitting comfortably in my recliner, I closed my eyes and rewound the worn tape in my graying head.

I don't recall anything that happened the first few years of my life. With the exception of several random snapshots that my mind filed away, the film in my brain must have been exposed somewhere along the line—or perhaps someone forgot to load it? I smiled to myself. *Either way, my memories come in fuzzy bits and pieces; I'm guessing they're fragments of a truth I experienced with my own underdeveloped senses, coupled with collaborating stories that I've been told by my family through the years.*

The first thing I can remember is my mother. Maybe this isn't so much a thought or a picture as it is a feeling. Ma was there, always there. She had a distinct smell and that alone could stop the tears. Ma fulfilled my every need. Her dark eyes were gentle and kind. She was my protector, my light—my world. The thought made me smile again. *It's funny how some things never change, no matter how many years pass.*

Early on, Ma began to share her faith, teaching me and my brothers how to love God and pray to Him. "Now I lay me down to sleep, I pray the Lord my soul to keep. If I should die before I wake, I pray the Lord my soul to take." I believe that simple prayer was the first time I ever experienced a sense of panic. What do you mean, "If I should die before I awake?" I questioned. While I'm sleeping? To make matters worse, Aunt Phyllis told me and my brothers, "They say if you die in your dreams, then you actually die in real life."

I stopped. *Childhood is filled with terrors,* I thought, *the perfect training ground to learn how to face life as an adult.* I returned to my scattered recollections.

Those days were normally marked by events and not by calendars. Aunt Phyllis scolded me for chewing my food with my mouth open. It was a grilled cheese sandwich and I was laughing hard when she let me have it. "Shame on you, Herbie. You've been raised better than that." When the words spewed from her crooked mouth, I could feel my face burn red. I knew better and, for the first time, I felt embarrassed. And the worst part—the witch was right. Ma had taught me better. Aunt Phyllis seemed to enjoy putting my mother down every chance she could. I made sure to never chew with my mouth open again.

My family didn't have much and, without anyone ever announcing it, I knew we were poor. One winter day, Pop dragged home a huge card-board box and left it in the bedroom I shared with my brothers. Within two days, Ma cut out a door and two windows, using the extra material to fashion a chimney. From there, she colored everything from furniture to pets on the interior walls. Suddenly, Wally, my big brother—by fourteen months, Alphonse, my baby brother, and I had our own clubhouse. On that very day, I realized we'd been blessed with so much more than money.

There were some Fridays when Pop came home from work with fish and chips from Higson's Seafood. My brothers and I giggled from the excitement of being able to stay up late. We'd sit in Pop's lap and listen to the tall tales of his own childhood. Nothing felt better than to fall asleep on my father's chest, his deep voice turning to a drone. It was even better to awaken in his arms when he carried me off to bed. I never opened my eyes, pretending I was fast asleep. I knew I'd grown too old to be held in my father's arms and really missed it.

Some nights, visions of monsters and devils would force me out of my bunk bed and into my parents' bedroom. Unlike Alphonse, who still wet the bed on occasion, my mother would place me between her and my snoring father. On those nights, when the wind beat angrily against the windowpanes, I enjoyed the sleep of angels. I almost looked forward to the vivid nightmares in those early days.

My eyes snapped open. *Nightmares of monsters and devils hiding in our bedroom closet or under our bunk bed*, I recounted. *And how did I react? I slid into my parents' bed.* I thought about that. *But I was really young then and being allowed to hop into their bed didn't last long.* I hurried back to my memories.

From that point on, every time I had a nightmare I was exiled to the hard, green chair in the corner of their room. I've never forgotten the feeling of sitting cross-legged in that uncomfortable chair. Many nights, I sat silently, counting off the seconds until the morning sun arrived to chase away the darkness. While my father snored, I felt safer just being in his presence. Sometimes, I'd fall asleep sitting straight up, but on most of those long nights I'd just sit there in the darkness, trying not to pay attention to the shadow of the tall tree dancing outside of their bedroom window—immediately followed by a hundred horrific scenes conjured up in my overactive imagination.

I contemplated getting up to grab myself a drink but decided against it. I was on a roll and, although the memories felt a bit random, I was really enjoying the trip back.

My Uncle Arthur—everyone called him Skinny, even though he was two biscuits away from having to wear Velcro sneakers—usually rocked in his chair, entranced in the words of some voice that hid inside of a small radio. I sat with my knees to my chest and listened too. With my eyes closed, I could picture every word. When it was over, he'd pat me on the head and sneak me a sweet. He wasn't married and worked hard in a factory, so my brothers and I figured he must be rich. He even got Wally, Alphonse and I each a heart-shaped box of chocolates for Valentine's Day every year.

I was probably six when my Memere, Aunt Phyllis and my mother took Wally and me shopping for school clothes. Ma and Memere smelled of flowers; Aunt Phyllis reeked of mothballs. Men, passing by on the sidewalk, smiled and tipped their hats to them. I couldn't wait until I was old enough to do the same. Once we finally reached Zayre's Department Store to get Memere some new "unmentionables," my mother gave Wally and me the usual warning, "Look, but don't touch!" And we didn't, for fear that she'd have to pay for everything in the store. As Pop would say, "Don't let her fool you, your mother's piss broke." Instead, Wally and I raced up and down the long aisles until Aunt Phyllis yelled, "Don't be actin' like retards!" I didn't understand what the word meant, but I knew it couldn't be good. "Don't you ever call my boys that again!" Ma screamed, scolding her with the same disappointed tone she used with us. "Not to mention, you're really showing off your ignorance by using words like that, Phyllis." I decided right then that even as an adult, I was never going to like Aunt Phyllis. I might have only been six, but there were still a few things I did know.

It was Easter and I was still suffering a toothache from all of the candy Uncle Skinny sneaked us. Ma had me in the tub and was washing the day's mud out of my hair when Pop stumbled through the door. He was leaning on Uncle Skinny's shoulder and singing a song—though I couldn't make out most of the words. He told Uncle Skinny to leave and staggered into the bathroom. I smelled it right away. He'd been drinking "booze." I didn't think anything of it until he gritted his teeth. "He's old enough to wash himself!" he yelled, scolding my mother. For the first time,

I saw fear in her face and I instantly accepted my share of it.

Christmas quickly became my favorite time of the year. Besides Santa being the most generous person I'd never met, I loved walking down Pleasant Street during the first snowfall. It was usually dusk when Pop would take us into Pleasant Drug Store to see the newest tree decorations we could never afford. He always bought Ma something special at Jack & Harry's Department Store, had Mrs. Marques wrap it and then told us, "Shut your pie holes." It was thrilling to know something our mother didn't, especially since it was sure to make her happy.

It was my first day at school when I asked my teacher, Mrs. Cabeceiras, to use the bathroom. She told me, "Okay Herbert, you can go to the basement." I remember walking around in circles, frightened that I'd never find my way back to the classroom, never mind "the basement."

Without ever relieving myself, I ended up back in the classroom where I stood in horror—as I urinated all over myself. Long after the class had finished laughing, my mother brought in a new set of clothes for me. They were old, though, and didn't have the new smell that I'd spent the entire morning enjoying. I never wanted to go back to school again.

Church was mandatory every Sunday, though I could never understand why. According to Ma, "Saints are just sinners that keep trying." As she listened attentively to the back of a man who rambled on in some foreign language, Pop usually nodded off. When it was done, everyone lied, talking about how much better they felt because of it. The only thing Wally, Alphonse and I ever got out of it was ice cream. Having to sit still for that long hardly seemed worth a fudgesicle.

I was seven when my mother got sick and went to the hospital. Memere stayed at our house so she could take care of Wally, me, and Alphonse. Though no one ever explained Ma's illness, I was consumed with worry. Pop finally told us that she was getting better and took us to Woolworth's Five and Dime to "buy her something special to give her when she gets home." Although I didn't understand the concept of a five and dime because everything in the store cost more than a nickel or a dime, I picked out a knick-knack, a green ceramic parrot. Two days later, my mother came home. She was thinner than I'd ever seen her, and I cried at the sight of her. I think it was a combination of joy and sorrow. As she began to unwrap my gift, she grimaced at the slightest movement. I thought I was going to jump out of my skin from the anticipation of her certain joy. When she finally pulled the treasure out of the box, the bird's head was completely broken off its body. I cried more. Aunt Phyllis mumbled something mean and Ma snapped back, "Herbie's a sensitive soul and I wouldn't want him any other way!" Looking at me, she added, "I love the parrot, sweetheart. We'll fix him up as good as new, okay?" I loved Ma more than anyone in the world.

I took a break from memory lane to grab a drink. *Wow,* I thought, pouring out a glass of cold coffee milk, *Like Alex, I cried a lot when I was young.* I took a long sip. *But Pop broke me out of that soon enough.*

Back in the recliner, I quickly picked up where I'd left off. *I must have been eight years old when my mind began recording memories again. Pop joined Wally, Alphonse and I in a game of catch. Alphonse—we called him Cockroach in those days—kept throwing the ball over my head when Pop wasn't looking and laughed each time. Fed up, I went after him. My father broke it up before giving us a speech that would become famous. "He's your brother. You shouldn't be fighting with him. Someday, you'll realize how much you mean to each other." I doubted it. "If you have to fight, make sure it's with someone else," Pop finished, "but never with each other." Unfortunately, these were words that fell upon deaf ears for many years.* I laughed, thinking, *Fighting was our favorite pastime.*

I smiled, thinking of my own boys.

Ma and Pop began playing cards with Aunt Phyllis and Memere every Saturday night. Uncle Skinny would usually sit in the corner, content to be alone with his beer. Wally, Cockroach and I—choking on the heavy cigarette smoke that filled the room—stayed just the same, in search of pennies that fell from the kitchen table onto the floor. Most times, we'd just hide under that table and listen, knowing that the adults would eventually forget we were there and begin discussing things that only adults discuss. I learned that Grandpa was "a real bastard" in his day, but nothing compared to the murderer that had raised him, that Santa Claus was a bigger hoax than the politicians that Pop insulted, and that Aunt Phyllis' niece had turned into "a filthy slut." And then I learned why.

I took pause to laugh. *I learned nearly everything I ever needed to know beneath the table of some heated pitch games.*

When I was ten, Pop got promoted from driver to warehouse foreman at work. It was a special occasion, and a rare one, so he treated the family to a fancy sit-down dinner at a restaurant called Rustler's Steakhouse in Dartmouth. For Wally, Cockroach and me, it was beyond exciting. Usually, we only skimmed through restaurant menus after our parents' tax return came in. Anyway, we'd never stepped foot into a place like Rustler's before. "You boys can order anything you want," Pop told us.

"Anything we want?" we responded, pretty sure that we'd heard wrong.

Smiling wide, he nodded.

I tried to start at the dessert side of the menu, but Ma wouldn't have it. Outside of holidays and Uncle Skinny's discreet passes, Wally, Cockroach and I were forbidden to eat sweets or drink soda pop. "It'll rot out your teeth," Ma would remind us. But when the waitress came over to take the order, Pop told her, "Give each of these boys a large Coca Cola."

Exchanging excited glances, my brothers and I felt like we'd just hit the lottery.

A few months later, I blew out eleven candles on the chocolate cake that my Memere had baked. Life was good. The whole family was there and we'd even made it the entire day without Wally breaking any of my new toys—the Partridge Family drum set, included.

That very next week, however, my brothers and I arrived home from school to find both my parents waiting. How unusual, I thought. Something in my gut told me it wasn't good. With tears in his eyes—something I'd never seen before—Pop announced, "Your grandpa just passed away." I looked at Wally and Cockroach, who were also in shock. "He had a massive heart attack," Pop explained.

"Oh, no," I yelled when Ma went to her knees to pull each of us in for a hug. "At least he didn't suffer," she said, speaking with more compassion than my father could muster. This can't be true, I thought, we just saw Gramps two days ago. How unfair! My grandfather was a good man with a great laugh. For me, he walked on water.

Pop threw the three of us into his work truck and took us out for Coney Island hot dogs. "Your grandpa died a wealthy man, boys," he explained. "He gave away everything he had . . . even his last nickel." He searched our eyes. "Remember that it's not how much you accumulate in this world, it's how much you give away." He nodded. "That's the only real way to measure a man's success."

Cockroach's face went white.

"Your grandfather's lucky he still has one shirt left to be buried in," Pop added.

I knew right then and there that I wanted to be generous and kind, too.

By the time we got home, I think each one of us felt a little better. Pop understood our loss and the time we spent together somehow made the loss more bearable.

For the next few days, we sat redneck shiva, listening to Ernest Tubb and the Troubadours while eating a mix of Ma's casseroles and take-out food. The entire time, my father and Uncle Skinny drank Grampa's favorite beer—Schlitz—which Pop claimed, "tastes like skunk piss."

During Pop's mournful drunken stupor, he offered a stammering spiel that I've never forgotten. "You boys may not like it or . . . or even understand," he slurred, "but . . . but I refuse to raise lollipops." He shook his head. "And we don't need any snowflakes floatin' around this house neither."

"Lollipops?" Wally repeated, confused.

"Suckers," Pop explained.

For a moment, I pulled myself out of my head to recognize that I was now "Pop," and that I needed to impart the same lesson on my sons. *Though it's probably best for everyone that I choose different words to teach it,* I thought, returning to my family's story.

"Okay, Walter," Ma said, "maybe now's not the best time to teach the . . ."

"No!" he roared, interrupting her, "they . . . they need to hear it, Emma."

Although Ma shook her head, she never uttered another word.

"Just like your grandfather gave to me and Uncle Skinny, my job's to . . . to teach you to be respectful and . . . and accountable." He started counting off on his massive fingers. "If you don't make the baseball team this spring, then . . ." He burped. ". . . maybe you'll practice more, right?"

We started to nod before realizing it didn't matter.

"If you get into trouble with the law," Pop continued, having trouble maintaining eye contact with us, "your mother and I ain't . . ."

He stopped to take a sip of beer. "We ain't bailing you out, got it?"

We stared at him, wide-eyed.

"And . . . and being a man sometimes means helping people who can't help themselves." He burped again; this time, it sounded like he was ready to vomit. "You got it?" He stared off into space for a few awkward moments. "If you can't do that, then . . . well, it's hard to call yourself a real man, ain't it?"

Uncle Skinny nodded. "Amen to that, brother," he muttered, slapping Pop on the back.

It's the strangest thing, but I seem to have lost time around then— maybe from the incredible, nauseating grief of losing my grandfather; the world would never be the same again and I knew it. There was a big hole left behind, a pit of darkness that could never be filled.

In complete stillness, I sat in the recliner for a long while when it suddenly hit me. *February vacation, one week in the winter of 1984.* I laughed aloud. *If I live a hundred years, I'll never forget that outrageous week.*

I quickly returned to my memories.

I was twelve and, although I had no clue how I'd ever pay for it, I was waiting on the delivery of Van Halen's newest release, 1984, The initial investment cost me one penny, a deal I couldn't pass up. I'd signed up with Columbia Record and Tape Club—ten albums or cassettes for one penny, with the agreement to buy four more titles at full price in the next two years. I completed the form and mailed in the shiny penny I'd found under the kitchen table, with no idea of how I was going to pay for the other four albums. It doesn't matter, I'd thought, at least not right now.

I smiled. *Ahhhh, the winter of 1984,* I thought, *a time when everything was so damn scary. Every time my brothers and I overcame one fear, we were forced to face a bigger, more terrifying one.*

Raising the chair's footrest, I folded my hands behind my head and—with a sense of nostalgic longing—completely surrendered my thoughts to the glorious 80s.

CHAPTER 2

FRIDAY

It was the afternoon of Friday 13th, 1984, the last day before February vacation. *A whole week off from stupid middle school*, I thought, excitedly.

From the moment I stepped onto the bus, the atmosphere felt electric, everyone happy for the much-needed winter break.

Many of the bus's green fake leather bench seats were split and duct-taped. As I made my way down the narrow aisle in search of a seat, I heard the usual remarks offered to most eighth graders from the high school kids who'd already claimed their territory.

"You can't sit here, dufus."

"This seat's taken."

Even on such a joyous afternoon, I was quickly reminded that riding the bus was a hard kick in the teeth. It didn't matter whether they were wearing black leather vests and chain wallets or Swatch watches and turned-up collars on their pastel IZOD Polo shirts, the high school kids were just plain mean.

As I made my way farther down the line, the objections got even stronger.

"Oh, I don't think so, dweeb."

"If you even think about sitting, you dink, I'll beat you to a pulp."

Eat shit and die, I replied in my head, but never uttered a word aloud.

I hated sitting with the nerds or the kids that smelled like spoiled lunchmeat, but after receiving enough rejections I began to wonder, *Maybe the older kids see me the same way?*

Although school had its social order, this mobile environment was even less forgiving. At a time in life when the mind is impressionable—constantly worrying about what others think of you, even about what you think of yourself—the bus's sadistic hierarchy created scar tissue that would help to define many lives for years to come. It was a cruel testing ground for survival, where the tougher or more popular kids claimed the back of the bus. Those coveted seats were sacred territory that most of us spent years aspiring to. On the big, yellow school bus, physical threats were the least of our worries. *This is psychological warfare,* I realized early on.

Besides having to deal with the pecking order, there was incredible peer pressure to do things most of us would have never dreamed of doing—like distracting the elderly driver, Mr. Gifford. Given that the bus had no seat belts, this daily practice seemed pretty insane to me. I'd never actually seen Mr. Gifford's eyes; the two narrow slits were usually squinting into the rear-view mirror. "Sit down!" he constantly yelled.

There was always the smell of smoke wafting from the back, though I was never really sure it was cigarette smoke. Usually, there were two kids making out—a boy and girl—and it wasn't always the same couple. The bus had its own sub-culture, a microcosm of the twisted society we were growing up in.

It's amazing Old Man Gifford can keep this giant bus on the road and not in one of the ditches we pass on our way home, I thought.

As I claimed my seat beside another outcast Junior High-Schooler, I spotted my brother, Wally, sitting toward the middle of the vessel. Wally had straight brown hair, serious brown eyes and the chunky Bloomfield nose. He looked like my father. Unfortunately, a terrible case of acne was in full bloom, taking away from his rugged handsome looks. Our eyes locked. I nodded toward him. Although he returned the gesture, he was much more subtle in his action. *You're such a butthead*, I thought.

A cold breeze tapped me on the shoulder. *It's freezing in here*, I realized, turning around to see that the windows were open in the back of the yellow torture chamber. As I turned, I caught a whiff of my bus mate. *And thank God they're open*, I thought, trying to place the unusual smell. *Fried Spam?* I guessed, before noticing that the stinky kid was wearing a Smokey the Bear sweatshirt that read, *Only You Can Prevent Forest Fires*. I had to do a double-take. *No way*, I thought in disbelief, *it looks like Mr. Potato Head, here, has a death wish . . . wearing a lame pullover like that. I'm surprised he doesn't have a Just Say No campaign button pinned to the front of it.* I chuckled aloud, drawing a look from my new best friend. *I pity the fool*, I thought, quoting Mr. T. in my head.

I'd just popped my last Luden's cherry cough drop into my mouth when I heard it. There was a commotion behind us, much louder than the usual ruckus. *What the hell?* No sooner did I turn in my seat to investigate the ruckus when my heart plummeted past my stone-washed jeans straight into my worn Chuck Taylor high tops.

Owen Audet—the most feared enforcer on Bus 6—was standing toe-to-toe with Wally. He was more than a head taller than my poor brother. *Oh no*, I thought, *Wally's gotta be shittin' bricks right now.* I swallowed hard. *I know I would be.* Owen was big, dumb and mean—and heavy on the mean.

"I need to borrow another book," the Missing Link barked, looming over my brother.

There were a few laughs from the bully's brain-dead minions.

My mouth instantly went dry, while my heart began to race. Although my brother was on the "big-boned" side, built like a Sherman tank, he looked so small next to Owen. *That dude's a Clydesdale,* I thought, *and Wally's road pizza.*

"Sor . . . sorry, but I can't do it," Wally refused, his voice three octaves higher than normal. Even though he sounded like a yipping dog, he somehow stood his ground.

Owen's face turned beet red. He obviously didn't appreciate being challenged in front of his captivated audience.

It's Friday the 13th, I remembered, *and Jason's back.*

Owen grabbed for Wally's backpack, who pulled away violently.

"Ooooh," the crowd groaned.

"You must be out of your damn mind, loser," the aggressor hissed.

"I . . . I would be if . . ." Wally stuttered, looking like a terrified Kindergartner, " . . . if I let you take another book."

I didn't blame him. *After the way Pop reacted the last time this same nightmare happened,* I thought, *Wally has no choice.* My mind quickly flashed back.

• • •

A month earlier, Owen had snatched one of Wally's school books, opened the bus window and tossed it out—while everyone laughed nervously, hoping they weren't next.

This could never happen to me, I realized, priding myself on the fact that I never took home a book. This wasn't because I wasn't supposed to or didn't need to. I'd simply decided early on that if the material couldn't be learned in the classroom, then there was no way I was going to "get it" at home.

When we got home, Wally explained that he'd been "bullied on the bus."

Our father's reaction was even worse than the crime Wally had reported. "Bullied?" Pop roared, addressing Wally, me and our little brother in the living room, "there's no such thing as being bullied unless you allow it, right?" He didn't wait for an answer. "Lions are not bullied by sheep," he barked, "and I hope to God I'm not raising sheep!"

"Okay, Pop," Wally mumbled at a little more than a whisper, "I get it."

"There's only one way to set a bully straight," Pop added, staring my older brother in the eye.

Any one of us could have recited his next words by heart.

"Punch him square in the nose as hard as you can."

"Walt!" my mother yelled from the kitchen, clearly opposed to the harsh lesson.

Pop peered even harder into Wally's eyes. "As hard as you can," he repeated through gritted teeth.

Three heads nodded.

Message received, I thought, *loud and clear.* When teaching us, Pop never gently peeled back the onion. He always sliced it right down the middle, cutting straight to the bitter tears.

As if that wasn't bad enough, Wally had heard two earfuls over the missing book—not just from our father but from his teacher, as well. My brother had reported that his book was missing; that he'd lost it. It was better than the alternative. *If he'd told the truth, it would have been so much worse.* Owen would have been enraged and Wally's classmates would have labeled him a stool pigeon. And Pop, well, Pop would have thought he was a coward—*a fate worse than death itself.*

Yup, it's so much better to lie sometimes, I decided.

• • •

Back on the bus, the crowd grew louder. "Ooooh..." they sang in chorus; everyone was now up on their knees to witness the inevitable pummeling.

I'd always looked up to my brother. Now, I just felt bad for him.

As Owen's jaw muscles flexed violently, his beady eyes darted back and forth—his baby brain clearly considering his options. He looked toward Mr. Gifford, whose squinted eyes were looking into the giant rearview mirror positioned directly above his head.

"You're lucky, you little queer," Owen spat at my brother.

Wally kept his ground. "Why don't you pick on . . . on someone your own size?" he stammered.

I couldn't believe my ears. It was like experiencing a scene from Karate Kid. *Wally's sticking up for himself, even though Magilla Gorilla's threatening to bash his squash in.* Although my brother had found the courage to stare the predator down, I knew he wasn't crazy enough to accept the giant's invitation to tussle.

Owen laughed, cynically. "Oh, you're my bitch now," he said, "and I'm gonna take care of you good when we get back from vacation. You got it, bitch?"

The crowd didn't laugh this time; everyone feeling bad for Wally. *It could be any one of us at any time,* I thought. Owen was an equal opportunity bully who didn't discriminate.

"I'm gonna beat you down," Owen promised Wally, "and it's gonna be like that for the rest of the year." He chuckled. "And next year, too." By now, his putrid breath was inches from my brother's crimson face, spittle flying with every terrifying word he spouted.

I'd never felt so freaked out in my life, and the scumbag wasn't even talking to me. *I don't know how Wally's staying on his feet,* I thought, proud that my brother's eyes never left Owen's.

As the bus screeched to a stop in front of our house, Wally turned to leave. The brakes weren't done squealing when Owen pushed him in the back, collapsing him to the filthy floor.

Eyes wide, Wally looked up from his prone position.

"Say one word," Owen growled, "and I'll kick your friggin' teeth in right here."

Wally scrambled to his feet and glared at him again before marching off the bus, hyperventilating from either fear or anger. *Most likely both,* I figured.

As the bus's folding door closed and the air brakes belched out a sigh, I turned to Wally. "Do you think the Sleestak will actually . . ." I began to ask.

"Shut your damn mouth before I kick *your* teeth in!" he barked.

"Well, okay then," I mumbled. My big brother was the master of wedgies and Indian sunburns, with years of experience under his belt, so I thought, *I hope you get yours after vacation.*

We lived at 602 State Road in the second-floor apartment of a two-tenement house, with a real estate office located on the first floor.

This set up was incredibly rare in a town consisting of single-family homes, defining our socio-economic status amongst those who were financially better off. Fortunately, the suit-wearing realtors never used the cellar, so we were able to claim that space, as well—even though we needed to access it from outside.

As we entered the apartment, Ma was at the stove, making a vat of hot dog stew. "How was everyone's day?" the short woman asked. She had the kindest eyes and most loving smile—except on those moody days when it seemed like she'd eaten a bowl of spiders for breakfast.

"Just great," Wally said, storming toward our bedroom.

"Better than his," I said, pointing at my brother.

Wally stopped at our bedroom's plastic accordion door, spinning on his heels to stare me into silence.

The menacing look worked. "I had a good day," I told my mother, prepared to quell any questions she might have. "Mr. Timmons, my science teacher, nearly choked to death on an apple in class today," I told her, laughing.

"And you think that's funny, Herbie?" she asked, disgustedly.

I shrugged. "You would have too, Ma, if you'd been there," I told her. "He was just starting to turn blue when he coughed it out."

"Dear God," she said, "that's enough. I don't want to hear another word about it."

I smiled. *Mission accomplished*, I thought, knowing there was no way she'd remember my comment about Wally. "Oh, and we're on vacation all next week," I reminded her.

"I know, I know," she said, her face incapable of concealing her disappointment. "When Alphonse gets home, I want the three of you to clean up that pig sty you call a bedroom."

"Why would we clean it now, before vacation week?" I asked. "It doesn't make sense, Ma. We're only going to mess it up all week."

"Because I said so, that's why." She stared at me for a moment. "Or if you want, I can have your father . . ."

"Fine," I quickly surrendered, "we'll get started when Cockroach gets home from school."

My younger brother was still in elementary school and took a later bus. *I have a half hour to play Atari*, I thought, *and that new Donkey Kong game is mint.*

The Atari gaming system was the best Christmas gift my brothers and I had ever received. Although I'd begged for Rock 'Em Sock 'Em Robots, Ma adamantly refused. "Not on your life," she told me. "The last thing you guys need is more encouragement to fight." Instead, we received a much better—and completely unexpected—Christmas present.

The Atari 2600 came with two joystick controllers with red buttons, a conjoined pair of paddle controllers, and black game cartridges that looked a lot like Pop's 8-track tapes.

Wally stormed out of the room just as I was entering.

"Where are you heading?" I asked him.

"To do my paper route."

"Can I come with you?"

"No."

"Come on, Wally," I said. "I can help you and . . ."

"I said no," he barked. "Besides, I need to hurry today and get it done quick."

"Why?"

"None of your business." He stepped through the kitchen, heading for the front door.

"Be back for supper," my mother told him.

"I will, Ma," he said, walking out of the house and slamming the door behind him.

"What's wrong with Wally today?" my mother called out, just as I was starting to control the block-headed ape on the small black-and-white TV screen.

Nice try, Ma, I thought, confident that I'd never make the same mistake twice. "He's just wiggin' to get his paper route done, so he can veg out tonight," I told her. "The Dukes of Hazzard are on and he's in love with Daisy." I smiled, thinking, *We all are*.

"Well, there'll be no Dukes of Hazzard, if you boys don't get that room cleaned up."

"We'll get it done, Ma," I yelled from the bedroom. "Me and Cockroach will tackle it when the space cadet gets home."

I returned my attention to the TV screen and began jumping barrels with my two-dimensional video ape.

Our bedroom door opened and closed like a cheap accordion, catching Cockroach's fingers within its folds. "Ouch!" he yelled out.

I laughed. I couldn't help it. In fact, each time my little brother screamed out in pain, Wally and I laughed like it was the first time he'd ever hurt himself. *Cockroach's injuries never get old*, I thought.

As soon as he stopped his belly-aching, Cockroach and I went straight to work. "Either that," I told him, "or Ma won't let us watch Dukes of Hazzard."

"She wouldn't do that," he said.

I shrugged. "You wanna risk it?"

"What about Wally?" he asked. "Isn't he gonna help us?"

"He's on his paper route." I thought about it, surprised that I still felt bad for my older brother. "Let's just get it done, you little cabbage patch kid."

He flipped me the bird.

Our bedroom consisted of single bed and a set of bunk beds that was also used as a fort, a stagecoach, a spaceship, or anything our cross-wired brains could conjure up—with a bed sheet draped down from the top bunk. There were two bureaus, Cockroach's padlocked toy box and a tiny black-and-white TV that sat on a rickety fake wooden stand, the Atari console and joysticks lying in front on the shag carpeted floor. Three beanbag chairs helped to complete the cluttered room.

Cleaning was not as simple as it sounded. Not long ago, Ma had insisted, "You guys are gross and, from now on, you'll be doing your own laundry and making your own beds." I had KISS-themed bedding that once belonged to Wally. Although Cockroach liked to pretend he was sleeping on Star Wars sheets, he enjoyed my hand-me-down astronaut set. It wasn't easy changing the bedding on a bunk bed, but we finally got it done.

For the next hour, while we put away clothes and moved things around—mostly kicking everything under the beds—Steven Tyler from Aerosmith wailed away on Cockroach's massive silver boom box. Although we each owned a portable stereo system, Cockroach's was in the best shape. *He takes good care of his stuff,* I thought, *in case he ever wants to unload it to the highest bidder.* It was in pristine condition, with no stickers or corroded battery compartment. He barely used it, so this was a treat.

When we were done straightening up, I turned to Cockroach. "Looks schweet, huh?"

He nodded in agreement. Without a proper inspection, the place looked immaculate—or at least as clean as it had been in a very long time. "Schweet," he repeated.

It was amazing to me how different my brothers were. Being stuck in the middle of them, I usually played the family diplomat. Cockroach's real name was Alphonse, after our Pepere—but we always called him Cockroach. *I wasn't sure if it was because of the way he scurried about, or because no matter how badly Wally and I beat on him we couldn't seem to kill him.* I learned later on that he'd actually been nicknamed after a character on one of Pop's all-time favorites, Hogan's Heroes.

Cockroach was more like a skeleton wrapped in olive skin, while I was built on the sturdy side like my older brother. Although we also shared the small potato-shaped nose, I had blue eyes with curly blonde hair, which made more than a few people confuse me for a girl when I was young. Cockroach had darker eyes and a nose as slender as his build, making him appear like the one piece that didn't quite fit into the family portrait. My little brother could have easily been mistaken as the offspring of Face, the good-looking soldier on The A-Team.

"What do you want to play?" he asked me once we'd finished cleaning. His deep dimples framed a grin that was sure to make most females crane their necks.

"We could play with your Stretch Armstrong doll," I teased.

His handsome face went white.

I laughed, remembering that ridiculously violent day.

• • •

My brothers and I had enjoyed a few rare days of peace, until a small disagreement escalated into our usual slugfest. During the melee, Wally grabbed Cockroach's Stretch Armstrong doll, who ended up getting the worst of it.

Wearing blue bikini underwear, the bare-chested, blonde-haired rubber doll could take a real thrashing. We could stretch him and even tie him into a knot before he went back to his original bulky form. Whether catapulted high into the air or used as the rope in a heated tug of war match, the action figure was reputed to be indestructible.

Screaming for mercy, Cockroach watched on in horror, while Wally and I put that poor doll to the test. We pulled and pulled, both of us ending up on our backsides, digging in our heels to create more distance between us.

As the first break in the skin revealed itself, Cockroach cried out, "You're hurting him!"

That's when something came over me and Wally (who was also known as the Mangler). We pulled harder, mutilating Mr. Armstrong beyond recognition and dispelling the fact that he could never be destroyed. As Wally and I finished ripping the arms off of old Stretch, a clear gel that looked a lot like Crazy Glue oozed out.

"No!" Cockroach wailed.

"That's weird," Wally commented, nonchalantly, "the jelly doesn't seem to have any smell to it."

Inconsolable, Cockroach went down on all fours to mourn the death of his favorite playmate.

• • •

"You guys suck," Cockroach said, back in the present.

I couldn't argue with him. *Our job as big brothers is to toughen you up*, I thought, justifying the cruel act. I then realized that Wally the Mangler destroyed everything in his path. *The new Merlin six-in-one, hand-held electronic game I'd gotten for Christmas a couple of years ago, the table-top motorcycle game he unwrapped last year . . . everything.*

"You want to play Operation?" Cockroach asked me.

"Nah."

"Perfection?"

"Half the pieces are missing," I reminded him.

"Battleship?"

I shook my head. "Can't, the batteries are dead." I smiled. "What about Twister?"

"No way," he said, "it just turns into a pig pile with me on the bottom."

I laughed. *That's right.*

His eyes went wide with excitement. "What about G.I. Joe's, Herbie?" he asked. "We haven't played war in a long time."

I was well beyond the cusp of being too old to play soldier but making Cockroach happy was the perfect excuse for me to play. *It's the least I can do after helping to murder Stretch Armstrong*, I thought. *Besides, war is not an individual sport.*

Wally and I had received the entire G.I. Joe Command Center a few years earlier when we'd both gotten our tonsils removed. "It's for all three of you to share," our mother had announced, referring to the large gift. In recent months, Cockroach claimed the cool play set as his own, and Wally and I were good with it.

It didn't take long for my little brother to set up everything on the floor we'd just cleared. The grey G.I. Joe Headquarters Command Center was walled in the front and wide open in the back, allowing for the tank to drive in and out of its bay and the Jeep to enter the Motor Pool. Multiple G.I. Joe action figures manned the communication tactical station with colorful stickers illustrating the security monitors. An armory, filled with weapons, was located directly beneath the Heli-Pad—home to the awesome Dragonfly Helicopter. A holding cell for captured enemies was normally empty—as Cockroach and I rarely took enemies—while machine guns and cannons defended strategic positions on top of the spot-lit wall.

For the next hour or so, we fought—and defeated—battalions of imaginary enemies.

"Come in, Flying Squirrel," I called into a damaged walkie-talkie, "this is Swamp Yankee. How copy, over?"

"I read you, Swamp Yankee," Cockroach called back on his matching broken walkie-talkie. "The enemy has been neutralized."

I laughed. *Cockroach is too smart for his age,* I thought. *It must be from all the TV he watches.* It didn't really matter that our walkie talkies had been broken since we'd gotten them. We were kneeling side-by-side only a few feet apart.

"So, you really like this girl, Donna Torres, huh?" Cockroach commented, parking the Jeep in front of our perimeter.

I wheeled the tank through the Headquarters compound. "Like totally," I said, never looking up. *Donna's different,* I thought, *she's beautiful. Most girls aren't too hard to look at, but Donna's in a class all her own.*

"Help, I've fallen and I can't get up," Cockroach joked, mimicking the funny commercial of an elderly woman pushing a panic button on her necklace.

That's clever, bro, I thought. After a few moments of tank patrol, I blurted, "I think she's the one."

Chuckling, my little brother took the plastic helicopter into the air. "Sure she is, Herbie. You said the same thing about Abby Gerwitz last summer."

He's right, I thought. For as long as I could remember, I had a huge crush on Abby Gerwitz. *But who hasn't?* I thought. "She likes Richard Giles and everyone knows it," I told him, and because of that my feelings for her had died a very cruel death. "Donna's the one," I repeated, hammering my point home.

Cockroach stopped playing. "Have you told her?" he asked, giving me his undivided attention.

"Sort of."

"Sort of?"

For weeks, I couldn't stop thinking about exchanging valentines with Donna; giving her those small chalk hearts that said everything I didn't have the courage to tell her: *Be Mine* and *I Love You.* I decided that these colorful messages of affection were much safer to give than a greeting card or a box of chocolates. *But what if she doesn't like me?* I kept thinking, torturing myself. *I'll be a laughing stock at school.* I began getting heated, picturing Paul Roberts laughing at me, and then me punching his smug face over-and-over-and-over again. Even young, I sensed that love never went unpunished.

On Valentine's Day, I got to homeroom early and left a box of the chalk hearts in Donna's desk. I signed the gift, *From Herbie.* While my heart pounded out of my chest, I watched from the back of the room as she found the candy. She looked back at me and smiled. "Thank you," she said, and I nodded—my face feeling like it was on fire.

The more I thought about it, the more I realized that Donna had never gotten the real message I was trying to send.

"I gave her a valentine," I explained to Cockroach, "but I'm not sure if she thinks I gave it to her as a friend."

"Oh . . ." He thought for a moment. "That's pretty lame."

"What do you know?" I snapped back. Cockroach was still too young to understand the risk and devastation associated with being rejected by a girl—*especially a girl as perfect as Donna.* It was like being picked for teams in gym class—no big deal unless you were picked last. *And you only have so many shots in Middle School,* I thought. *If you're rejected by more than one girl, then you're destined to be stuck in Loserville for life.*

"So, what are you going to do?" he asked, bringing me back into the moment.

"I think I'm going to write her a letter."

"Really?"

"No question."

While we played, I began to daydream about my crush. I could picture Donna as plain as the bearded G.I. Joe doll I was holding.

Donna's so choice, I thought. She had the prettiest chocolate-colored eyes and a smile that made me feel like I was the only eighth-grade boy walking the earth. Every day at school, she either wore Jordache or Sergio Valente jeans; these were skin-tight right down to a pair of jelly shoes or clogs. Unlike most of the other girls who wore big hair with bangs—mall hair, as we called it—or tied up in a scrunchy, Donna's dirty blonde hair was parted in the middle and feathered back. *Just like Farah Fawcett on Charlie's Angels,* I thought. She usually wore a shirt with shoulder pads and her jewelry was simple; gel bracelets and friendship beads. I'd only seen her in leg warmers and a colorful headband once, realizing she'd look good no matter what she wore.

Yup, I thought, *I definitely have to write her a letter. It's the only way she'll ever know that I . . .*

"Herbie!" I heard someone scream.

I looked up. Cockroach was gone and I was sitting on the floor alone. *Wow, that's weird*, I thought.

"Herbie!" I heard again, struggling to register reality.

It's Ma, I realized. "Sorry, Ma, I didn't hear you."

"How could you not hear me? I've been yelling for you for ten minutes."

Now there's an exaggeration, I thought. "Sorry, Ma," I repeated.

"Your father's home from work. Go get cleaned up for supper."

"Okay."

"Now," she said.

When I pulled my chair out from the kitchen table, Pop was already sitting at the head of it—wearing his faded dungarees and graying crew-neck t-shirt. Thankfully, his same-colored handkerchief—which he used to blow his nose and then yank out our loose teeth, sometimes one right after the other—remained in his back pocket.

Wally was also there, his face ruddy from the cold.

"How was school today?" Pop asked, blowing on his hot bowl of stew.

"Fine," Wally mumbled, his eyes on his steaming meal.

"Good," I added, "we're on vacation next week."

The old man looked across the table at his wife. "Lucky Mom," he said, grinning.

"And we cleaned our room," Cockroach reported.

"Well, what do you know," he said, "it's a winter miracle."

For the next half hour, besides the occasional grunt or groan, we ate in silence. "Lots of hot dogs tonight," Pop commented, dunking a slice of buttered bread into his bowl. "Did we hit the lottery or something?"

Ma grinned. "They were on sale, Walt."

As they discussed the expensive price of groceries, my mind drifted off again. I couldn't help it. *I don't even care that Donna has a crush on Kevin Bacon*, I thought, shrugging to myself. *All those hearts on her Trapper Keeper, with his initials written inside each one—who cares.* I inhaled deeply. *I love it when she wears that Luvs Baby Soft perfume.* I could actually smell the liquid baby powder when I closed my eyes. *Ahhhh . . .*

"I'm done," Wally announced loudly, bringing me back to the table. After placing the plastic bowl into the sink, my brother grabbed his heavy winter jacket and put it on.

"Where are you going now?" Ma asked him.

"The cellar," he said.

"Good," she said, getting up, "while you're down there, why don't you throw a load of towels into the wash?"

Although Wally's face contorted, he nodded in surrender. "Fine, Ma."

Within seconds, she was back in the kitchen with an overflowing laundry basket of mismatched towels.

"Bo and Luke Duke are on tonight," Cockroach reminded him.

"I'll be back by then," Wally said, wrestling the bulky basket out the front door.

My father was finishing his second bowl of soup when he asked, "What the hell's he do down there, anyway?"

"Laundry," Ma said, standing to fetch him another bowl of stew.

At eight o'clock, Wally, Cockroach and I watched our favorite show—the Dukes of Hazzard. While we sat entranced by Bo and Luke's insane car jumps in the General Lee—as well as Daisy's wonderfully short cut-off jeans—Ma treated us to our favorite Friday treat: hand-cut French fries, salted and shaken in a brown paper bag. *There's no better snack on a Friday night*, I thought. *Hold the vinegar, please.*

Once the show was done, the TV belonged to Ma—who watched Dallas at nine o'clock, immediately followed by Falcon Crest. For two full hours, she snubbed out one cigarette butt after the next into a giant ashtray that rested atop its decorative wrought-iron stand beside the couch. In no time, the living room was engulfed in smoke, a low-clinging fog that had quietly crept in. While Pop snored on and off in his worn recliner—a half-empty beer can in hand—my brothers and I decided to call it a night. We'd already second-hand smoked a full pack that day.

My brothers and I wrapped up the night with a lively game of Atari Pong.

Cockroach preferred the longer paddles, while I was a bit more skilled and liked the shorter rectangles. I loved it. With virtual reality, there was much less need for actual reality.

Once Cockroach turned out the light and we retired to our beds, I called out to Wally, "Goodnight, John-boy . . ."

My big brother normally responded, "Night, Erin . . ." like we were part of the Walton family. But there was no reply tonight. There was no laughter—just silence.

It suddenly hit me. *Wally's still buggin' out*, I thought, realizing that my brother's fear was swallowing him whole. *All because of that bullshit on the bus today.* I shook my head. *He just needs to take a chill pill. I mean, we're off from school for an entire week!*

CHAPTER 3

SATURDAY

I awoke at nine o'clock, very early for a Saturday morning. Overnight, both bedroom windows had turned to blocks of ice. *Wally's gonna have some real fun on his paper route today*, I thought. *Maybe he'll let me go with him?* I considered the possibilities. *Nah, I doubt it.*

As my brothers and I rose from the dead, wearing just underwear or faded pajama bottoms and holey t-shirts, we took our bed hair straight into the living room for our usual Saturday cartoon marathon; Bugs Bunny, Porky Pig, Tom and Jerry, The Flintstones and Road Runner were all on the list. "Meep . . . Meep . . ." One show blended into the next until the entire morning was an exercise in deep hypnosis.

We laughed when the Mr. Microphone commercial came on. A curly blonde teenage boy, riding in the back seat of a convertible, spoke to a passing girl through a plastic microphone. "Hey good lookin', we'll be back to pick you up later!"

Everyone looked at Cockroach.

"What," he said, "I don't want that."

"Good," Pop said, yawning, "because that thing's junk." He shook his head. "You can get the same results by talking into an empty paper towel tube."

I laughed, thinking, *Now there's something that would really help score with the ladies.*

Decorated in flowered wallpaper and framed family photos, our living room had a real 'lived in' look to it. There was a brown couch and love seat, the fabric slightly softer than burlap—which was ideal for three growing boys. Both pieces of furniture were as worn as Pop's burgundy recliner. The carpet was a tan shag, which Ma never stopped vacuuming. A bulky walnut-paneled Hi-Fi stereo sat in one corner of the room, while a three-layered shelf—cluttered with Ma's knick knacks and Pop's beer steins—sat in the other. This shelf was our nemesis when playing the forbidden game of catch in the house. The best hands always stood on the side of the shelf, defending the green ceramic parrot with its head glued to its body, amongst other priceless treasures.

The floor model 25-inch Zenith TV was the shining jewel of the room. A set of rabbit's ears—topped with balls of aluminum foil and no longer used—sat atop the bulky console. For years, Pop had complained, "I spend half my life adjusting these damn rabbit ears." Even with his best efforts, there were times when we could barely make out our programs through the haze of buzzing snow. *But that was before the miracle of cable TV*, I thought.

Hissing, steel radiators—painted silver—hurt like hell when you were pushed into them during a heated debate. But they threw off plenty of heat, fighting against the drafts that whipped through the old windows. According to Pop, "The windows are fine. It's the caulk in the sills that's been dry rotted for years." To combat the terrible drafts, old rolled-up bath towels were placed at the base of the apartment's lead-painted windows and doors; most days, it was a fight that the towels lost.

A few months earlier, Ma had announced that we could eat in the living room on the weekends, "Just as long as you use the TV trays and pick up after yourselves." It was like hitting the lottery, something Pop was yet to accomplish with his scratch tickets.

After chomping on a Flintstones chewable vitamin that impersonated a Pez candy, the silent breakfast bell was rung and the feeding frenzy commenced. Whenever it was cold outside, Ma said, "You're much better off eating Cream of Wheat." She clearly bought into the commercial pitch. "It's a hearty way to start the day," she added.

I hated Cream of Wheat; it was a texture thing. *It tastes like wallpaper paste.* Instead, I gorged on Lucky Charms from a small pail that I'd claimed as my cereal bowl. *You can keep your Cream of Wheat,* I thought, as my brothers and I tore through boxes of cold cereal like we were shoveling coal into three runaway locomotives. Although Ma bought fake Oreos and other generic foods, she was yet to bring home fake cereal. "I get whatever's on sale," she announced each week, replenishing a shelf lined with colorful boxes. Thanks to coupons, we'd not yet been reduced to Fruity O's—and I was grateful.

Wally liked to hang out at the Honeycomb hideout, while Cockroach was cuckoo for Cocoa Puffs. I preferred a sweeter breakfast cereal. Although I enjoyed Count Chocula, Frankenberry and Booberry turned the milk pink and blue, and I loved that. Of course, there was always the same dilemma when eating sweetened cereal. It all came down to maintaining proper milk levels. *You finish your first bowl and there's milk left. You add cereal, but halfway through that bowl you need to add more milk. You finish that bowl and, once again, there's milk left. It was the sweetest milk—mother's milk—and you'd be insane to dump it down the kitchen sink. So, you do the only thing you can; you add more cereal, understanding that you're now at risk of slipping into a diabetic coma. The forehead becomes sweaty, the hands jittery. What to do? And let's not even get into the short window of opportunity between carving up the roof of your mouth with a fresh bowl of crunchy cereal, or sucking mush through your teeth because you've waited too long to dive in.*

"Where's the Beef," an old lady asked on TV, the comical commercial breaking me out of my trance.

Wally looked at Cockroach, who was sitting on the couch in his underwear. "Not here," he mumbled, grinning.

I laughed.

The next commercial featured a jingle. "Lite Brite, making things with light..."

"I want that," Cockroach announced, as he did during most toy commercials.

"Is there anything you don't want?" Pop asked him from his recliner.

"Mr. Microphone," Cockroach answered.

"He won't admit it," I said, quickly jumping in, "but Cockroach wants that Easy Bake Oven, too. I know he does."

"I do not," my little brother yelled.

Pop laughed.

Although I also liked seeing the new toy ads between cartoons, I felt a deeper connection to Tony the Tiger and Toucan Sam.

Throughout the morning, we also watched Conjunction Junction and Bill on Capitol Hill. It was as much learning as I was prepared to do on vacation. *School House Rock's pretty cool, though.*

After dumping all of our empty bowls into the sink for Ma to tackle with her giant green Palmolive bottle, we headed back to the living room for round two of our morning programming schedule—which included a rerun of my favorite family, The Brady Bunch.

Wally declined to join us, throwing on his coat and heading back down into the cellar.

"Does he have a girlfriend down there or something?" Pop asked.

I looked at Cockroach and smiled. "A boyfriend, I think."

For the next two hours, Pop, me and Cockroach watched all of the wrestling greats: Chief Jay Strongbow, Ivan Putski, George "The Animal" Steele and Tag-Team Champions, Mr. Fuji and Mr. Tenaka. In my opinion, these were all undercard matches, leading up to the big show.

When Andre the Giant stepped over the top rope and into the ring to face off against four midget wrestlers, even Pop slid to the edge of his seat. "This is gonna be a good one," he predicted.

I agreed, thinking, *I love when they all swarm Andre the Giant.*

Although the match went back and forth a few times—each opponent getting the referee to slap the canvas twice—the pack of angry little men proved victorious. It was rare. With my mouth hung open, I looked to Pop for some sort of explanation.

"Your grandpa used to say that God never put the heart of a lion into an elephant," he said, grinning. "Sometimes you just gotta want it more than the next guy."

Nodding, I immediately thought about Wally. *I hope that's true.*

I wasn't sure whether professional wrestling was real or fake, but Pop treated it like it was the real deal. *That's good enough for me,* I thought.

Ma stepped into the room to find me and Cockroach lying on the floor like cord wood, flat on our bellies. "After lunch, you guys are getting out of this house. You're wasting the day away."

"Ugh . . ."

"Do you want to go sledding today?" Pop asked us out of the blue.

"Yes!" Cockroach squealed and was already on his feet, ready to get dressed.

"That'd be awesome, Pop," I said, trying to act more mature.

Smiling, Ma left the room.

"Okay," he said, before looking toward the living room door and lowering his voice to a whisper, "but we have to run an errand first, okay?"

"Awww . . ." Cockroach started.

Pop locked eyes with him. Within a millisecond, my brother was stared into silence.

"Your mom's birthday is next week and we need to get her something nice. She doesn't know it yet, but Memere, Aunt Phyllis and Uncle Skinny are coming over tonight."

Saturday's usually the night Ma shampoos her hair, I remembered, *now what's she gonna do?*

"Ugh . . . Aunt Phyllis," Cockroach complained.

Although Pop spared my brother the stink eye, I knew he understood. Having to kiss Aunt Phyllis was inhumane; her upper lip felt like a push broom, and her breath was a mix of stale tobacco and sour clams. The holidays were the worst, requiring several kisses. It was a heavy price to pay for a barrel of plastic monkeys, a cardboard kaleidoscope or some pair of cheap handcuffs that drew blood.

"They're just going to show up?" I asked.

Pop shook his head. "Memere's gonna call later and ask if Mom and I want to play cards." He smirked. "Your mother's never turned down a game of pitch in her life."

"Cool," I said, excited at the opportunity to see my mother surprised. *If anyone deserves it, it's her,* I thought.

"We'll tell Mom that we're going sledding, but keep the rest of it to ourselves, okay?" He looked directly at Cockroach.

"Okay, Pop," he promised.

"Good boy."

As we finished our clandestine conversation, Wally emerged from the cellar—his new favorite place—with a basket full of dried laundry for our mother to fold. Although Ma required that we wash and dry our own clothes, she still folded everything and put it away for us.

Ma entered the living room, complaining, "I don't know how you boys can lose so many socks."

My brothers and I avoided eye contact with her—and each other.

"I'm going to take the boys sledding," Pop announced, before looking to my older brother. "You coming with us, Wally?"

Wally shook his head. "Can't, Pop. I have to get my paper route done."

My father smiled proudly. "A working man," he said, "I get it."

"That's fine, Walter," my mother said, "but don't be there all day. My mother's coming over with Phyllis tonight to play pitch."

"Really?" he said, playing stupid. "Isn't she throwing an Avon party or something tonight?" His eyes immediately went to Cockroach, who was wearing the perfect mask of ignorance.

"It's been rescheduled to next week," Ma said.

The old man smirked. "So sweet Phyllis is coming over, huh?"

Ma slapped his arm. "She's my sister, Walter, and she's welcome here any time."

"Of course," Pop said, kissing her neck, "what are you making to eat?"

My ears perked.

"We'll see," she said. "Why don't you invite your mother? I'm sure she'd like to get out of that house for a while."

Pop half-shrugged. "I will, but I doubt she'll come. She lives like a spider now, holed up in her cave." He grinned. "But I'm sure Skinny will come over."

"Skinny?" Ma repeated, her tone clear that she'd rather not see him.

"He's my brother, Emma, and he's welcome here any time," Pop said, echoing her very words.

Ma slapped his arm again.

"Might be nice to have them all over, I guess," he mumbled, ". . . the in-laws and the outlaws."

I laughed.

As I was getting dressed, Ma caught me alone—like a sick gazelle that had strayed from the pack. "Before you go sledding, I need you to run to the corner store for me," she said, before rattling off a list of items to be placed on her tab. "Two loaves of bread, two gallons of milk, and two packs of cigarettes—Carlton 100s, the red pack." While the first two items were intended to keep us alive, she claimed that she needed the cigarettes to keep her sane. It always made me laugh that she specified the brand of cigarettes, like I hadn't shagged hundreds of packs of Carlton 100s for her over the years.

"Can I get something for myself, Ma?" I asked.

"Fine," she said, "but no candy. It'll rot out your teeth." She locked eyes with me. "And don't tell your brothers. I'm not made of money, you know."

No kidding, I thought. Long ago, I'd realized we were poor and that we were essentially hillbillies. For a while, I didn't know what to think about either. In time, I decided to embrace both. *I am what I am,* I thought. *Besides, not everyone can enjoy cucumber sandwiches and English muffin pizzas.*

"Oh," she added, "and grab me a couple of Sky Bars. I need something sweet today." Although Ma had her rules, they normally didn't apply to her.

Sure, Ma, I thought. *Do as I say and not as I do. I get it.*

It wasn't just cold outside; the world was frozen solid with no sign of thawing any time soon, so I hustled as fast as I could to run my mother's errand.

The corner store—R&S Variety—sat on the corner of State Road and Wilbur Avenue, the place where we got our discreet fix for a bad sweet tooth. Outside, a Coca Cola machine and an ice machine stood guard on either side of the front door, while a padlocked Sunbeam Bread bin—with a young, red-headed girl painted on the front—sat on the side of the small, brick building.

The heavy door swung open, triggering a brass bell that warned Mr. Sedgeband that—like it or not—he had a customer. It was dark enough in the store that it took my frozen eyes a few seconds to adjust. The store's windows, papered in old advertisements, were so filthy that only a few shreds of sunlight were able push their way in.

I hated being alone in the place with Old Man Sedgeband and his silent sidekick, Oscar. In record time, I grabbed all the items on my mother's wish list—along with a Charlston Chew and Yoohoo for myself, and a pack of watermelon Bubble Yum for Cockroach—and placed them onto the cloudy glass counter. *What Ma doesn't know won't hurt her,* I thought. As usual, I ignored my mother's double standard, accepting that although hypocrisy was a huge part of childhood I didn't need to abide. "And two packs of Carlton 100s," I told the hairy-eared store owner, "all on my mother's tab."

Old Man Sedgeband allowed tabs for the adults in the neighborhood. Though the shrewd businessman charged interest—always calculated in his favor, causing many arguments to take place when a debt was settled—Sedgeband sometimes threatened to cut off the tab if it wasn't paid in full. Most folks, including both my parents, refused to return until they needed something and had no choice but to send their runners back into the old-codger's extortion ring. *It's an ingenious scam*, I decided. Sedgeband knew everyone's business, allowing the neighborhood kids to run cigarettes, beer and other items home to their lazy parents. No one liked the old crook, but when they didn't have to see his scowling face he did a pretty fair volume of business— the neighborhood kids providing the free home delivery to boot. For us same kids, though, it was strictly cash and carry.

The old man surveyed the items on the counter, nodded once and then scribbled the tally into his green, spiral notebook. After double-checking the figures, he placed the goods into a paper bag. "Tell your mother her tab's getting up there."

"I will," I said, happy to get out of the place.

Sedgeband returned to his checker game with Oscar, his simple-minded partner.

On my walk home, I drank the pint of chocolate water, while tucking the long candy bar up my sleeve for later.

Returning home, I smelled fried bacon and bound up the stairs that led to our second floor apartment. The narrow wooden staircase, encased in horsehair plaster that was in a constant state of crumbling, was dirtier than anything I'd just stepped on outside.

I burst through the front door to feel a wave of heat hit my face and to also discover that it was feeding time again. *Ma made BLTs,* I thought excitedly, *a stack and a half of them.* She'd used two pounds of bacon, a loaf of bread, a head of lettuce and three tomatoes sliced thin. After emptying half the jar of Miracle Whip, we were in business.

I love BLTs, I thought, my mouth watering over the smell. I threw off my coat and placed the paper bag onto the kitchen table.

"Did you get everything?" she asked.

I nodded, my mouth already stuffed with a giant bite of the sandwich.

"Cold out?"

I shook my head. "Worse than that," I told her between chews. "It's freezing."

The family sat together, tearing through that small mountain of sandwiches like it was our last meal.

Oh . . . I thought. "Ma, Old Man Sedgeband told me to tell you that he needs a payment on the tab."

She sighed heavily. "The tab that never ends," she muttered.

Probably because I'm in there every day, charging things for you, I thought.

As my little brother and I got dressed for our sledding adventure, Ma helped Cockroach get ready. "Layers," she kept repeating, "you boys have to dress in layers." Donning two pairs of pants, as well as multiple shirts and sweatshirts, we were as mismatched as our mother's glassware.

"What if the hill's too steep?" Cockroach asked, his voice quivering with fear-based anticipation.

"Your father wouldn't put you in danger," Ma said, trying to soothe his dark imagination. "You know that, right?"

We slid bread bags—Sunbeam or Wonder Bread—over our socks to provide a second line of defense against the cold wet snow.

"What if I get hurt, Ma?" Cockroach asked, clearly not listening to her.

"You're a big boy now, Alphonse. You need to try new things."

We then squeezed black rubber boots over our sneakers; these had steel clips which, by the time I received Wally's hand-me-downs, were mostly broken. Although the boots remained the same size, our feet grew faster than Pinocchio's nose, so the boots fit like seal skins and were nearly impossible to get on.

"What if . . ."

"Enough, Alphonse!" Ma snapped, her forehead glistening in sweat from wrestling the welded boots.

I shook my head. *Cockroach is afraid of everything,* I thought, *earwigs, roller coasters and those Sleestaks from Land of the Lost. He hates mice, the Boogie Man and Mr. Peanut's monocle.* I chuckled aloud. *Snakes and bridges and heights . . . oh my!*

Two drab green snorkel jackets later—creating tunnel vision for both of us—and we were ready to go birthday gift shopping in Bradlees' overheated department store.

Pop's four-door station wagon was olive green, with fake wood paneling that had started peeling long before our father picked up the gem for three hundred dollars, a "real steal" that he took great pride in. The fenders were a rust color because they were rusted. The tires were retreads, with chains that Pop put on for the winter—steel links that probably saved our lives, given the lack of tire treads.

Cockroach and I climbed into the back seat. There wasn't just dirt on the car's rugs, it was frozen mud. There was a giant hole in the back floor, nothing but asphalt racing beneath our feet.

Atop an inch of dust on the dashboard sat several crumpled packs of Carlton 100 cigarettes and one Slim Jim still in the wrapper. According to Pop, "It's survival food, in case we ever break down. You gotta always have a game plan, boys . . . a game plan." There was also a broken pair of sunglasses, missing one arm, that Pop still wore if he forgot his good ones, a pen and small pad of paper, which I never saw him use, and some old yellowed receipts.

Pop turned the key in the ignition. The old wagon whined terribly to start, choking and sputtering in the frigid cold. As it fired up, Pop slapped the steering wheel in a show of affection. "You're too good to me, sweetheart," he said, equally surprised that it ran once more.

As we pulled out of the driveway and onto the road, the wagon sounded mean and throaty. *It's no wonder*, I thought. A few months before, Pop had dragged the exhaust pipe for as many miles as it took for it to finally give up and separate from the car.

Walking around Bradlees was a blur in the sweltering heat. While Pop located the item he had in mind, a new microwave oven, I became so hot and sweaty from my winter gear that I began to cook in my own juices in my maroon-colored Levi's corduroys.

The microwave was huge, maybe a quarter size of our refrigerator, and the box it came in was giving me some ideas. *Maybe we can use it to start a fort in our bedroom?*

As we headed to Sampson's Potato Farm for the best sledding in town, Pop made a quick stop at Lee's Market to pick up a bag of microwaveable popcorn.

"I don't know what the hell else your mother can cook in that damn thing," he said, returning to the station wagon. "I suppose she'll have to figure it out for herself." He paused. "Shit, I forgot to get her a birthday card." He peered into the rear-view mirror. "You boys will have to make one when we get home."

"Okay Pop," we said.

"You have what you need, markers and paper?"

"Yeah, Pop."

"All right then, let's go freeze our tails off."

We sat at the top of the snow-covered potato farm, where young Labrador retrievers were trained during the other three seasons. The snow was hard-packed, making it feel like ice beneath our backsides. I sat on the Flexible Flyer, a wooden sled with red steel runners. The idea was to steer the sled with your feet, while holding onto a frayed rope. Gravity, however, was the one in charge. Cockroach sat atop an inner tube that bounced down the hill more than it slid. I watched as he rode that thing like a bucking bronco, screaming right up until the moment he got tossed off and landed face first. I laughed so hard I thought I was going to pee through my layers of pants.

For the second run down the hill, and every run after that, we switched sleds. *I wish Donna was here sledding with us,* I daydreamed, *or I was with her—wherever that is.*

We didn't stay long. Both of us were suffering a permanent flow of snot that froze just above our top lips like pistachio ice cream moustaches.

"So gross," Pop said, waiting for us at the top of the hill.

"What, Pop?" Cockroach asked, breathing from his mouth.

Pop shook his head. "Just make sure you scrub your mugs when you get home and thaw out."

"Did you boys have fun?" our father asked on the ride home.

"Yes, thank you!" Cockroach squealed, trying to score his points for the day.

Pop looked directly at me in the rear-view mirror.

"It was okay," I said, shrugging.

"Someone's getting too old to go sledding?" he asked, grinning.

I shook my head. "I don't know, Pop. Other kids my age are starting to do much cooler stuff now and I . . . ."

"Don't be in such a hurry to grow up, Herbie," he said, cutting me off. "There's plenty of time for that." He held his grin. "Besides, if someone tries to tell you the Kool-Aid tastes that good, then you probably shouldn't drink it."

I had no idea what Pop meant. *All we ever drink is Kool-Aid,* I thought, picturing one of us yelling, *Hey Kool-Aid!* and the giant red pitcher crashing through the side of the station wagon. *Oh yeah!*

Pop slowed the wagon, causing me to search out the windshield for the reason. An elderly man was standing beside a parked car in the breakdown lane; he was holding a red metal gas can.

Oh no, I thought, *this is exactly what Ma warned Pop about.* I could still hear her voice. "Don't ever stop to pick up anyone with the kids in the car, Walt. With the nuts that walk this earth, you never know . . . and it's just not worth the risk."

As the station wagon skidded to a sideways stop, I was already wigged out.

"You think I can get a ride to the nearest gas station?" the wrinkled stranger asked, his head stuck inside the passenger-side window.

"That's why we stopped," Pop said. "Jump in. It's a little cold to run out of gas, ain't it?"

He nodded. "That's what I get for not checking the fuel gauge after the old lady took it to run errands."

"They can be thoughtful," Pop joked, obviously referring to women—*Ma included.*

Both men laughed. I found it too funny to be insulted for my mother and laughed along with them, making me feel like a man.

"Women," the older man said, sighing heavily. "My old lady used to be hotter than fish grease."

"Sure," Pop said, "but fish rot from the head down, am I right?"

"Ain't that the truth," the geezer said, laughing harder. "You from around here?"

"We are," Pop said.

"You hear about Charlie Potter?"

"I know Charlie," Pop said. "What about him?"

"He dropped dead yesterday."

"You're shittin' me?"

"I shit you not."

Pop whistled. "Well, when it's your time to go, it's your time to go."

"Sure, unless his wife helped him toward the light," the old man said.

We all laughed. *Maybe we didn't pick up a serial killer after all,* I thought, feeling relieved. I looked to my left. Cockroach's face was bleached white from having the unwelcome visitor aboard. *Poor little guy,* I thought, before shrugging it off. *At least his booger moustache is starting to thaw. That's something, anyway.*

"Poor Charlie," the old timer said, breaking the silence. "Loved his beer and scratch tickets."

"Sounds like he might have been my soul mate," Pop joked.

The old man chuckled before nodding a couple times. "I do appreciate the ride," he said, looking around the car.

Pop grinned. "This baby cost me three hundred bucks," he said, proudly—patting the steering wheel.

"Quite a steal," the old-timer mumbled, and I couldn't tell if he was being sarcastic.

Pop spotted me in the rear-view mirror, listening. He jerked his head back toward me. "The guy in the back seat, the bigger one, we could have named him asphalt." He smiled. "His mother's ass, my fault." He looked back in the mirror at me and smiled. "Then again, I guess each one of my boys could have taken that name."

Great, thanks Pop, I thought.

The old-timer laughed hard. "I'll have to remember that one," he said, "I'm sure the boys down at the Vets Club will get a kick out of it."

We stopped at the closest gas station a few miles away, filled the stranger's can and gave him a ride back to his car.

"Can't thank you enough," he told Pop, shaking his hand.

Pop nodded. "Happy we came by when we did."

As we drove away, Pop looked back into the rear-view mirror. "Now that's what you call a hot shit," he said.

We nodded in agreement, as brighter colors than white returned to Cockroach's face.

"No need for your mother to hear about him, though," Pop said. "Am I understood?"

We nodded again.

"I don't need to hear her bitchin'."

• • •

SATURDAY NIGHT

After a long visit to the bathroom, I stepped into our bedroom and smelled crayons—a much more welcoming scent. *I wish I could still color and get away with it*, I thought, before realizing Cockroach was working on Ma's birthday card. "How's it going?" I asked.

"Almost done," he reported. "You've been in there forever, Herbie, and I was tired of waiting."

"Good man," I told him. "You color better than I do, anyway."

Shaking his head, he added a few scratch and sniff stickers that he'd gotten from school onto the front of the card.

At my age, nothing smells good any more, I thought, feeling jealous.

Ma fed us before the rest of the family arrived. I had no idea what was on the adult menu, but I didn't care. My brothers and I felt like kings, eating TV dinners on TV trays, watching DEVO "Whip it good!" on MTV in the living room. Although we were one of the last families I knew to get cable, we'd finally reached the Promised Land: a box was placed on top of the floor console with an actual cable that ran from the box to a remote control. *Cutting-edge technology,* I thought. We now had access to MTV. *We now have everything.*

Prior to that, my brothers and I served as our father's remote control. While one of us would shag his beers, another would change the TV channel from McHale's Navy, Hee Haw or Gilligan's Island to Pop's favorite—M.A.S.H. "That Klinger's something else," Pop always commented, laughing hysterically.

There was no longer a need to adjust the rabbit's ears and fight the static that rivaled our father's beloved programs. All Pop needed to do was yell, "Boys!" in his loud voice and we were running; it was a tone that would send ice water through the veins of those who'd never heard it.

Fortunately, the old man's programs weren't on, so we were able to watch MTV. This new world felt like a miracle to me. Although Michael Jackson's music wasn't my jam, his Thriller video was absolutely mind blowing. *I never realized people could dance like that,* I thought, learning that I'd never be able to moon walk no matter how long I practiced, and that VJ Nina Blackwood was really opening up my universe. From Cutting Crew, The Buggles, and Bertie Higgins to Men Without Hats, Billy Squier and Thomas Dolby, I was hypnotized by these unique styles of music. Of course, the big hair bands—Poison, Ratt, Warrant—were thrown into the glorious line-up, as well.

We ate and we watched, everyone enjoying the silence that MTV commanded.

The first to arrive at our house was Memere, smelling like Jean Nate and looking as pretty as a winter lily.

"Hi Memere," we yelled out, rushing toward her with the usual onslaught of hugs and kisses. It didn't matter how old we got, our sweet grandmother's loving smile always reduced us to toddlers that needed hugs.

"Here's my angels," she purred, giving each of us a long squeeze.

"Oh, they're angels, all right," Ma mumbled.

Memere's head snapped toward her. "That's right," she said, defending us, "they're *my* angels."

The next to show up was Uncle Skinny, and the celebration continued. Although we weren't allowed to eat candy or drink soda, except on holidays, Uncle Skinny sneaked it to us every chance he could. "Here's my demons," he teased, palming us each a Bit O' Honey bar as we lined up to hug him.

We loved the generous man. We were sugar addicts—not one of us capable of ever knowing how many licks it took to get to the center of a Tootsie Pop—and Uncle Skinny was our dealer.

"Thanks, Uncle," Cockroach said, garnering a suspicious look from my mother.

"Oh, you don't have to thank me," Uncle Skinny said. "it's just a hug, and I've got plenty where that came from." He offered a subtle wink.

Satisfied, Ma looked away—never seeing Wally sock Cockroach in the arm for running his big mouth.

The last to arrive was my mother's older sister, Aunt Phyllis.

Wearing my best fake smile, I took a deep breath and stepped up like a man to receive my punishment.

Aunt Phyllis' lips felt like a cold snail on my cheek. She held it there just long enough to cause goosebumps, before slowly sliding it down my face like the mollusk was heading for home.

Please God, I thought, *make it stop*. I spotted Cockroach's eyes go wide with terror. *You're next*, I thought, trying to focus on that small shred of joy. *You're next, little brother.*

I loved when our family gathered and it always happened at Ma's kitchen table. Although I'm sure it wasn't her dream kitchen, she still loved the space. The wallpaper was a mix of vegetables and roosters, a real country motif. A large wooden spoon and matching fork hung on the wall, as though people wouldn't know it was a kitchen otherwise. The rotary phone, with its green-spiraled cord that reached the living room, hung on the opposite wall. The cord was so long that Ma could multi-task while watching her shows. The kitchen floor was covered in worm yellow linoleum, curling up and chipping at the corners. A few patches were missing—the high traffic areas where everyone walked or dragged kitchen chairs out from under the table—revealing the dark wood beneath it. There was a white gas cook stove, an old refrigerator and some scarred pine cabinets filled with the odds and ends Ma had collected over the years. The centerpiece of the room, however, was the Formica kitchenette table surrounded by six faux leather chairs, two of them mended with black electrical tape. Ma called it, "The family hub."

Before the card game started, Memere lit a few candles on top of the chocolate cake she'd concealed since arriving.

"Oh, you guys," Ma said, blushing, while everyone sang Happy Birthday to her.

I wasn't sure how old my mother was, but I knew that if my grandmother had lit the correct number of candles, she would have melted the cake—*maybe even burned down the apartment.*

While Pop left for a few minutes, Cockroach handed her the homemade card, making sure that she knew he was the lone artist.

"Oh, thank you, Alphonse," she said, "you're so thoughtful."

Although he smiled, he was smart enough to avoid eye contact with me and Wally.

Pop returned from the car with the frozen microwave. Without any great fanfare, he plopped the unwrapped monstrosity down on the table in front of his shocked wife. "Happy Birthday, hon," he said, bending to kiss her on the lips.

"Oh Walt," she squealed, "it's beautiful!" You would have thought Pop had just given her the world. "I love it." She jumped up from her chair and kissed our father again before hurrying to wrestle the contraption out of the box.

Goodbye Jiffy-Pop, I thought, thinking that we'd just entered a new era and feeling a little conflicted about it.

Even out of the box, the microwave was giant, with a timer-type dial located on the front and a dark mysterious window to view whatever was cooking inside. Ma put in the popcorn first. Within seconds, it smelled like we were sitting in the middle of a cinema, getting ready to watch *Red Dawn* or *Fast Times at Ridgemont High*.

"It cooks so fast," Memere commented, as Ma removed the inflated popcorn bag from the box. "There's no way that can be good for anyone."

Ma opened the steaming bag and we all dove in like a pack of hungry dingos.

"It's delicious," Uncle Skinny commented. "Never tasted popcorn so good in my life."

Excited, Ma grabbed a loaf of frozen bread from the freezer. "Let's see how good it defrosts." She threw in the bread, closed the door and set the timer. The moment she pressed *Defrost* and the loaf began to spin, I knew something wasn't right. Sparks began flying inside the microwave.

"Shut it off, Emma," Pop yelled. "Shut the damn thing off!"

Ma did.

Carefully, Pop removed the bread and inspected it. "It's the twist tie," he reported. "The twist tie has a strip of metal in it."

"And you can't put metal in a microwave?" Ma said; it was more of a question than a statement.

Pop looked at her until it became awkward. "You should probably read the instruction booklet before you kill us all, Emma."

"Best damn popcorn I ever tasted," Uncle Skinny repeated.

Once everyone had stepped away from the microwave's window and lost interest in the great science experiment, Pop fired up his Hi-Fi stereo, alternating between his record albums and 8-tracks. *Either way*, I thought, *his music really sucks*. From Ernest Tubb and Hank Williams to Elvis Presley and Jerry Lee Lewis, halfway through the song the track would jump to the next song with a distinct *kathunk*. Although it drove me nuts, no one else seemed to mind. *Pop needs to come out of the dark ages and start playing cassettes*, I thought.

Wally was doing his own thing in the living room and I figured, *He's probably still sulking about being bullied on the bus*. I felt bad about it, though not bad enough to miss out on the adult conversation. Cockroach and I sat in the shadows of our bedroom—with the plastic accordion door cracked open—quietly listening.

Uncle Skinny got up from the table and headed for the bathroom.

"Make sure you hit the bowl this time, Skinny," Pop said, laughing. "I swear he's got the bladder of a canary and the aim of a fruit bat."

"It's not funny," Ma said, before yelling toward the bathroom. "I'm so sick of cleaning boys' piss off that floor."

I looked at Cockroach and shrugged.

"Hey, did you hear about those two kids that were reported missing yesterday in Fall River?" Uncle Skinny asked, returning to the kitchen. "They did a full neighborhood search and the cops found them walking in the woods behind Earl Street. I guess both kids were naked. They were screaming and crying and . . ."

"Lower your voice, Skinny," Ma said. "The boys might be listening." She glanced toward the bedroom, but Cockroach and I were sitting completely still in the shadows so she didn't see us. We'd learned long ago that even the slightest movement could give us away.

Uncle Skinny lowered his voice to just under his normal scream. "The kids reported that they were walking home from the corner store when a man in a white van pulled up in front of them and offered them candy."

I quietly closed the door a few more inches and turned my ear to concentrate.

"Piece of garbage," Pop hissed.

"I heard about this on the news," Memere said. "It's so terrible. Honestly, what has this world come to?"

"I guess the kids tried to run, but he pulled them into the van where he held them at knife point. He then tied them up, beat and raped them—threatening to kill them both if they ever told," Uncle Skinny added.

I swallowed hard and looked at Cockroach. *He looks like he's going to faint,* I thought.

"They should take that knife and skin the freak alive," Pop said, bringing me back to the conversation.

"Those kids are lucky he set them free in the woods behind their house."

"Yeah, they're lucky, all right," Aunt Phyllis chimed in.

"Last I heard," Uncle Skinny concluded, "the cops are asking for help in locating the white van."

There was silence for a moment, enough time to hear my heart beating out of my chest. I looked at my little brother again. As expected, he was wide-eyed and nearly hyperventilating.

"We should keep an eye out," Pop said.

I was preparing to hyperventilate, myself, when my father saved me.

"Hey, did you hear about Michael Jackson?" he asked, changing the subject. "He was filming a Pepsi commercial when his hair caught on fire."

"That's terrible," Ma said, alternating between her microwave popcorn and sucking on a Carlton 100. The room was engulfed in a cloud of heavy smoke.

"And grease fires are tough to put out," Uncle Skinny added, sipping from his beer.

"I heard they just launched the Space Shuttle Challenger a few weeks ago," Ma chimed in.

"Wasted money, if you ask me," Memere said.

"Not surprising, Ma, coming from someone who doesn't believe that we actually walked on the moon," my mother said.

"I'm telling you, the whole thing was one big hoax."

"I agree with you, Ma," Aunt Phyllis said.

"Of course you do," Pop muttered under his breath. Ma cleared her throat prompting him to change the subject again. "And gas just went up to a dollar ten a gallon," he said. "Can you imagine that?"

"I remember when it was a quarter a gallon," Uncle Skinny said.

Shaking his head, Pop finished another beer. "This guy, Reggie, at work is looking at a brand-new pick-up truck. It's gonna cost him nine grand for all the bells and whistles. Isn't that crazy?"

"That is crazy," Uncle Skinny agreed.

There was quiet for a few minutes, while they played out their hands.

"It's awful," Memere commented, breaking the silence, "that subway vigilante, Bernhard Goetz, shooting four black kids on a Manhattan subway."

"I don't think they were kids," Uncle Skinny countered, "and for all we know . . ."

"That's enough, Arthur," Memere said, stopping him from saying something incredibly ignorant.

"I heard that the Russians are boycotting the Los Angeles Olympic games," Uncle Skinny said, attempting to save face.

"That's right," Aunt Phyllis said, "but it's in response to the US boycotting the Moscow Olympics. You know that, right?"

"Well, the recession hasn't gotten any better, I know that," Pop said, getting up to grab another beer.

"That's what you get with trickle-down economics." Ma added, cynically. "The one-percenters don't even want to throw us their scraps."

"Reagan's a jackass," Aunt Phyllis said.

"But he looks dapper in those brown suits he wears," Memere said.

Dapper? I thought, stifling a laugh. I couldn't tell if she was joking.

They played more cards, the shuffle making its way around the table.

"Hey, what'th the differenth between an actor and a politi-than?" Uncle Skinny asked in a pronounced lisp.

"I don't know, Arthur, what is it?" Memere asked.

"You got me," he said. "I'd thay they're one and the thame."

Everyone laughed, except Ma. "What's with the lisp, Skinny?" she asked.

My warped uncle chuckled. "Some queer just started at my work and I want to be able to . . ."

"Knock it off," Ma scolded, "the boys could be listening."

"Is there any group of people you don't make fun of?" Memere asked him.

"Nope," he said, proudly, "that would be called discrimination."

As they continued to play cards, I realized, *It doesn't take a village to raise children in our family, it takes an asylum.* I turned to Cockroach. "Do you wanna play Atari?"

"Which game?" he asked.

"Either Combat or Air Sea Battle," I told him.

"I don't like Combat."

"Air Sea Battle it is then." It was a game we both enjoyed.

The screen appeared in layers of blue: baby blue on the bottom where the ocean was depicted, getting darker with each line going up until reaching the sky, which was navy blue. We controlled small canons, shooting at targets— from airplanes to fish—that passed by.

"Just one thing," he said.

"What's that?"

"Can we close the door all the way?" he asked.

"Good idea," I said, "there's some really bad influences sitting at that kitchen table."

Once our eyeballs started to itch after a few hours of playing video games and Cockroach turned off the light, I slid our bedroom door open just enough to hear the adults. There was no better feeling or sense of peace than to fall asleep to the drone of familiar voices— people who instilled love and security—*no matter how nuts they are.*

To the distinct sound of cards being shuffled, my small world slowed to a crawl. *I can't wait to learn how to shuffle like that,* I thought, before nodding off.

CHAPTER 4

SUNDAY

There were nightmares and then there were nightmares. This one was a doozy, making my body twitch from some terribly vivid details...

We met Clarence at Victor Pavao's eleventh birthday party. The bash was hosted at one of those arcade-style pizza joints. As Pop waited patiently for the festivities to end, he approached the establishment's happy clown. "What the hell's a man your age—40 plus—doing making a living dressed in big shoes and a red nose?" he asked, kicking off a crude line of questioning.

The clown honked his horn. "I do adult parties too."

Pop gritted his teeth. "Go near my kid and I'll kill ya!"

An odd-looking, middle-aged man with beady eyes approached Pop, laughing. "I wath wondering the thame thing," he said in a heavy lisp. "I'm Clarenth," he added, extending his hand.

They shook hands.

"Good to meet ya, Clarence. I'm Walt." Pop sized him up. "So how'd you get roped into this shindig?"

"Well, it'th only Reggie and I now," Clarence said, pointing toward a young boy who was playing on a Woody Woodpecker pinball machine. "My wife pathed away a year ago." A spray of saliva escaped his lips with each word spoken.

Pop twisted his mouth in sympathy, slowly wiping the spittle from his face. "Oh, I'm sorry to hear that."

Clarence nodded his appreciation. "I'm here for more punithment, I gueth," the quirky man said, before looking at me and grinning. His jagged teeth appeared sharp—at least the ones that remained—like a Swiss Army knife.

Goosebumps covered my body. *What a super creepy dude,* I thought.

As the spit-machine went on, Pop took a half-step back. "I got Reggie a hamthter for hith birthday a while back. He named the rodent Mr. Templeton." He shrugged once. "Anyway, a couple of weekth ago, the week it wath hotter than hell, I went into the kid'th room and notithed that Mr. Templeton wath trembling. I thcanned the cage and thaw that the water bottle wath empty. Poor Mr. Templeton did not look good at all. He'd clearly gone blind and couldn't even walk."

"Oh, that's not good," Pop said.

Clarence nodded. "I think he wath having a theizure, tho I filled the water bottle, put him near the nozzle and hoped for the beth-t. I figured if the rat made the night, then it had a real will to live, you know?"

Pop snickered.

"In the morning, I went in and tapped on the plexi-glath," Clarence explained, "The little fur ball didn't move. I tapped again. Nothing. I picked up the cage and gave it a good thake. It never woke." He shrugged. "Tho I broke off the tube and put the whole cage—Mr. Templeton, and all—into a trash bag, leaving it out on the thidewalk. I told Reggie there had been a wonderful little theremony. Of courthe, he wanted to know why hith pet died. I told him,

'Becauthe God called him home.' I never let on that it wath proba-bly 120 degreeth in that plexi-glath cage, with no water for the poor thing." He grinned the eeriest grin. "I kept that one to mythelf."

Pop laughed, surprising me. "You're quite a storyteller," he told Clarence, and I knew then that my father was going to become friends with the weirdo.

Big mistake! I screamed in my head. *Let's just leave, Pop. You shouldn't be talking to this monster.*

"You gotta keep laughing," Clarence said. "It'th the only med-ithine that heal-th the thoul." He grinned at me again. This time, his crooked smile appeared anything but friendly.

Oh . . .

"You should come by the house some time with Reggie," Pop said, "I'm sure the boys would love to play with him."

Are you crazy? I thought. *We're not even sure that Reggie's his kid.*

As if he were reading my mind, Clarence looked straight at me. "We'd love to come by, Walt," he said. "I've been dyin' to get out of the houthe."

I swallowed hard.

• • •

My eyes flew open. My sheets were soaked in sweat, my heart, thump-ing like Tonto's war drum. I sprung up to a seated position in bed, trying to catch my breath. *What the hell,* I thought, trying to make sense of the twisted dream. As I began to calm my breathing, it started coming back to me in fragmented bits and pieces. I wished it hadn't.

I thought about Clarence, the frightening man in my dream. I could still picture every detail of him: the beady eyes, the Jaws-inspired grin, with those serrated teeth. *Think of something else*, I told myself. *That's the only way to get Freddie Kruger's smile out of your head. Think of something else.*

I jumped out of bed in search of my personal adviser—the Magic 8 Ball. For the past several years, the shiny plastic ball was responsible for most of my major decisions.

Our cousins sometimes played with a Ouiji board for a peek into the future, but I was too scared to open any door I might not be able to close. *The Magic 8 Ball is as far as I'll take it,* I decided. *Ouija boards scare the hell out of me.* I definitely missed my grandpa and would have loved to communicate with him, but not enough to crack open some invisible portal and allow a less-than-friendly spirit through. *I saw Poltergeist,* I thought, *I'm all set with that.*

I shook the smooth ball three times "Does Donna like me?" I quietly asked the plastic sage.

I took a deep breath before looking into the circular window.

My answer appeared on the small triangle floating in purple fluid—*Reply hazy, try again.*

I did exactly as instructed. "Does Donna like me?" I whispered.

I shook it three more times—harder this time—and took another deep breath before looking into the tiny window.

Concentrate and ask again.

I closed my eyes. *Come on, now,* I thought, *I need to know if Donna is the one.* I shook the swishing ball multiple times. *Is she?* I turned it at different angles. When I finally flipped it over, I couldn't believe my eyes.

The message read, *Don't count on it.*

Nope, I don't think so, I told myself, refusing to believe the prediction. *We'll try again later.*

Sunday morning began a little slower than the day before. Our parents had been playing cards for a jar of pennies into the wee hours of the morning, so we had the complete run of the house to either sleep in or create mayhem.

We quietly closed Ma and Pop's bedroom door and turned on the TV—spinning the volume down to low. While Popeye and Brutus fought over Olive's affections, I ate a half box of Capn' Crunch cereal. *Maybe we should just relax in front of the TV today?* I thought. The Jetsons buzzed around in their flying car, as I committed to finishing off the rest of the cereal in the box.

Still stuck in silent mode, Wally finished his sugary breakfast and hurried to get dressed. The Sunday newspaper—nearly twice as thick as the daily paper with all its heavy inserts and advertisements—had to be delivered in the morning.

I couldn't help it. Every time Wally returned from his paper route on his ten-speed Schwinn, his face ruddy and wind burned from the bitter cold, he shared a new story that was either funny or scary. I always felt jealous that I couldn't experience the same big world out there. "Let me tag along, Wally," I pleaded. "The newspapers are so heavy on Sunday and I can help carry some of them for you."

For the first time ever, my big brother paused to give it some thought.

Please . . . please . . . please . . . I begged in my head.

As if he were deciding whether I should live or die, he finally nodded. "Fine," he said, "but you'd better keep up with me."

"I will!" I squealed, overwhelmed with excitement.

Trying to calm myself, I tiptoed into my parents' bedroom and tapped my mother on the shoulder until one eye opened. "Wally said I can tag along with him on his paper route today," I told her. "Can I go . . . please?"

She yawned once, making me do the same. She then gazed at me with a blank stare.

"Can I have your permission to go?" I asked, hoping she was too tired to object.

"Ummm, I don't know, Herbie," she said, reluctant to give me the free pass. "It's far away and you'll be on your bike . . . I . . . I don't know." Yawning again, she turned to my father and pushed him. "Walt, Herbie's asking if he can go with Wally on his paper route." She looked toward the window at the frozen world outside. "And I don't know if it's such a good idea. Maybe it'd be safer if he went in a few weeks when the weather's a little more . . ."

"Just be careful, Herbie," Pop moaned, without ever opening his eyes.

I couldn't believe it. "Thanks," I said, kissing my mother's cheek and sprinting out of the room before either one of them could change their mind.

It took me and Wally no time to get dressed in multiple layers against the cold, leaving the bread bags at home for this run.

"It's not fair," Cockroach complained, pouting at our bedroom door.

"Life's not fair," I called back to him, as if I'd just passed through some invisible threshold into adulthood.

Thick bundles of newspapers were piled in front of R&S Variety for Wally and Richard Giles, the neighborhood paperboys, to collect. The yellow plastic strap, which was supposed to be wrapped tightly around the bundle, was loosely blowing in the wind.

"Shit," Wally said, immediately going to his knees to count the stack. "Shit," he repeated, "I'm short two."

"What are you gonna do?" I asked, oblivious to the vicious game.

My snarling brother shook his head. "I got no choice. I have to go buy them back from Old Man Sedgeband."

"Buy them back?"

Wally nodded. "If the old bastard gets to the bundles first, he always snatches one or two off the top."

"Are you kidding me?"

Shaking his head again, Wally slid the remaining papers into his soiled canvas bag with the thick orange shoulder strap.

Evidently, the newspaper distributor was a smart man to dump the bundles in front of the corner store. It didn't take long for Wally and Richard to learn that if they didn't get to their packages in a timely manner, then Old Man Sedgeband was going to steal from their bundles and cut into their meager profits.

"You should tell Pop," I suggested. "He'd strangle the old crook."

Wally flung the bag over his shoulder and across his chest. "Yup, he would," he said, "and then I'd be out of a paper route." He stepped into R&S Variety with me on his heels.

Furious, Wally never addressed Old Man Sedgeband as we entered the darkened store.

The silence was too much for me. "Hello, Mr. Sedgeband," I said nervously.

The old timer looked at me, but never replied.

Old Man Sedgeband was a scarecrow of a man, with serpent eyes that peered out from Coke-bottle glasses. His long-sleeve flannel shirt smelled like our shed. Atop three stacked milk crates, he sat behind a smudged glass case that he used as a counter, playing checkers with his mute partner—Oscar.

Oscar had a pronounced twitch and, with the exception of a few odd jobs that he performed around the store, he worked as often as he spoke. Though he and Sedgeband played game after game of checkers, I'd never heard them exchange a single word.

Arms crossed, Old Man Sedgeband gawked at me, filling his tiny store with clouds of blue pipe smoke.

Although I hated the place, it was our one-stop-shop for satisfying our daily cravings.

Beyond the candy case, old plank floorboards led to outdated displays that offered even more outdated goods. The short stacks of cans and bottles were covered in several seasons of dust. The magazine rack was ancient, though it hardly mattered when it came to the comic books. A toy selection included paddle balls, jacks, yoyos, and whiffle ball bats. For last minute gifts, you could choose from nail clippers, plastic combs (though no one bought them because they looked used), nylons, playing cards, or corncob pipes. The one-shelf pharmacy offered feminine supplies and condoms, causing embarrassed giggles. There was also aspirin, band-aids and rubbing alcohol. For some of the neighborhood parents, Sedgeband carried rolling papers and cheap wine. For our parents, he was kind enough to stock quarts of Narragansett, Schaeffer and Miller High Life beer, as well as cartons of Carlton 100s. *Our family's probably paying the light bill in this dump,* I thought.

For my brothers and I, as the years passed, YooHoos competed with Slush Puppies. This didn't last long, though. Old Man Sedgeband skimped on the syrup, and a cup of ice for fifty cents just didn't cut it. Half-filled bags of stale popcorn and nuts sat unsold. A full ice cream cooler housed Nutty Buddy cones, ice cream sandwiches, strawberry shortcake bars, Creamsicles and Fudgsicles. If Cockroach and I weren't buying from the candy case, we were investing our scanty allowances in the ice cream cooler—regardless of the season. Wally, the working man, bought whatever he wanted, whenever he wanted. I was so jealous, thinking, *He always gets to do everything first.*

Wally slapped two newspapers onto the counter.

The old man smirked. "That's a shame, boy," he grumbled. "I got screwed out of two papers myself today."

"What a coincidence," Wally countered, his face crimson red.

The creepy man's smirk turned into a full-blown smile.

I wished it hadn't. I wouldn't have been surprised to watch a centipede climb out from behind his yellowed, broken teeth— just like the Grinch who stole Christmas. I did a double-take. *Those are the same exact teeth I saw in my dream last night,* I realized. *Those are Clarence's teeth.*

I eyed the half-empty box of wax red lips and black moustaches sitting in the candy case beside a handful of Mr. Bones candy coffins, leftover from Halloween. For whatever reason, flavored wax played a big role in my life. Back then, I also enjoyed those wax bottles, where you bit off the tip and sucked out the few drops of colored sugar water. It didn't hurt that there was no shelf life on these taste-less beauties. Sometimes, they were still available at R&S right into the summer.

I placed twenty-seven cents—mostly pennies I'd discreetly claimed under the kitchen table while my parents played cards—on the counter and bent to gaze into the penny candy case. "I'll take one of those wax lips. And give me three root beer barrels, two pixie sticks, five Swedish fish, five fireballs and two Bazooka bubble gums." Although the gum lost its flavor after three or four chews, I loved the tiny Jughead comics that were folded inside the wrapper.

Abandoning his checker game, Sedgeband snatched up the change with his gnarled fingers and threw it into his massive, brass cash register. Annoyed with the interruption, he snapped open a small, brown paper bag and quickly began to fill the small order, recounting twice to ensure that he wasn't on the losing end of the deal.

Wally turned to me. "Let's go," he said, leading me back into the driving wind.

We weren't ten feet from the store when my big brother gave me a sideways look that suggested he wasn't pleased with me.

"What?" I asked him, tossing a fireball into my gob.

"That nasty old bastard just stole from me and you turn around and give him another twenty-five cents." He shook his head. "Nice brother, you are."

"Give me a break, Wally," I said, quick to defend myself. "You'll be in there this afternoon spending ten times what I just did on full-size candy bars." I shook my head. "Besides, it was twenty-seven cents," I added, happy to burrow even deeper under his skin.

"Whatever," he said, jumping on his Schwinn to head out on the trail.

Placing the wax red lips between my teeth, I hurried after him. *You need to schelax, Lil' Walt*, I thought.

Wally's paper route encompassed Davis Road, Gifford Road, Rock Street and Faulkner Street straight up to Wilbur Avenue, where Richard Giles' territory began. Navigating the icy roads on our bikes was treacherous. We didn't own helmets; those were only used by the kids whose parents could afford new bicycles. We rode miles from our apartment in the driving wind, while our parents snored peacefully in their bed. Given the terrible weather, I thought, *I can't believe Ma and Pop are okay with me being out here delivering newspapers. They must be insane.*

At one point, we reached the auto repair garage on Davis Road, an old filling station that still had a soda pop machine. It was freezing, so Ronny, the head mechanic, let us sit on our bikes in the warm bay to enjoy our well-deserved break. With the sound of air guns removing lug nuts, we sipped two Cokes from green glass bottles—Wally's treat.

"Thanks," I told him.

He nodded "You earned it."

For the first time, I felt the pride of having actually worked for something; it was a feeling I very much enjoyed and intended to experience again, many times over.

Wally smiled at me. "Just so you know," he announced out of the blue, "I've been looking for another paper route so I can give you this one."

"Really?" I said, completely blown away.

He nodded. "I heard that Dewey's thinking about giving up his Herald News route and I told him that I want it when he does."

"Really?" I asked, too excited for other words. My mind began to race with the opportunities this would afford. *I could trade in the Bazooka bubble gum for a pouch of Big League Chew.* It's what Wally chewed. Even if I saved my allowance for weeks, Big League Chew was still too expensive for my taste.

"Yes, really. It can be a real pain in the ass out here, especially when the weather sucks," he said, taking a swig, "but it's awesome not having to go to Ma and Pop for money."

"Wow," I mumbled, my whirling mind still imagining how life-changing this would be. *Maybe I can even pay off the Columbia Record contract and keep myself out of jail? Of course, I'd have to trade in this old banana seat bike for a ten speed. But it would sure beat picking drops at Del Mac Apple Orchards this summer for twenty-five cents a crate.*

"Can you keep a secret?" Wally asked.

From his face, I could tell he was going to let me in on it either way. I nodded.

"Ma's borrowed money from me twice already for cigarettes."

"Really?" I said, regretting the overused word as soon as it left my lips.

He smiled proudly before taking another sip of his hard-earned soda. "Yup, but that stays between us, okay?"

"Of course," I said, impressed with how grown up Wally seemed to me now. For whatever reason, I was equally excited at the possibility of being able to lend my mother money when she ran out of smokes.

As we prepared to ride back into the freezing cold, I said, "Hey, you've been quiet the last few days. I'm guessing it's because of that bullshit with Owen on the bus. If you need to talk about . . ."

"Don't worry about it," he said, taking off ahead of me. "I'm fine."

Although I didn't buy his answer, I respected it.

As we delivered newspaper after newspaper in the biting wind, I fantasized about making my own money year-round. *It'll be so much easier than having to hustle money in the summer*, I thought. Cockroach and I sometimes scoured R&S Variety's small parking lot, searching for loose change that may have fallen out of cars as people ran into the little shop of horrors for an ice cream sandwich or a pack of cigarettes. We also collected aluminum cans that went into huge clear plastic bags that were stored in the shed, stinking the place to high heaven. We cashed these in twice a year and, as a kid, it was an absolute windfall. *But there's no way to make money in the winter*, I thought, *unless Wally can give me his paper route.* I felt so excited that I wanted to scream—but I didn't.

For the rest of that dreadful morning, any exposed skin felt like it was being slapped hard. The farther we pedaled, the more it felt like my face was being stung by an angry swarm of killer bees—another illogical fear of mine. *I doubt I'll be asking Wally to tag along again any time soon*, I thought, *at least not until it gets warmer out.*

As we pedaled into our frozen driveway, Wally dismounted his bike and turned to me. "Thanks for the help today," he said, handing me a single dollar bill, "consider us square."

Wow, I thought, *my first real pay.* I immediately pictured myself standing at Old Man's Sedgeband's candy case, buying strings of Zotz candy. I could already imagine biting into the hard candy and hitting that sour fizzy center, a taste that could easily become addictive. I looked down at my dollar and smiled. *This should cover enough Zotz for a week.*

• • •

I was never so happy to come home, but we didn't even have our coats off when Ma announced, "We were up too late last night to make it to church today, but we're definitely going to start going again." She nodded decisively. "Yup, this family needs church."

"Sure, Ma," Wally said in a tone that represented everyone's doubt.

Smiling, I began to peel off the first frozen layer of winter clothing when Ma made her second announcement.

"Leave everything on," she told me and Wally. "We're going to Memere's house."

Oh no, I thought, *I'm gonna miss Casey Kasam's Top 40 countdown.*

"But we saw them yesterday," Wally complained.

"You didn't see Pepere," Ma reminded him.

"Ugh," Cockroach groaned from the shadows of our bedroom.

"We visit your grandparents on Sundays, Alphonse," she said, looking in his direction. "We always have and today is no exception."

Still exhausted, Pop raised an eyebrow in protest.

"Let's go," she said.

"Is she making food?" Pop asked, betraying his only excuse to surrender.

She gave him a sideways look. "When doesn't my mother feed us, Walter?"

"Fine," Pop said, throwing up the white flag. "Let's get a move on then."

So much for Casey's countdown, I thought, still ruminating over it.

"Ugh," Cockroach echoed.

Although the station wagon struggled in the cold, she still managed to transport us one town over to Memere's house.

Hustling inside to get out of the relentless cold, we were smacked with a wave of heat unlike anything we'd ever experienced in our apartment.

"They must be giving away free heating oil now, huh?" Pop teased.

Pepere grunted in response, his eyes still locked on the color TV set in front of him. To say that Pepere was a quiet man would have been a gross understatement. Essentially, he was silent. For better than thirty years—while wearing his soft hat and chewing on a soggy cigar—he worked at Lincoln Park, the local amusement park; he ran The Comet, one of the most feared roller coasters in New England.

I normally loved spending time at my grandparent's house. It was like being in an interactive museum. On their living room wall, looming over a long, flowered couch, was a velvet portrait of John and Bobby Kennedy sitting on twin hotel beds, facing each other. A fake fireplace sat dormant across from it, a row of ceramic knick-knacks lining the mantle like a squad of fragile soldiers.

Our Memere was a talented woman. She made clothes for our G.I. Joe dolls, most of her magic created from an old cookie tin that stored buttons, needles and thread—everything she needed. *She can do anything*, I thought, *cook, sew—anything.*

Given the lack of conversation between the adults, I knew right away that this was going to be a low-key visit. *They played cards for hours last night*, I thought, *so at least this'll be a quick one.* That's when I received the bad news.

"It's time to eat," Ma announced. "Memere made her split pea soup."

Although my Memere was an amazing cook—I loved nearly everything she made—her famous split pea soup, with giant pieces of fatty salted pork floating on top, triggered a gag reflex in me at the very sight of it. What made matters worse was that although my parents had only a few strict rules they refused to bend on, one of them was that my brothers and I were not allowed to leave the supper table until we finished our meal—or left for home.

I took a seat at the table and tried to eat the green slop. I really did. But I dry-heaved, as I did every other time I'd ever tried swallowing it. *Looks like I'll be sitting at this table alone for the entire visit,* I realized.

My poor grandmother, clearly feeling awful about it, offered to make something different for me. "Would you like a Gorton sandwich, Herbie?" It was her homemade French-Canadian pork spread, which I enjoyed with a little mustard.

"No!" my parents barked, refusing her kindness on my behalf. "What is he, special?" They gawked at me. "He can eat what the rest of us eat."

Shaking my head, I realized, *Memere can't feel that bad for me because she makes her split pea soup at least once a month.*

For the entire visit, I sat at that table, watching the loudly-ticking clock—the black cat's diamond-shaped eyes and long tail moving in sync—until we left. Every time my empty stomach groaned, I thought, *I'd love to rip that damn cat's tail off.*

By the time we left, I was starving. On the way home, we had to drive by the new Burger King. We'd only been twice before, but I still couldn't get the amazing flame-grilled taste out of my memory. Fast food was a new concept—at least for us. Even in the dead of winter, I could smell the perfectly-cooked meat through the frozen windows.

"Can we stop?" I asked my parents, knowing this was a long shot at best.

In my mind, I was already watching the greasy beef patties and toasted buns fall off the conveyer belt to become a Whopper with cheese—*my* Whopper with cheese, a rite of passage out of childhood.

Can I get the Whopper? I asked my father in my head.

As long as you finish it, he replied in the fantasy.

"Are you nuts?" Pop barked, answering in the real world. "Oh, I don't think so. Nope, we have plenty of food at home," he said, complying with Ma's shaking head.

"And if you'd eaten what the rest of us ate," Ma began, "then . . ."

"Then I would have thrown up," I blurted.

"You watch your mouth," Ma said, jerking sideways like she was going to come over the front seat after me. "Your Memere is a great cook."

"I didn't say she wasn't, Ma, but I can't eat pea soup. It makes me sick to my stomach."

"Starve then," she muttered under her breath, lighting a new cigarette off of the one she was finishing.

"We have food at home," Pop repeated, "but you're on your own to make it."

I nodded, knowing better than to utter another word.

"Ugh," Pop complained, a half mile up the road, "I hate it when people drive so slow."

We finally passed the other driver to see that it was an elderly woman.

"Now apologize to God," Ma told Pop.

He snickered. "God's got bigger things to worry about."

I gave it some thought. *That's probably true.*

It was quiet for a few moments.

"I can't wait to get back to work so I can relax," Pop told Ma, breaking the silence.

Ma shook her head. "Not me," she said, jerking her head toward us in the back seat, "I have them all week."

Pop chuckled. "I know," he said, "and you're a brave woman."

When we got home, I headed straight to the fridge and swung open the dented door. Besides a pitcher of Kool-Aid and two gallons of milk, there were two jars of pickles, a jar of pickled eggs, some pickled onions and pickled peppers. *Ma and Pop really enjoy their pickled products*, I thought. As I surveyed the shelves from top to bottom, I decided, *Screw it, I'll just make a sandwich.*

Famished, I ate one fluffernutter after another until I began to sweat from sugar overload and risk childhood diabetes.

Before I'd finished my gorging, Wally slithered out the front door to head down to the dungeon. Cockroach headed in a different direction, settling into the living room to watch TV with Ma and Pop. *He can have them all to himself tonight,* I thought, wanting nothing more to do with my parents. *I'd rather be alone with my marshmallow fluff,* I thought. Suddenly, Donna's beautiful face popped into my head. *I wonder if she has to eat fluffernutters because she gags on a spoon full of pea soup?*

With Donna in mind, I headed for my bedroom, deciding to listen to some music on my boom box. The giant beast required 8DD batteries, which was ridiculous, so I only used it when I could plug it in. The portable stereo was silver with round black speaker covers. The cassette deck on the left side was broken, so I couldn't tape my favorite songs off of the radio onto a blank cassette tape any more. *Even though the mix tapes are out,* I thought, *this baby still kicks.* I threw in Journey's *Frontiers* cassette and began listening to *Faithfully*—over and over.

"Lower it," Pop yelled from the living room.

As I took it down one notch, Donna smiled at me in my day-dream. *Hi babe*, I thought, while Steve Perry continued to wail away.

The boom box was covered with a few rock band stickers that came with their albums, as well as a bumper sticker from 94 HJY, the local rock station; all of these were plastered over some faded Garbage Pail and Whacky Packy stickers.

". . . faithfully," Steve Perry crooned.

"Keep it down, Herbie," Cockroach called out from the living room. "We can hardly hear the TV."

My blood pressure instantly rose, making me feel like my head might shoot right off my shoulders. *Keep it down?* I repeated in my head. *Wait until I get you alone, you little bastard. We'll see if you can keep the screaming down.*

I pictured Donna again. *This is crazy,* I told her in my head, *but I really feel like I'm in love with you. I've never felt this way about anyone. You're so beautiful and sweet and . . .* I scrambled to find my Bryan Adams *Reckless* cassette, having to rewind it and hit *play* a half dozen times until I found the start of the song, *Heaven*. After finishing the song, I thought, *This could be our song, Donna.* I rewound the tape six or seven more times until I found the start of *Heaven* again.

I unfolded the cassette insert to sing along with the lyrics, think-ing, *Maybe I should listen to Summer of '69.* I read the song list. *Damn it*, I thought, *it's on the other side of the tape.* Ejecting the cassette, I began rewinding it with my pinky finger because I couldn't find my number two pencil. After hitting *play* a half dozen times, I finally found the beginning of the new song.

"If I have to tell you to lower it again, Herbie," Pop screeched, "I'm taking that damn radio away from you."

Geeze, I thought, *what's it gonna take to get some alone time with Donna?* Jumping off of my bunk, I began searching for my yellow Walkman.

• • •

Cockroach shut off the bedroom light and catapulted himself into his top bunk like he was being chased.

I chuckled before calling out to Wally, "Whatchu talkin' about, Wally?" We both loved the show Different Strokes and I was sure this one would get a response from him.

Once again, there was silence.

Damn, Wally, I thought, *you're in a worse place than I thought.*

A moment or two passed when Cockroach replied, "Da plane, boss . . . da plane."

"Nice try," I told him, "but wrong show." As I laughed, I could hear my older brother doing the same. But still, he remained silent.

Goodnight, Oscar the Grouch, I told him in my head.

It took me a while to fall asleep that night. Besides having way too much marshmallow pushing its way through my digestive system, my thoughts were consumed by Donna.

Then I pictured Clarence, his knife-like teeth smiling at me. *Not again,* I silently begged, *please God, just let me sleep tonight.*

CHAPTER 5

MONDAY

Right from the start of our vacation, we planned on bumming around in t-shirts and flannel pajama bottoms all week. We were okay with changing our underwear and brushing our teeth, given that Ma told us to. *We're not complete animals*, I thought. Combs, however, were deemed unnecessary. It didn't matter, anyway. Our haircuts were as unstable as most of our family. Although we wore buzz cuts in the summer, we were as unkempt as three shaggy mutts in the winter. Wally and Cockroach wore long mullets, while my coif puffed out like I was the Jackson 5's pale brother.

Pop hurried off to work, whistling on his way out of the house.

Mom offered her usual fare of Cream of Wheat for breakfast. "It's good for you and the maple and brown sugar is delicious," she said. "It'll stick to the ribs and keep you full for more than a half hour."

"No, thanks," I said, opting to eat three full bowls of Kellogg's Sugar Smacks. I liked the cool-looking frog on the front of the box, and there were always a few games to play on the back.

Halfway through my feeding, I discovered the wrapped prize. *A pair of baseball cards*, I guessed, rubbing the foil wrapping between my fingers. *No big deal*, I thought, *I find three or four cereal prizes a week*. I was just placing the new prize into the blue Danish cookie tin on top of the fridge when Ma returned to the kitchen and placed both hands on her hips. *It's announcement time*, I thought.

"If you guys think you're staying in this house all week and driving me crazy, then you're out of your minds," she said.

We looked at each other.

"I want you dressed and out of the house," she added. "There's plenty for you to do outside."

"What, freeze?" Wally muttered under his breath.

She glared at him. "Not if you dress for it, Wally." She exhaled deeply, like she'd been dreading this speech for a while. "It's your vacation, boys," she added, softening her tone, "so get out there and have some fun, okay?"

We exchanged glances again.

"Can we at least watch TV for an hour?" Wally asked.

Very clever, I thought. *Ma's soaps don't start until later this afternoon and we can probably turn that hour into two...maybe three.* I looked at my brother and nodded my respect. *Stellar move, Wally,* I thought. *Stellar.*

"Fine," she said, "but one hour and then I want all three of you out of this house."

"Thanks Mama," Cockroach said.

Wally and I both sneered at him. *Brown-noser.*

After sneaking in a couple of half-hour episodes of The Three Stooges, which Ma forbid us to watch, we began wrestling in the living room. Ma's brown pleather hassock was home base for everything—a game of tag or wrestling—but today it was high ground to launch a surprise attack from. I was airborne, aiming for Cockroach's head, when Ma walked into the room.

Oh no, I thought, knowing right away, *We've made too much noise.*

"Outside now," she roared, "and I'm not telling you again."

"Okay . . . okay," we said, nice and primed to head out into the yard and maim each other.

Donning our drab green snorkel jackets, with bright orange liners, we slid the plastic bread bags—Wonder Bread, Sunbeam or a mismatched pair of both—over our socks before grappling with our hand-me-down boots. The bread bags were great in theory, but only lasted so long. *Once the snow gets in,* I'd learned, *it gets trapped*—until melting and becoming ice water.

In order to combat this, we either used good rubber bands or duct tape. "Who cares about blood circulation?" Wally commented, as we finished preparing to go into battle.

Ma couldn't have cared less. In between folding laundry and preparing dinner, she needed to get caught up on her "stories"— As the World Turns, All My Children and General Hospital. We weren't allowed in the house until late afternoon when all three were done.

"Go out and play," she repeated, "it's nice out." She spouted those same words whether it was mid-summer or twenty below zero. "And stay out of the cellar," she warned. "They're working downstairs and we don't need . . ."

"Awesome," Wally interrupted. "No more laundry!"

"I'm talking about not playing down there, you smartass." She peered at him. "You know what I meant."

Nothing's going to come between Ma and her soap operas, I thought.

"And I want you in before the street light comes on," she concluded.

"We know, Ma," we replied, as we had a thousand times before, "we know."

So much for lunch, I thought.

Although my brothers and I dreamed of owning fast cars to take pretty girls to the drive-in movie theater or the roller-skating rink— with its black lights and neon colors—the future didn't exist beyond our next meal time. We lived in the moment with vigor and total disregard for most situations, regardless of the danger or the terrifying consequences to follow. It was glorious.

Our backyard was nearly a football field in length but only half the width. From the top, it pitched down and left. It was wide open with nothing to block the wind or the snow from drifting in the punishing New England winters.

I looked at the covered swing set at the bottom of the yard, picturing it in the summer—my brothers and I tackling it like baboons, the poles lifting up out of the ground. *I can't wait for summer*, I thought, happy to suffer more bruises from our worn Slip and Slide or the potential disfigurement of throwing lawn darts into the air as high as we could.

For a moment, I just stood there. Although I couldn't put it into words, there was no other quiet like the quiet after a fresh snowfall in New England. It was as though a giant white blanket, heavy and wet, had been draped over the entire world. Every sound was deadened, absorbed into the high, glistening drifts.

"Wanna play tag?" Cockroach asked, disturbing the peace.

"You mean frozen tag?" Wally asked.

Although we both laughed, we declined. *Tag's only fun when other kids come over to play*, I thought. My brothers and I knew every rut and divot in our yard. There was a moon crater—'the ankle breaker,' we called it—toward the left side, putting our unaware opponents at a serious and dangerous disadvantage when playing chase or tag.

"It's no fun unless we can watch other kids wipe out," I told Cockroach.

He nodded.

"We could build an igloo?" I suggested.

"No way," he said. "I'll never help build another igloo in my life!"

Wally and I both laughed. *Poor Cockroach was buried alive last winter and the mental scars are still fresh.* I remember frantically digging him out. *That one actually scared me, too,* I thought, before glancing toward the shed.

Wally shook his head before I could even suggest it.

Pop's shed was at the top of the yard. Playing on or around it usually required immediate medical attention. With all the rusty nails sticking out, it was like a medieval torture chamber.

"I'd rather head into the cellar than the shed," Wally said. "There's a lot more room."

"I hate the cellar," Cockroach said. "It's so scary down there. Besides, Ma said . . ."

Wally snickered. "You're scared of everything, Alphonse."

"Not everything," he said, looking at me.

"Almost everything," I said.

He shrugged. "Can't we just play outside?"

Wally was starting to shake his head when Victor, my best friend, arrived. "Hey guys," he said, dressed for a light autumn day, "what are you up to?"

Vic was Portuguese or what I called "Porch Geese." He lived four houses down in a pink raised ranch that was as much a mystery to me as any Scooby Doo plot line. He was my age and, at only twelve-years old, he already sported a full moustache. I couldn't decide whether it looked cool on him—*or creepy*. He also wore a fake gold chain that left a green ring around his neck.

"You smell like fried fish," Wally told him, kicking off the usual insults.

I laughed, knowing that my friend wouldn't dare talk back to my brother. *Vic always smells like fried fish*, I thought.

Even though Vic's family had eight kids, most of them working full-time and surrendering their money to their parents, Vic dressed like a hobo with worn clothes and even rattier shoes.

"We're still trying to figure it out, Vic," I told him.

"What about hide-and-seek?" Cockroach suggested.

I cringed.

"Sure," Wally said, surprising me, "but me and Herbie will hide. You and Vic will try to find us."

"Where's home base?" Vic asked.

"The willow tree," Wally said, pointing across the yard. "Count to ten Mississippi to give us time to hide."

They both nodded.

"But only the yard is in bounds, right?" Cockroach wisely tried to clarify.

Both Wally and I nodded.

Smiling, the two of them took off running. Once they reached the bare willow tree, they leaned against it and covered their eyes. "One Mississippi," Vic screamed out, "two Mississippi . . . three Mississippi . . ."

"Suckers," Wally whispered, taking off for the cellar door to hide behind it.

"Ten Mississippi," Vic screamed out, "ready or not, here we come!"

Both fools began scouring the barren yard. This went on for quite a while, making Wally and I giggle like school girls.

"Look at Starsky and Hutch," I whispered, "except they don't have a clue."

"More like Cagney and Lacey," he said.

We stifled our laughter.

Vic and Cockroach continued the search, their body language betraying their frustration.

As they drew closer to the cellar door, Wally and I ducked down—trying to hush our laughter.

"Where the hell are they?" Vic asked, his voice muffled by the door between us.

"Who knows," Cockroach said, "but I know they'll make us search all day before they surrender."

They turned to walk away when Wally sneaked out the door, formed a snowball and threw it at Victor, clipping him right off the top of his head.

They both turned, shocked to find us standing there—clearly unsure of where we'd come from.

"Oh, it's on," Vic yelled, laughing.

All four of us scattered in different directions to amass our icy arsenals. The entire yard was open game, so for the next hour there was lots of running and laughing and screaming.

"Ouch!" Cockroach yelled out, getting pelted by one of Vic's fastballs.

I started to laugh when I caught the next one right in the chest. *Damn*, I thought, *that does hurt*. I looked down and spotted a black rock where Vic's snowball had fallen and broken apart. "Are you packing rocks in the snowballs, numb nuts?" I yelled toward Victor.

He giggled. "Stick your head up just a few more inches and find out, Herbie," he yelled back.

"He's throwing rocks," Cockroach screamed, "I knew it. Vic's throwing rocks!"

Brain dead Victor's been digging up rocks from the driveway and hiding them inside his snowballs, I surmised. *We should bury him in the snow for being . . .*

"That's it, I'm telling Ma!" Cockroach screamed, waddling toward the house. "I'm telling Ma!"

"No, you're not," Wally called after him, stopping our little brother cold. "You say one word to Ma and I'll rip your tongue out."

Victor started laughing, until he spotted Wally running straight at him. "I'm sorry," he screamed, collapsing to the frozen ground. "I . . . I'm sorry!"

Vic's done for, I thought, hurrying over to help Wally. *Vic's my friend, but the idiot hurt my little brother.* Pop had taught us well—*blood's thicker than even Memere's nasty pea soup.*

Cockroach did an about-face and hustled over to take in the show.

Wally was suddenly on Vic—knees resting on the screaming kid's back—his arms locked forward, shoving Vic's face into the frozen snow. "You throw another rock at any one of us, wingnut, and it'll be the last time," he roared. "You understand?"

"Yeah, yeah," Vic yelled back, turning his face just enough to be able to speak. "I'm . . . I'm sorry, Wally. I won't do it again. I . . . I promise . . ."

Wally released a war cry that shocked us all. "Oh, I know you won't," he screamed, spit dripping from his blue lips.

"Okay, Wally," I told him, grabbing his arm, "that's enough. He gets the idea."

Wally jammed Vic's frightened mug into the ground again.

I yanked on my brother's arm as hard as I could, rolling him off my friend. "That's enough, Wally," I yelled. "Damn!"

Wally's flaring nostrils threw off plumes of steam, making him look like a raging bull. For a moment, he just lay there while reality slowly registered in his eyes. "Okay, okay," he muttered, as though he were waking from a dream. "I'm done," he panted.

Scrambling to his feet, Vic wiped the snow off himself. "Damn, Wally," he said, "I shouldn't have done that, but man . . . you didn't have to . . ."

"Just leave the rocks in the driveway, fish stick," my brother told him, "and we'll be fine."

Fish stick, I repeated in my head, grinning.

As Vic brushed more snow off his pants, he looked at me. "What the hell, Herbie?" he whispered.

I shrugged. "You had it coming, Vic," I told him. "We can punish Cockroach . . ." I grinned, ". . . but nobody else can. You know that."

Smiling from ear-to-ear, Cockroach nodded proudly.

I looked back at Wally. *This is all because of Owen humiliating him on the bus*, I realized. *He hasn't been himself since Friday. He's been so quiet and . . . and angry.* I knew my brother. I could read him well. He was suffering the kind of fear that stole your breath away and made your mind race out of control. *Having to face that bully is hanging over Wally's head like one of Wiley Coyote's giant anvils*, I thought.

To make it up to Cockroach, we took him sledding around the flat yard; basically, this meant pulling the tattle tale on a sled like some panting Saint Bernard.

"It's your turn to pull," Wally told Victor.

"But I just had my turn," Vic complained, sweating profusely.

"It's your turn again," Wally said.

"Fine."

Occasionally, the sled's steel rails—waxed with a bar of soap—ran over the back of Vic's ankles like a derailed locomotive. "Yow!" he screamed out.

Every time he yipped out in pain, my brothers and I laughed uncontrollably. *That's what you get for messing with our little brother*, I told my best friend in my head.

It wasn't long until we were exhausted from watching Vic huff and puff around the yard. "Do you wanna build a snowman?" I asked.

Although no one was enthusiastic about the idea, everyone pitched in.

We were looking for something to use as a nose—the final touch—when Wally the Mangler ran full-steam at Frosty, tackling the poor snowman at the waist and turning it into a giant cloud of white powder.

"No!" Cockroach hollered, unable to conceal his rage.

"Relax," Wally told him, "this is lame, anyway." He thought about it. "Let's head down the railroad tracks to the clubhouse."

We all looked at each other.

"I'm in," I said.

With matching nods, Vic and Cockroach followed our lead.

The trees bent in toward the railroad tracks, leaning into the sun and creating a natural tunnel of bare, ice-covered branches. It was an active railroad; the cargo train ran twice a day, but there were never any passenger cars for us to moon.

We walked in single file along the tracks, trudging through the deep snow. "This sucks," Cockroach complained.

"It's either this or the igloo," Wally teased.

"Are we there yet?" my little brother asked after a few more yards. He was breathing heavy like a Nepal Sherpa.

Wally stopped and turned to the group, causing our small rag-tag patrol to halt. "We'll be there when we get there, okay?" He headed off again.

Wow, he sounds just like Pop, I thought.

Another quarter mile down the tracks and a hundred feet inside the thick woods, we arrived at the neighborhood fort—affectionately known as *the clubhouse.*

The entire area was eerily silent. The birds that usually sang in the trees were missing; there was no chirping or rustling of leaves, evidence of squirrels and chipmunks scurrying about in their world.

The elevated shack was constructed of splintered boards and rusty nails stolen by neighborhood kids who'd claimed this sacred ground long before the four of us had ever come along. Some of the building materials included stolen road signs, a grape Nehi soda pop advertisement, and even a section of white picket fence that appeared in better shape than the rest of the place. *I wonder where that came from?* I thought, knowing better than to question it aloud.

Wedged into the forked trunk of an ancient oak tree, the fort was built nearly ten feet off the ground. A frayed and dry-rotted length of rope hung from the hole in the clubhouse floor, which was once the only way in and out. *Unless you get tossed from the window, which I'm told has happened,* I thought. Many moons before, the rope had been abandoned, replaced by different lengths of scrap wood that had been nailed to the trunk at staggered climbing levels. Besides a committed effort, it took some real thought and effort to ascend into the belly of the beast. *We should get Tetanus shots just for climbing into this place.*

Wally was the strongest and the only one who could pull his own body weight up and in, so he went first. Laying flat on his belly, he then hung one of his hands over the edge for us to grab onto. "Let's go," he yelled down.

Vic was the second to go. With me pushing and Wally pulling, he flew in through the hole.

I looked at Cockroach. "You're up next," I told him.

He shook his head. "I'm thinking about staying on the ground, Herbie," he said, crafting his first excuse. "I could be the lookout for you guys."

"We don't need a damn lookout!" Wally bellowed from above.

"Relax, Cockroach, it's easy," I told him. "I won't let you fall, I promise."

He searched my eyes for a moment before believing me.

"Just get on my shoulders," I told him, "but this time, face the same way." I could hear Wally's laughter from above. Cockroach looked at me like a moon bat; there wasn't a whole lot of understanding behind his dull eyes. "Just go," I told him, interlocking my ten fingers for him to step into.

He took a deep breath and started to climb. I stood one step behind my little brother, prepared to catch him if he fell—*or at least break his fall.* With me pushing on his backside, and Wally pulling on his stick of a forearm, we finally managed to toss his quivering legs into the clubhouse.

"I told you that you could make it," I heard Wally say.

"I'd still rather play lookout," Cockroach mumbled from above.

"Good," Wally said, "then go look out the window."

I laughed.

Wally looked down at me. "Let's go, Herbie. My arm's getting tired."

Being the last to go, I was surprised at how strong my brother was. From the moment Wally grabbed onto my hand, I knew he wouldn't let go until I was safe. *He'd better not,* I thought.

As my head broke the plane and my eyes struggled to adjust to the darkness, it was like discovering a whole new world. A Boston Red Sox pennant as well as a few curled posters of half-naked pinups papered the walls. There was a broken lava lamp, which didn't make sense as the treehouse had never been wired for electricity. Two bean-bag chairs had been patched with silver duct tape, while the rest of the roll had obviously been used to help hold the dump together. The front seat from an old Chevy Camaro—the leather ripped, the steel springs exposed and free floating—completed the furniture.

Very few of the sun's rays made it through the thick snowy canopy; those that did created shadows inside the clubhouse.

An ancient Playboy magazine, soaking wet under a swag of carpet, served to teach many of the neighborhood's pre-adolescent boys about the birds and the bees. Although many of the pictures were faded, they still served their purpose.

In our neighborhood, the clubhouse was the inner sanctum. Not everyone was invited or welcome, so it was a crucial to one's social status to get in. To us, it meant everything.

"Feels warmer in here," Cockroach noted, sitting against the back wall.

He's right, I thought, *it's definitely not as cold up here.*

"It's only because the walls are breaking the wind," Wally explained before looking at me and winking. "If you hadn't been adopted, you'd have some meat on your bones like me and Herbie and you wouldn't be cold all the time."

I concealed my laughter.

"I haven't been adopted," Cockroach said, his bottom lip a few minutes from quivering.

"Is that what Ma told you?" I asked him, playing along.

He looked at me.

Wally shrugged. "You should ask Pop, Alphonse. He'll tell you the truth."

"He might," I said, half-shrugging.

Cockroach shook his head. "I'm not adopted," he repeated; this time, he was speaking more to himself.

"You guys are brutal," Vic commented and his eyes went wide as he did—realizing he'd just made a grave mistake.

"Why are you speaking pork and cheese, Vic?" Wally asked him, busting his chops. "You know we only speak English, right?"

"Whatever," he muttered.

I laughed. "Hey Vic, if your brother Manny had been born a girl, would he have been named Womanny?" I asked, wanting in on the fun.

"Why don't you go ask him, Sherbet, and see what he says," Vic replied, smiling.

I immediately shut up, Everyone knew that Manny was the toughest dude in the neighborhood and nobody screwed with him— *nobody*. I thought about it. *I hope Vic doesn't send Manny after Wally, He's got enough to worry about.*

"What's up with that new kid, Scott, on Rock Street?" Cockroach said. "I'd really like to kick his ass."

Every head snapped around to see if he was serious.

"*Kiss* his ass?" Wally teased.

"Kick," Cockroach clarified, "kick!"

"I don't know, Alphonse," Wally said, "I watched you fight a stuffed animal once and lose."

"That's not true."

"Ayyyy!" Vic said, mocking him with two thumbs up.

Even Wally laughed at that one. We sometimes called Alphonse, Phonsey—after Fonzie on Happy Days.

"Ayyyy," I joined in, giving him two thumbs up.

Cockroach just shook his head. Although he hated the nickname, he'd learned that the more he complained, the more relentless we were.

As my little brother tried to laugh it off, I thought, *Good for you, Cockroach. You're starting to learn.* I then realized, *In the short time we've been in the clubhouse, both Cockroach and Vic have already been picked on . . . which means I'm next.* That's how it went; we worked our way up the pecking order, with the guy at the top sitting safe and sound.

"So Herbie, what's up with the new girl you're in love with?" Wally asked.

And there it is, I thought.

"You don't honestly think you have a shot with her, do you?" he said.

Watch what you say about my future wife, I thought, not daring to reply. Like Cockroach, I simply turned into a smiling bobble head. *If you don't fight it,* I told myself, *then it can never beat you.*

Having lost track of time, it was already getting dark when we started for home.

"We'd better motor," Wally said, taking off at a gallop with the rest of us at his back.

We were almost at the end of the tracks on Davis Road when I decided to take a short cut the rest of the way home. Vic and Cockroach followed me. As I reached the wire fence, I picked up the pace and—feeling like the Six-Million Dollar Man—attempted to hurdle it. But I never accounted for all the extra clothes and landed right on my crotch. "Ahhhh," I moaned, trying to breathe through the piercing pain. "I think . . . I think I tore my Hyman," I gasped.

"What's that?" Cockroach asked.

With both hands on my family jewels, I took a few deep breaths. "Nothing you'll ever have to worry about," I managed, unwilling to pass up on any opportunity to mess with my little brother—no matter how much pain I was in.

I looked at Vic. His face was blank. *He's got no idea, either,* I thought. *Another wasted joke.*

We reached home a few minutes after the streetlight came on, but still a few steps in front of Wally. *Beat ya,* I thought, looking back at my brother's hulking silhouette.

Roscoe, our neighbor's dog, barked at us from inside his doghouse. *Poor thing,* I thought, *stuck out here in this wicked cold.*

"Ma's gonna be mad at us," Cockroach said, grabbing my attention.

"Relax," I told him, shaking my head. "General Hospital just finished."

Eight rubber boots were removed right at the kitchen table. There was screaming and swearing, but nothing compared to Cockroach's dizzying fit of rage as he convulsed on the linoleum floor—trying to kick off his boots like they were on fire.

"You need real help," I told him, laughing.

"But you're not going to help him, are you?" Ma asked from behind me.

I spun on my soggy heels to watch her drop to the floor in Cockroach's aid.

"That's not the kind of help I meant," I told her.

"Oh, I know what you meant, Herbie," she said, grunting to get one of Cockroach's boots separated from his extended foot. "And I also know that you could have helped him, but you didn't."

"Because he's old enough to do it for himself, Ma," I snapped back.

Blowing a strand of hair from her eyes, she paused to look up at me.

"It's true," Wally said, "Cockroach isn't gonna do anything for himself until he has to."

Although she shook her head, she didn't argue the point.

Now that's rare, I thought.

While Ma returned to the battle of boot hill, I headed off to our bedroom to thaw out—and play Atari Street Racer. Vic went with me.

I loved Street Racer, where the cars looked like different colored puzzle pieces. A thick line divided the racers, the cars racing side-by-side from the bottom of the screen to the top.

A few minutes—or hours—went by before our plastic accordion door snapped open and Ma stood there, darkening the doorway. I glanced up from my video trance to see her step into the room, positioning herself between me and the small black-and-white TV. "We'll be having supper soon and I need Victor to go home now," she announced, talking as though my moustache-wearing friend wasn't sitting right there beside me. "He doesn't live here, you know," she said.

Trying to look around her, I coughed a few times. "Well, he kind of does, Ma."

"No, he doesn't," she said.

"Well, I kind of do," Victor added.

I laughed more, happy to toy with the annoying distraction that was still blocking my view.

"Goodbye Victor," she said.

With a single nod, he got up and placed his joystick down. "See you tomorrow, Herbie," he said, stepping out of the room.

"Not if I see you first," I called after him, never looking up.

Ma peered down at me. "I don't mind if your friend eats here once and a while, Herbie, but not every night, okay?"

"That's okay, Ma," I told her, coughing. "Vic loves his mother's fried codfish anyway."

"Cover your mouth when you cough," she scolded me before walking out of the room.

I reset Street Racer and switched to one player. *Finally, a real challenge,* I thought.

Although my father enjoyed such delicacies as deviled ham and jellied Spam—even considering Slim Jims and a spray can of Easy Cheese as suitable proteins—my brothers and I felt a bit more entitled. We expected only the best for supper.

"Fried bologna again?" Wally complained, as we dragged our feet to the kitchen table.

Vic couldn't stay over for bologna? I thought, hacking into the back of my hand.

"Your father likes fried bologna," she said, flipping the curled luncheon meat in the sizzling frying pan.

"And pickled beets," Pop said, reaching for the bowl in the middle of the table.

"Alphonse is going to help me make biscuits, too," Ma added. "Aren't you, sweetheart?"

Without complaint, Cockroach got up from the table to make our mother smile.

Grabbing the Pillsbury dough cardboard tube from the fridge, Ma began unwrapping it.

Oh, here we go, I thought, thrilled at the possibility of a comedy show.

A second or two later, there was a loud pop—the tube of raw biscuits exploding open. Cockroach hit the deck like he'd just been shot.

I started laughing and couldn't stop, alternating between fits of coughing and laughter. Wally was also hysterical. Even Pop couldn't contain himself. "I'm gonna pee my pants," I blurted, hurrying off to the bathroom.

"Make sure you wash your hands when you're done," Ma called after me, not nearly as amused as the rest of us.

As we ate, I could feel myself getting sick; I was stuffed up and the cough was getting worse.

"So what did you boys do today?" Pop asked.

"Freeze," Wally said, drawing a bad look from our mother.

"It was a cold one out there today, that's for sure," he said, dunking his fried bologna in ketchup, "and the forecast doesn't look any better for the rest of the week, either."

Oh great, I thought, *a whole week of survival training. I should definitely have pneumonia by the end of it.*

"We played in the yard for a while," Cockroach reported, "and then we went down to the . . ."

Wally shot him a look that stunned him into silence.

"Down to where?" Ma asked, getting up to fry the final batch of German bologna.

"Just . . . just down the road . . . to . . . to see how high the snow-drifts are," he babbled.

"That's good," Ma said, without paying any real attention.

Pop looked around the table and grinned. "Wherever you guys go this week, make sure you're dressed for it, yeah?"

"We will, Pop," Wally said.

Cockroach lifted a slice of curled bologna with his fork and looked at me. "Pardon me," he said in a horrendous British accent, "but do you have any Grey Poupon?"

Everyone laughed—but Ma.

Too bad Ma didn't serve fish sticks with the fried bologna, I thought, continuing to feed my face. *There's nothing better than welfare surf and turf after a long day on the open tundra.* I chuckled aloud.

"It wasn't that funny," Ma said, preferring to get after me than her little angel.

I shrugged. "It kind of was," I mumbled, covering another cough. Although we weren't on welfare, I often thought, *We probably should be.*

"Well, I hope you guys are full," Ma announced, "because we're out of bologna."

I looked over at Wally, who rolled his eyes.

"I'm stuffed," Pop said. "That really hit the spot, hon."

How did we run out of bologna? I wondered. Even at my young age, it seemed like lunacy. *And if we have to eat lunch meat for supper, then how in the hell can we run out of it?* I popped the last pickled beet into my mouth. *Maybe it's a good thing Vic didn't eat over.* I chuckled again, drawing another look from Ma. *I'm sure he got fish sticks.*

Like clockwork, every night at seven—although I could never understand why—Ma talked to Aunt Phyllis for about an hour on the phone. Some nights, whether I liked it or not, I caught my mother's side of the conversation—while she paced from ashtray-to-ashtray, smoking one cigarette after the next.

"Yeah, we had fried bologna," Ma said into the olive-green receiver, "I told you, Phyllis, we're still playing catch up from the holidays." She took a drag. "Our Christmas club at the credit union didn't quite cut it this year." She paused. "Well, I don't care if we have to starve for another month," she added, her tone more firm and committed, "Walt and I decided a long time ago that our kids were gonna get the Christmases we never had." She took a long drag on her cancer stick, nearly choking on a snicker. "Give me a break, Phyllis! My boys are hardly spoiled. And I don't care what you say . . . I don't see a damn thing wrong with me and Walter giving our boys everything they want . . . even if it's only once a year."

Thanks Ma, I thought, and meant it.

We were getting ready for bed when Ma came into the room again. "Still coughing, huh?" she said.

I nodded. "I'm not feeling too good, Ma," I told her, putting on my best sick voice. Although it was a long shot, I hoped, *Maybe she'll let me stay in bed tomorrow?*

She automatically headed out of the room in search of old faithful, Vic's VapoRub.

Minutes later, she was rubbing the thick menthol on my bare chest. "You'll be as good as new tomorrow," she promised, "You'll see."

Yeah, I thought, *so I can get out of this house and out of your hair.*

Although we smelled like a Calamine lotion and mercurochrome throughout most of the summer, in the winter we traded in those medicinal colognes for Vicks VapoRub.

"Here," she said, handing me two orange-flavored Saint Joseph's aspirin tablets, "sit up, so you don't choke."

I did and, as I chewed away, I realized, *These things taste better than Pez.*

Cockroach shut off the light and sprang up into his bed.

Once the bunk bed stopped rocking, I broke the silence, asking, "Who ya gonna call, boys?"

There was silence.

"Ghostbusters!" Cockroach replied—but only after giving Wally enough time to answer.

"That's right, Cockroach," I said, coughing, "you're starting to get it."

The silhouette laying in the single bed on the other side of the room remained still—and completely silent.

CHAPTER 6

TUESDAY

The kitchen door creaked open, revealing Clarence standing there—and smiling. Instantly, my skin crawled.

"Reggie couldn't make it," Clarence told Pop. "He'th at hith aunt'th houthe until Friday. I thought it would help him heal. I hope you don't mind that I thwung by alone?"

"Oh no, not at all," Pop said, shaking the freak's hand and stepping aside for the man to step into our kitchen, "it'll give us some time to get to know each other."

"That thoundth good," Clarence said in a spray of spit. He turned to me and grinned.

It looks like a few more teeth are missing, I thought, my heart plummeting into my stomach. *I doubt that kid at the party was even his. I bet there is no Reggie.*

The cookout lasted well after the mosquitoes called it quits and headed into the wet grass. I was closing up the shed when I wondered, *What the heck happened to all the snow?* That's when I spotted Roscoe, our neighbor's dog, lying still on the green lawn. For a Labrador retriever, this wasn't unusual—it was impossible. *I've never seen Roscoe lying outside of his coop*, I thought. *. . . or lying still.* Hurrying over, I dry heaved at the sight of the dismembered animal.

By Roscoe's contorted position, I could tell that all four of his limbs had been broken. The dog's jaws had been pried so far back that the skin was completely torn, leaving behind a face that was nothing more than a grotesque gaping mouth. Worse yet, Roscoe's genitalia had been removed, where a bloody cavern remained. For whatever reason, I scanned the area for the dog's missing testicles. *Nowhere to be found.* I dry-heaved several more times until finally puking up a half-digested hamburger. *Roscoe would have loved the treat,* I thought, before reality sank in. *Go get Pop!* I took off at a sprint.

The police asked a few questions and took some pictures, but they were obviously too busy with more pressing issues than investigating the peculiar death of a four-legged animal. The dog officer removed Roscoe's carcass before we headed back into the house. Ma was a mess over it. As Pop tried to console her, she snapped. "I want him out!"

"Who?" Pop asked.

"Your new friend, Clarence," she said. "We don't know him, Walt. For all we know . . ." She stopped. "Besides, I'm tired of wearing his saliva and I don't want . . ."

"The poor guy just lost his wife, for God's sake!" Pop roared. "Sometimes, I don't even think I know you." My father slammed the door behind him to find Clarence standing there, who'd obviously overheard every word.

Clarence's red face said it all. "That'th okay, Walt," he said, shrugging, "I think I'll be taking off now."

Pop shook his head violently. "Nonsense," he barked, "if you leave, then I'm goin' with you. This is my home, too." Thinking further on it, he quieted his tone. "Emma's just upset about that poor dog. It'll pass."

Clarence nodded. "Okay," he said, "I'll thtay on one more night then." He glanced at me and smiled.

Is that blood on his teeth? I wondered.

• • •

I awoke from the recurring dream in the middle of a terrible coughing fit. I tried to catch my breath. It took more time than usual. *That was awful,* I thought. The inability to control my reality was absolutely maddening. *Change your mind,* I thought. *You need to change your . . .* It came to me again. *Concentrate on Donna,* I told myself.

Although I'd crushed on Abby Gerwitz for a very long time, it was all about Donna Torres now. *She's definitely the one for me,* I thought, imagining myself kissing Donna like it was the first time I'd ever kissed anyone—*and the last.*

Until falling for Donna, the only thing that ever took my breath away was that blue rubber nose sucker that Ma used on us when we were young and stuffed up. I feared that dreadful booger sucker worse than Clarence. It was so bad that I couldn't go anywhere near a turkey baster for years.

I pictured Donna's beautiful face. *I can't wait for the next school dance,* I thought. *With any luck, we'll be going out together by then.* I imagined holding her warm body against mine, as we swayed to Led Zeppelin's *Stairway to Heaven,* or another lengthy favorite, *Always and Forever.* Those slow songs always required great courage to approach a girl and risk rejection. *But not if you're going out with someone,* I realized, *then it's just expected.*

Clarence's face popped into my head, his twisted smile dripping with bloody saliva. I shook my head, trying to clear away the monster's hideous shadow.

Write Donna's letter, I told myself, getting up to grab a pen and some paper.

I'd started the letter a dozen times, crumpling it up and tossing it into the trash each time. *It has to be perfect. Every word has to count,* I realized, making me curse myself for not paying closer attention in English class.

Dear Donna, I wrote, coughing a few times, *I hope this letter finds you well.*

"Ugh," I sighed, quickly tearing it up. *I hope this letter finds you well?* I snickered. *I just saw her a few days ago. Of course she's well. She's fine.* I shook my head. *Besides, it's 1984—not 1884.*

I started over. *Dear Donna, it's Herbie . . .*

"Ugh," I repeated, tearing off the sheet of paper, balling it up and missing the overflowing trash can with the free throw.

Dear Donna, I wrote, staring at the white-lined paper until the lines became blurry.

Coughing, I shook my head again. "Maybe it'll come to me after a big bowl of Cookie Crisp?" I thought aloud, making a beeline for the kitchen.

As we munched through breakfast, Ma announced, "I'm telling you again, you boys aren't staying in this house all day."

I coughed in response.

She looked at me. "You're fine."

After depositing our empty bowls into the sink, we hid in our bedroom and played with Cockroach's electric racetrack. Both cars traveled at the same speed, round-and-round. It was almost cool for about three minutes.

The plastic door snapped open. "Nice try," Ma said, "but I want you out of this house now."

Oh no . . .

In preparation of heading into the great outdoors, we donned our heavy winter clothing—still damp from a mix of snow and sweat from the day before. With fresh, mismatched socks and a layer of dry bread bags in place, we yanked on the seal skins we called boots and hurried to get out of the warm apartment.

Our mother was smiling, as she watched us go. "Be home before the streetlights come on," she reminded us.

This routine's already getting old, I thought, *and it's only Tuesday.*

We stood outside for a few minutes to discover that it was easily as cold as the day before, but that the winds had grown much stronger. *This isn't good,* I thought. Huddled against the house with my brothers, I asked, "What do you guys want to do today?"

"We could head back to the clubhouse," Cockroach suggested.

"Nah, it's too long of a walk," Wally said. "They might find us frozen to death halfway there."

"Yeah, once everything thaws out in the spring," I said.

Wally chuckled.

"Another snowball fight?" I said.

"Okay, but without rocks this time," Cockroach said.

Rain or shine, my brothers and I usually made up games to stave off the boredom. Sometimes we made each other run a violent gauntlet, testing each other's mettle like we were going into combat and needed to make sure everyone could hang tough. That was the thing about growing up in New England. The weather was so bad, so often, that it was absolutely necessary to develop creative imaginations. Other days, we'd play king of the mountain or muckle, or even set up ramps, jumping over each other with our bicycles—Evel Knievel-style. *But it's too cold for any of that today*, I thought, surrendering to the fact that Mother Nature was a hell of a lot tougher than we were.

"We could build an igloo?" Wally suggested for the second day.

As if scripted, Cockroach shook his hooded head. "No way," he said, "I'm out!"

Wally and I both laughed.

"This will be different," Wally said. "No roof this time. We'll build a snow fort."

The little guy looked at me for confirmation.

I nodded. "No one's gonna have to dig you out this year, Alphonse."

"Better not," he said, as if he even had a say in the matter.

We worked and worked, gathering snow and packing it into four glistening walls. The higher the walls grew, the more we were inspired to work harder. The constant movement helped us to keep warm—*or at least alive*. Although the sun was strong, making my eyes strain against the light bouncing off the stark white snow, it didn't provide much heat.

Victor's silhouette suddenly appeared out of nowhere, making Cockroach jump at the sight of him.

"Where have you been?" I asked him, squinting to make out his face.

"I had to finish my chores before I could come out and play," he said.

I looked at Wally and shook my head. Vic didn't just do chores, he suffered forced labor—without the allowance we received.

"How 'bout we hang out at your house today," I suggested. "There's no way Ma's letting us back in the house, so . . ."

"Are you nuts?" Vic said, shocked—looking at me like Max Headroom. "That's never gonna happen, Herbie, and you know it."

He was right. Mrs. Pavao despised having a stranger in her house, no matter how long she knew the person. The few times Vic had sneaked me in, she was off food shopping—which was the only time she ever really left. I was stunned to see that their furniture was covered in clear plastic.

"We're building a snow fort," Wally told him, "and we could use some more muscle."

"Sounds like fun," Vic said.

Wally half-shrugged. "I don't know how much fun it'll be, but we definitely need the shelter."

An hour and a half later, although our red-neck ice castle would have been uninsurable by any industry standards, it still broke the wind—just like the clubhouse on the railroad tracks—if you hunkered down low enough in one of the corners.

"Vic was right. This has been a blast," I said over the howling wind.

Everyone laughed.

Although the shabby igloo lacked a roof, all four walls—constructed of hard-packed snow and ice—created the perfect cover for a heated snowball fight. *It's a life-sized G.I. Joe Command Center*, I thought, and took off running to build my arsenal.

"And if you use rocks again," Wally yelled at Vic, "we're gonna bury you alive."

"Yeah, we are!" Cockroach said, making me chuckle.

We played until we could no longer feel the sting on our faces—Mother Nature's constant backhands. We played until our red cheeks turned ashen and our eyeballs felt frozen. Our fingers, shriveled like raisins from the snow that crept into our cheap cotton gloves, turned a pale blue. We wore double pants—the inside pair becoming soaked—making me wonder, *Did I accidentally pee myself?* At some point, my body was starting to fail me physically, evidenced by the chattering teeth and involuntary convulsions, my limbs twitching to circulate blood and stay warm.

Normally, these symptoms didn't matter. There was always one more snowball fight to be had, one more hill to sled down. *But not this time. Not today,* I thought. *I'm gonna get even more sick than I already am.* I gave it some thought. *Maybe even as bad as last winter.* My mind immediately went back to picture every vivid—and nasty—detail.

• • •

It was a terrible pulsating pain, almost mind numbing.

Ma stuffed a white cotton ball into each of my ears, deadening all sound. "It looks like a double ear infection," she said, confident in her diagnosis. "We'll go see Dr. Schwartz tomorrow to get you some penicillin." She patted my chest. "Try to get some sleep."

I did, but the throbbing in my ears sounded a lot like pounding footsteps coming down a metal staircase. At first, it was faint. But the harder I tried to sleep, the louder the footsteps became. Being stuck within the dream-like state was terrifying.

Although it took me forever, I finally nodded off.

In what seemed like seconds, I heard a pop in my left ear, immediately followed by the warm sensation of a syrupy flow that brought the first hint of relief. I pulled the sticky cotton ball out of my ear and looked at it. *So gross*, I thought, but the intense pain on the left side of my throbbing head was all but gone. *Not a bad trade off*, I thought. Sounds were now amplified.

I lost another five hours of sleep until the right ear popped, saturating the second cotton ball to egg yolk yellow.

The following day, I sat in Dr. Schwartz's waiting room for two full hours—listening to other kids hack and threatening to make me even more sick—until I was called forward to receive my bottle of pink liquid antibiotics.

"I can pay you half for the office visit today," Ma whispered to the doctor, "but I'll have to . . ."

He placed his wrinkled hand on her forearm. "You'll pay me when you have the money, Missus," Dr. Schwarz said with a smile, "that's fine."

Too bad Pop just bought his beer for the week, I thought, picturing three cases of shiny gold cans stacked on the side of the fridge, *or we'd have the money to pay you.*

On our way home, Ma and I made a quick stop at R&S Variety. "Get me three packs of . . ."

"Carlton 100s," I finished for her, jumping out of the car to run up her tab.

She nodded. "Smart boy."

I was back in the car within minutes, handing over the three packs while concealing the blue bag of Razzles I'd scored for myself. *First, it's candy,* I thought, *and then it's gum.*

"I'm more stressed than usual," she explained, half-shrugging.

Sure, Ma, I thought, *I have a double ear infection and you're the one who's suffering.*

· · ·

I returned to the present to see Cockroach's sad eyes looking up at me. "I'm starving, Herbie," he said.

"Me too," Vic said.

"We have to eat," Wally agreed, with the concern of a true leader. "Ma can't say anything if we go in to eat. And if we . . ."

"Keep quiet," I said, finishing his thought, "we might be able to hang out in our room."

"Exactly," Wally said, preparing to stand.

I looked at all three of them and grinned. Even in the vortex of winter, Cockroach still wore a full Kool-aid mustache. Wally was growing a real mustache, a blonde one, and it looked pretty good, too, if you caught it at just the right angle in the light. And Vic, well, he looked like Burt Reynolds in Smokey and the Bandit. *Not me, though*, I thought, shaking my head. I was as hairless as a baby piglet and filled with worry that I might stay that way for the rest of my life.

As we headed for the house, I turned to Vic. "After you take off your boots, sneak right into our bedroom and close the door."

"Quietly," Wally added.

"I'll bring you something to eat," I told him.

"Good," he said, "'cause I'm starving."

"Yeah, you might have mentioned that already."

Wally whipped up tuna fish sandwiches, as much as two cans could make, while Ma stayed in the living room. *So far, so good,*

I thought. *As long as we stay within our own territories . . .*

We finished lunch, devouring every last bit of the canned fish. Suddenly, I remembered that Vic was waiting patiently in our darkened bedroom. *And for almost an hour,* I thought, looking at the kitchen clock. *He's probably eaten Wally's switchblade comb by now.*

I whispered my problem to my older brother.

"I don't know what to tell you," Wally said, shrugging, "we're out of tuna."

"Can you make him a couple PBJ's?" I asked, hoping he wouldn't laugh at me.

"Nope, but you can," he said. "What am I, everyone's personal chef?"

After Vic choked down his sandwiches, we agreed to play quietly in our bedroom.

"But it's gotta be a board game," Wally whispered. "It's the only option."

"No Atari?" Vic whispered, disappointed.

"It makes noise and we don't want to draw Ma's attention," Wally explained.

"Not if you turn down the volume on the TV," Vic whispered, still haggling.

Cockroach and I looked at each other.

"Board games," Wally repeated in a tone that announced the final decision had already been made.

"Monopoly or Parcheesi?" Cockroach whispered.

"Parcheesi," Wally said, "we'll only end up fighting if we play Monopoly."

He's right, I thought, *we've never finished a game of Monopoly in our lives. The board usually gets flipped over before we're done.*

As we played the safer game, Wally turned to me, smiled and then farted. "I feel like I just lost the best part of me," he said, trying not to laugh.

"That's so gross," I told him.

"At least I didn't blame the dog," he said.

"We don't even have a dog," Cockroach reminded him.

He smiled. "Exactly."

We were three games in when Cockroach complained, "This sucks!" It was what everyone else was thinking.

"Do you want to go back outside and freeze?" Wally whispered, farting again.

Vic stood. "I do," he said at a normal volume.

"Shhhhhh . . ."

"I don't think I can take any more of this," Vic whispered.

"You're leaving?" I asked him.

He nodded.

"Chew and screw, huh?" Wally said.

Vic ignored the comment. "I'm sure somebody in the neighborhood is outside playing."

"Who, Eskimos?"

He shrugged. "Whatever," he said, "anything's better than hiding in this stinky room like those poor refugees on T.V."

"Go freeze then," Wally told him.

As my friend reached for the accordion door, I whispered, "You'd better tiptoe out of here, Vic, and put your boots on once you're out of the house."

"Are you serious?"

"Yeah, I'm serious. If Ma catches you here, then we're busted too."

"Whatever," he whispered, tiptoeing out of the room.

Wally quietly slipped away to use the bathroom when I told Cockroach, "We might have to hang out in the cellar tomorrow, if this weather doesn't break."

"But Ma said . . ."

"Ma's not out there freezing to death, Alphonse," I told him.

He shook his head. "I don't like it down there, Herbie," he whispered, with real fear in his voice.

"Why?" I asked him. "What's there to be afraid of?"

Shrugging, he broke eye contact.

I shook my head, thinking, *Cockroach is afraid of everything . . . puddles he thinks might be over his head . . . monsters . . .*

"Monsters living in the basement," he admitted, matching my thoughts.

I couldn't understand why. "With the condition our cellar's in, don't you think a monster could find a much nicer place to live?"

"You never know, Herbie," he said, looking at me again like one of the puppets from Fraggle Rock.

"Alphonse, you're afraid of everything."

"Nah, ah," he said, "not everything." He thought about it. "Just sharks, the dark, rats, snakes, tunnels . . ." He stopped.

"Keep going," I told him, "sometimes it helps to talk about it."

He searched my eyes before making his decision. "Sometimes I'm afraid of someone looking into our bedroom window," he reluctantly admitted.

"But our bedroom's on the second floor."

"I know that," he said, shaking his head, "but I'm still afraid that if I look out our window, an old person's face will be looking back at me."

As I laughed, I saw his face change—with him retreating inward. I stopped. "What else?" I asked.

"Nothing," he snapped back, defensively.

"How 'bout I go next and tell you something stupid that I'm afraid of?" I suggested. Although I was older and a little more practical—fearing that Wally would use my toothbrush to clean the toilet, like he'd threatened a hundred times—I still carried around my fair share of illogical phobias.

As Cockroach's eyes came to life again, he nodded.

"I'm still terrified of the child catcher in Chitty Chitty Bang Bang," I admitted. "Augustus Gloop going up the chocolate pipe in Willy Wonka and the Chocolate Factory freaks me out. And the flying monkeys in the Wizard of Oz are pretty bad too. But that long-nosed kidnapper in Chitty Chitty Bang Bang is a whole different level of scary for me." I couldn't believe it, but it actually felt good to tell someone about it. I never had. "Now it's your turn," I told him.

This time, he couldn't talk fast enough. "I always think there's someone hiding in our bathtub. Every time I'm in there, it takes everything I have just to peek into the tub." He shook his head. "And after I take a bath, I hate looking into the mirror when I'm stepping out of the tub. I'm afraid that the steamy face in the mirror won't be mine."

"Wow," I said, nodding, "I . . ."

"And I'm scared of being left behind," he quickly continued.

"How do you mean?"

"Like when I get home from school, I'm afraid I'll find that no one's home and the whole family's left me."

I felt bad about that one. "I'm sure Wally and I teasing you all the time about being adopted doesn't help with that one." We constantly tried to convince Cockroach that it was a real possibility.

"It doesn't," he agreed, without a hint of anger or judgment.

I thought about it. *And Ma doesn't help with that one either.* Whenever we were misbehaving—which was always—Ma threatened that she and Pop were going to drop us off at the orphan's home. "Let's see if they can do something with you animals," she'd tell us, "cause God knows I'm at the end of my rope." Sometimes, she'd even pick up the kitchen phone and pretend to call the home, requesting that they come pick us up right away. Although this never worked on me and Wally, it straightened Cockroach out every time. To stop his crying so we could sleep, we'd always tell him that it was never going to happen.

"And like I said, I hate going down into the cellar," he said. "There's so many places for monsters to hide and . . ."

"Monsters?" I said, stopping myself again so he could go on.

"Sometimes I feel like I'm going to crap my pants, so I run up the stairs as fast as I can, hoping that something won't grab me by the ankles and drag me back down."

"Hmmm," I said, "that sucks." I placed my hand on his shoulder. "What about under the bed?" I realized he wasn't halfway through his fear list and I was already feeling bad for him—really bad. *It wasn't that long ago when I was afraid of everything, too*, I thought.

He nodded. "Still afraid of it."

Cockroach was convinced that something, or someone, had moved under our bunk bed—although they were only there at night. He would shut off the light switch on the wall before making a running leap into his top bunk, throwing the covers over his head on the way. For years, he refused to get up until morning. Given that I slept directly under him, I always asked him, "You peed already, right?"

"Yup."

Although I sometimes mocked my brother's child-like fears, I understood where he was coming from. When I stirred in the middle of the night and found that my hand or foot was hanging off the edge of the bed, I immediately pulled it back and stuffed it under the covers—a feeling of panic welling up inside me.

"I can understand that one," I told him, "you're not alone there."

His eyes brightened even more. "And let's not even talk about our bedroom closet."

This time, when I laughed, he laughed with me.

My little brother always made sure the closet door was open before turning in for the night. Although the door was right in front of Wally's bed, Cockroach still needed to see that there was nothing hiding behind it that could sneak up on him in the dark.

I can relate to that one, too, I thought. Our bedroom also had a tiny wooden door that led to a pink-insulated crawl space behind the wall. On more than one occasion, I wondered what might live inside that mysterious space. Then I'd have the worst, most detailed nightmares about a short, deformed creature with sharp teeth sneaking into our room through that door. I'd always open my eyes within the dream and see this hideous monster, silently beckoning me to come to him. Sometimes, I'd even wonder if that monster sneaked under our bunk bed when the light went out at night, putting me and my brothers in terrible danger.

Although I hated to admit it to myself, I thought, *And there's far worse than that.* I was still afraid of the tree beside Ma and Pop's bedroom window, its shadow dancing like some deranged woman. I feared finding deceased relatives standing at the foot of my bed when I was sleeping. Some nights, I had to leave a light on. And

I absolutely hated waking up and not knowing who I was and where I was. Nothing freaked me out more than being disoriented or feeling that lack of control. I also feared spiders crawling into my mouth while I slept. *Waking up with morning breath . . . maybe that's not so far-fetched?* And I hated watching horror movies. I'd obsess over them like they were completely real. *I still hate to leave the house when it's foggy out,* I reminded myself, *but nothing compares to the man with the lisp driving that white van.* It had become my worst fear, a recurring nightmare—Clarence in the same white van that supposedly drove around looking for children to abduct. *That one's a bad one.*

"I can't help it," Cockroach said, interrupting my own litany of fears. "I guess I am afraid of everything."

I looked him in the eye. "No more than anyone else your age, Alphonse," I told him, "trust me."

He nodded his appreciation.

"But it'll get better," I told him.

"It will?" His grin was filled with hope.

I nodded. "You'll grow out of it. I did," I fibbed.

As soon as Wally returned to the room, we went silent.

• • •

Pop brought home pizza for supper, answering some long-awaited prayers.

"You must have gotten a raise at work today," Ma said, sarcastically.

"What's that?" he asked, opening the first box and releasing the heavenly smell.

"Why are we celebrating?" Cockroach asked, innocently covering our mother's back.

"We're not celebrating anything," Pop said. "What's the big deal? I stopped by Nick's on the way home from work. It's just dinner."

"Can we *not* celebrate anything again tomorrow for supper?" Cockroach asked, getting up from his chair and starting to gyrate his narrow hips.

Although Wally and I both laughed, I couldn't tell whether he was dancing or having a seizure. "Go easy, Deney Terrio," I told him, "before you hurt yourself."

"Looks like someone's caught the dance fever," Wally added.

"If my cooking's that bad," Ma began to say, "then maybe you . . ."

"Not at all, Ma," Wally said. "You're a great cook."

"The best, Ma," I added.

Although she tried to fight it off, the corners of her mouth turned up.

Cockroach sighed heavily. "I don't know," he said, "this pizza's the best thing I've eaten since my last school lunch."

Just then, as though he were trying to save our little brother, Wally farted. "Excuse me," he said, "I honestly didn't see that one coming."

"Damn," Pop said, "that sounded like a mud flap in a bad rainstorm."

I laughed.

Ma didn't think it was funny. "Right at the supper table?" she asked Wally.

"I couldn't help it, Ma. It felt like something was inside me, fighting to get out."

I laughed harder.

She wouldn't let it go. "Are you sick?" she asked. "Do you have diarrhea?"

He nodded. "I don't know how to spell it, but I'm pretty sure I do."

"The Hershey squirts," Cockroach said, giggling. In a flash, he threw his left hand inside his shirt, placing it under his right armpit, and began flapping his arm like a sparrow taking flight. One fart after the other escaped his shirt.

Wally and I laughed.

"Stop!" Ma told him.

My little brother let a few more rip. It was impressive. Although Wally and I could make our armpits toot, Cockroach was gifted. When left to his own devices, he could make the skin behind his knee flatulent, as well as his neck. *And I've never known anyone else who can make their neck fart.*

"That's enough . . . all of you," Ma said, putting a stop to the foolishness that had already gone on too long.

There was a moment of silence, nothing but the sounds of chewing. "When does gas actually become a liquid?" Wally asked.

Pop looked at him and pointed toward our bedroom. "That's it," he said, "you're done. Clear your plate."

I choked on my laughter, careful not to join my brother in our bedroom. I was still hungry and there was pizza left. *And Wally's share is up for grabs*, I thought.

"What am I getting for my birthday?" Cockroach asked, out-of-the-blue. "It's only three weeks away, you know."

Pop looked at him. "Close your eyes," he told my baby brother.

Cockroach did as instructed.

"What do you see?" Pop asked.

"Ummm...nothing."

"Good," Pop said, "because that's exactly what you're getting."

Even Ma laughed at that one.

That night, while Pop snored away in his recliner—a beer can nestled safely between his legs—we started to watch Mork and Mindy.

"Turn it down," Ma said, flipping through the TV guide; it was a stark reminder that she controlled the programming in the house. At any point in time and, without a moment's notice, she could commandeer the television to watch her beloved shows: Knots Landing, Donny and Marie, Tony Orlando and Dawn, The Lawrence Welk Show with all its bubbles, and the very funny Carol Burnett Show. The only show we loved that she and Pop also enjoyed was Cheers. "Your dad's had a hard day," she added, looking up from the tiny magazine. This embellished truth threatened to become her daily mantra.

What about us? I thought. *Do you think trying not to freeze to death is a cakewalk?*

Wally was a little more vocal. "Sure he has," he muttered under his breath.

"What was that?" she asked.

"Poor Pop," Wally said, quickly covering his tracks.

"That's what I thought," Ma said, sure to get in the last word.

Pop's stinky stocking feet spasmed in the recliner.

We all looked at him.

It was impressive. Even when our father dozed, he never tipped his shiny gold can. The twelve-ounce beer was like an appendage he'd been born with. Occasionally, he'd wake up, guzzle down a generous sip and then nod back off—only to repeat the odd cycle long after the beer had gotten warm. *But God be with you if you accidentally touch his feet*, I thought. You'd face the wrath of an angry bear awakened early from hibernation. Even dazed, Pop was known to launch from his chair and seek out his attacker. *There's nothing more terrifying.*

My brothers and I got up, one after another, and headed for our bedroom.

"Good night, boys," Ma called out after us.

"Night, Ma."

It was later than usual when Ma talked to Aunt Phyllis on the phone.

"It couldn't have been that short?" Ma said, laughing. There was a pause, my mother getting in several drags on her cigarette. "Oh, we're fine," she said, "the boys are in bed for the night. They've been outside playing all day and they're . . ." She stopped. "I realize it's freezing out, Phyllis, but I also know that if I let them stay in the house this week, I'll be getting a call once an hour from downstairs about my three little animals making too much noise." She took a puff. "Imagine if we got evicted from this place? The boys would have to grow up in the city." The dread in her voice was palpable. ". . . which would be a whole lot worse than suffering wind burn." She took a heavy drag on her cigarette. "Besides, I don't want them stuck in the house all day, where they'll only melt their brains on those stupid video games."

Wow, I thought, my perspective of my mother instantly changing, *she's actually looking out for us.* I thought about her comments for a bit longer. *The video games aren't stupid, though.*

In our darkened bedroom, I called out, "May the force be with you."

Alas, Wally responded. He farted; it sounded like a wet slap.

"Oh, my God," Cockroach whispered from above, "I think he just crapped his PJs."

"I hope he did," I whispered back, making them both laugh. *At least Wally answered this time,* I thought, stifling a cough. *That's something, anyway.*

CHAPTER 7

WEDNESDAY

After devouring three bowls of Apple Jacks and just the right amount of pink, sweetened milk, Ma announced, "Be home before the street lights come on and not a minute longer."

She helped Cockroach get ready, complaining the entire time. "This is ridiculous, Alphonse," she said, "you're getting too big for Mommy to be dressing you."

"Or for him to be calling you Mommy," I muttered.

Wally laughed.

"Before the street lights come on," she repeated, staring Wally down.

I kissed her cheek. "Yes, Mommy."

We hurried out the door like three cackling hens heading straight for a walk-in freezer.

Cockroach and I tried to steel ourselves for another day on the Arctic circle, while Wally quickly ducked into the cellar. As soon as the frozen wind bitch-slapped my face, I turned to my little brother. "Alphonse, this is nuts," I told him. "If we keep hanging outside, we won't survive the week."

"I know," he said, his teeth already chattering.

"Let's head down into the cellar," I said.

"Wally probably wants to be alone," he replied, feeding into his fear of the eerie space.

"Good for Wally," I said, "and we probably want to stay alive today."

"I don't know, Herbie," he said, "I hate . . ."

"I know," I said, cutting him off, "but there's nothing to be afraid of down there, I promise." I grinned. "Well, except for Wally."

His eyes were filled with anxiety.

"Relax," I told him, "I'll be with you the whole time."

"Okay," he surrendered, sucking in a long deep breath.

A wooden slatted door, once painted gray, was unpadlocked and hanging on the steel latch. A narrow set of ancient stone stairs led down into the house's fieldstone foundation. *This place is even creepier than R&S Variety,* I thought. Even I had to duck my head, descending into the throat of the beast. After wiping away the cobwebs that stuck to my face and hat—hanging from the low ceiling's exposed beams and rusty nails—I looked back to make sure Cockroach was still with me.

"Maybe we're better off outside," he suggested, hoping I'd change my mind. "And Ma said . . ."

"Not today, brother," I interrupted, continuing on.

There were small windows up near the basement's ceiling—two on each side—allowing in enough natural light to view the abysmal conditions. *Disgusting.* As if that wasn't enough, a pair of pull strings hung from two bare bulbs located on opposite sides of the dank crypt: one above the washing machine, which made an awful ruckus because its drum was off kilter, and the other above our pathetic improvised gym. Both lights were on.

In the center of the grungy space was a giant black, cast iron oil furnace, a behemoth, that had been dormant for years. I looked back again. Cockroach's eyes were wide with fear, struggling to avoid eye contact with the iron giant.

"Relax, bro," I repeated, "you're fine."

The strong smell of mildew permeated the air, generated from swags of old discarded carpets that were soaked year-round. The cellar flooded during heavy rainstorms or thawing snowdrifts, the streams of water flowing through the cracks in the broken concrete floor and disintegrating foundation. The entire place was blanketed in cobwebs created by a community of daddy long legs that begrudgingly shared the space with us when we were trying to find a little bit of privacy from our parents—who very rarely visited the decrepit conditions.

Even above the banging washing machine—now on its last spin cycle—I could hear Wally grunting and groaning. *He's lifting weights*, I surmised, and made my way around the furnace to confirm.

A narrow weight bench, with enough plastic sand-filled weights to hurt ourselves, was located beneath the bare bulb in the corner. Wally was sitting on that bench, taking a breather between sets. *I hate that damn bench*, I thought. The last time I'd tried to work out, Wally kept adding more plastic plates until I couldn't budge the steel bar off my chest. *Wally laughed like a maniac, refusing to help me until my threats became pathetic cries for help.*

The moldy walls surrounding the low-budget gym were decorated with a few rock and roll posters—Def Leppard, Pink Floyd, REO Speedwagon—and my favorite poster of them all, Bo Derek running in a swimsuit down the beach.

Wally acknowledged us with a quick jerk of his head. Glistening in sweat, he got up to turn over the cassette—AC/DC's Back in

Black—on an old boom box that was missing two knobs. Although its rear compartment was corroded from the dried green acid of exploded batteries, it still somehow worked when plugged in.

Without a word, Wally returned to the bench, lay down and began bench pressing the weight, listening to "You shook me all night long . . ."

He's training for a fight, I thought, *a real fight, not like the one with Vic.* I contemplated whether or not I should talk to him about it.

He grunted like a wounded animal, pushing with all his strength and rage.

"What's going on?" I asked him.

He finished his set, racked the weights and sat up. "What's it look like, spaz? I'm working out."

"I can see that," I told him, "I meant . . ." I stopped.

He looked at me. "You worry too much, Herbie."

"Do I?" I asked, stripping off some of my winter gear.

"You do."

For whatever reason, looking at my big brother in the dim light, I felt really bad for him. As if adolescence wasn't cruel enough, Wally was in a fierce battle with acne—and losing badly. He'd been nick-named "pizza face" by some of the nastier kids in school. Although he did his best to combat it—his Clearasil tube always left on the side of the bathroom sink—given the lack of results, I always thought that the tube of Crest toothpaste might be more effective. *And if that's not bad enough,* I thought, *he's going to get beat down by Owen when we get back to school.*

Wally looked at Cockroach who was now wearing regular clothes and chewing gum. "Let me get a piece of that gum, little man," he said.

Cockroach shook his head, refusing to share.

"Give me a piece," Wally repeated, his eyes turning to cobra-like slits.

Cockroach grinned, singing, "Bubble Yum. Chew my bum. You don't get no gum."

"Don't be stupid," I told him, realizing that his cute little rhyme was missing a full syllable. "If it wasn't for me, you wouldn't even have the damn gum."

"Ma paid for it on her tab," he countered.

"Which she doesn't even know about," I snapped back. "I'm the one she sends to the store. And I'm the one who always grabs something for you."

"Not always."

"Most of the time."

He looked back at Wally and smirked. "Bubble Yum. Chew my bum. You don't get no gum," he sang.

"That's it," I told him, "you're shut off. No more freebees."

"Then I'll just tell Ma that you're stealing from her," he said.

"I'm not stealing from her!"

Wally held out his hand. "Give me a piece of gum, Alphonse." He stood up from the bench. "And I'm not asking anymore."

Feeling cocky, Cockroach maintained his smirk. "Bubble Yum. Chew my bum. You don't get no gum," he sang even louder.

After this third annoying verse, Wally dropped to one knee, grabbed our little brother by the waist and pulled him in for a hard bite on the rear end.

"Yow!" Cockroach screamed, jumping around like he'd been swarmed upon by fire ants. "He ripped my skin off, Herbie," he yelled, pulling his pants down to inspect the damage. "He ripped my skin off," he shrieked.

I crouched down behind him to take a close look. "Stop hollering, you big baby," I told him. "Wally didn't even break the skin."

"I'm telling Ma," Cockroach yelled, repeating the threat like a hyperactive parrot.

"Oh, I wouldn't," Wally warned, staring at him with the glare of a Mafia hitman. "I just wouldn't."

Cockroach swallowed hard.

You might want to listen to him this time, I thought.

Wally sat back down on the bench, preparing to do another set. "You wanna go with me on my paper route again today, Herbie?" he asked.

I looked up at the tiny cellar window to see the snow being whipped around by the relentless wind. "Nah, I don't think so. Not today."

He grinned. "I don't blame you."

"Any word on that other paper route?" I asked him, realizing it might not be the best timing.

He shook his head. "Not yet, though it's probably not the smartest move for you anyway."

"Why?" I asked.

He looked at Cockroach. "You'd better not repeat a word I say."

"I won't."

"You'd better not."

"What is it?" I asked, feeling like my newfound dream was about to be killed off right in front of me.

"Remember how I said I was letting Ma borrow money?"

I nodded.

"Well, she's talking about me starting to pay room and board every week," he reported.

"What?" I said, immediately thinking about Vic's parents, "Ma would never . . ."

"She's already mentioned it to me a couple times," Wally said.

"Word?"

He nodded.

No way, I thought, *that's so gaf.* "How much a week?" I asked.

"She's thinking half of what I make."

"Half," I repeated.

Cockroach whistled, causing both of us to look at him. "Half's a lot," young Ebenezer confirmed.

"You'd better not say a word," Wally told him again. "I swear to God, I'll . . ."

"I won't," Cockroach yelled.

Wally looked back at me, nodding again. "I told her that I need to start saving money for a car because there's no way that her and Pop are going to buy one for me." He laughed. "I mean, look at the junker the old man drives."

Of course they're not going to buy you a car, I thought, without judgement. *We should buy our own cars.*

"I've talked to Pop about it already," Wally added. "He agrees that I shouldn't pay half."

"But he thinks you should pay some room and board?"

Wally shrugged. "I guess that's what he and Ma did at my age."

Cockroach whistled again.

"That's so messed up," I said, still in shock.

"Tell me about it. Now I'm going to have to lie to them about how much I make."

I nodded. "You'd be crazy if you didn't."

"Ain't that the truth," Cockroach commented.

I stood there—frozen from shock this time—thinking about my future prospects. *I'm not sure getting a paper route would even be worth the time and effort, if Ma's gonna take half.* It made me sad. *But if I don't, I'll still need to figure out how I'm going to pay off that Columbia Record & Tape Club contract and get Police's Synchronicity album.*

"Something to think about anyway," Wally said.

I nodded. "I'm gonna hang out with him," I said, gesturing toward our little brother, "and make sure he keeps quiet."

"I'm not gonna say anything," Cockroach squeaked, annoyed by our lack of trust in him.

Nodding his gratitude, Wally lay back down, unracked the weights and began grunting again.

I turned to Cockroach. "Let's get out of here."

"Already?" he asked, excitedly.

"Yes, already. We'll sneak into the house and hide in our bedroom."

"Okay," he said, struggling to put his cold weather clothing back on.

Cockroach and I headed upstairs, much earlier than Ma would have liked. *As long as we're quiet,* I thought, *she won't kick us back out.* On the stairway leading up to the apartment, I warned Cockroach, "We need to be quiet or we'll be sent back outside to freeze. You don't want that, do you?"

"No, and I don't want to go back into the cellar either," he whimpered, tears welling up in his big brown eyes. "My butt hurts really bad, Herbie."

"Stop being a such a sally," I told him, "it was a little nibble. You're fine."

"I don't think I am," he said, rubbing his backside.

"Besides, you asked Wally to do it."

"I did not."

"Bubble Yum. Chew my bum. You don't get no gum," I sang in a whisper.

"Well, I didn't think he'd . . ."

"You had it coming, Alphonse," I interrupted, "and that's what you get for being selfish."

Like well-trained Navy Seals, we slipped into our bedroom undetected. The trick was to remove our winter gear once we'd closed the accordion door. While the TV played in the living room, I never realized how squeaky plastic could be until I needed it to be silent. As the door clicked, I smiled. *Mission accomplished!*

Cockroach went straight to the top bunk to sulk, while I pictured Donna's sweet face. *I wonder what my baby's doing today? Hiding in her room like me?* I snickered. *I doubt it.*

I searched for my Magic 8 ball. Finding it, I took it into the privacy of the bottom bunk. I shook the smooth plastic ball three times "Does Donna like me?" I whispered to the ball, my fingers crossed on the other hand.

I flipped the ball over to peer into the circular window filled with purple fluid.

The triangle read, *Cannot predict now*

Bullshit, I thought. *I need to know now!*

"Does Donna like me?" I said aloud, shaking it three more times.

"How should I know," Cockroach answered from above. "Why don't you ask her?"

"Good idea," I told him, "thanks." I flipped the ball again and looked into the fateful window.

Very doubtful.

Sighing heavily, I decided, *But that's not a no, is it? Let's give it one more shot.*

I shook the annoying toy harder and longer than I'd ever shaken it. *Will Donna and I go out with each other?* When I finally flipped it over, my heart sank.

My sources say no, the message read.

I whipped the ball toward the foot of my bed, where it skipped once before bouncing off the wall. *I hope it's broken for good,* I thought, joining Cockroach in the self-pity party.

After a few minutes of some serious pouting, I retrieved my letter to Donna and returned to my bunk. *It's been a while since I've looked at it.* I picked it up and read, *Dear Donna.* For whatever reason, I was surprised. *I thought I'd written more than this.* I shrugged. *Oh well.*

Using Queen's *The Game* album cover as my desk, I gripped my chunky three-ink Bic pen, ready to go to work.

I need to tell you a few things. I stopped writing, thinking, *You need to be careful about what you write next.* I sat there for a good thirty minutes, debating the next line. There were hundreds of options. *I can go with honesty, but if she doesn't feel the same way about me then . . .* I continued to contemplate my situation. *I could be a little more clever and hint about how I feel, so if she doesn't feel the same way, then . . .* It always came back to one single fear. *What if she doesn't feel same? I'll be humiliated.* But I also knew, *If I don't take a chance and let her know how I feel, then I'll never know how she feels—and I need to know.*

Cockroach moaned in pain.

I grabbed the pen again. Placing it onto the paper, I applied just enough pressure to pour out my heart. *I really like you.*

As though the pen had been slapped from my hand, it dropped from my fingers. I read the line. *I really like you.* I read it again and again. *Really,* I thought, *that's the best you've got?* I shook my head again. *Nope, I don't think so.* I shredded the piece of paper into white confetti. *Let's try it again tomorrow.*

Cockroach moaned again. "My butt really hurts me, Herbie," he complained. "Maybe Wally . . ."

"Do you want to play a video game?" I asked, trying to distract him and keep him from squealing on our brother. "Your pick."

"I get to pick?" he said, surprised by the offer.

"Yup."

He jumped down from the bunk like a new man. "Let's play Atari."

"I don't know," I said, "the noise might . . ."

"We can just turn down the volume on the TV," he said, proving again that he was much wiser than his years.

"Pac Man?" I asked, hoping against hope that he'd agree to it.

He shook his head. "E.T.," he said, grinning.

What a stupid game, I thought, *It's the worst.* "Okay," I said, preparing to take one for the team.

"It's my favorite," he said.

I nodded. *Maybe it's for the best,* I thought. *Ma hates the annoying sound that Pac Man makes and she'd probably pick up the slightest sound. And God knows, we don't need the heat.* I chuckled to myself, the irony hardly lost on me. *At least not that kind of heat.*

I looked at Cockroach to see that he was three knuckles deep in his nose, so deep that he could have probably scratched his own brain, placing his I.Q. back in question. "You're so gross," I told him.

"What are you talking about? You're always picking your nose, Herbie."

We turned off the volume on the black-and-white TV and, for the next few hours, played the dumbest video game ever designed— E.T.

"I love this game," he said, rubbing it in.

"Hmmm, hmmm," I responded, no longer able to access my vocabulary, never mind form full sentences.

We were well into our drooling marathon, when Cockroach opted to take a break and play with my Rubik's Cube.

I immediately switched the game to Pong, a riveting, more challenging game. It didn't take long before I realized that my head was bobbing from right to left, left to right, like a pendulum hypnotizing my brain into a state of numb oblivion.

"Look at what I did," Cockroach said, excitedly.

I reluctantly looked up at him.

He showed me the plastic cube; all of the colors matched up perfectly on each side.

"Sure, genius," I told him, knowing that my brothers and I were only smart enough to swap out the stickers.

"But I did it this time, Herbie," he said, still trying to sell his tall tale. "I really finished it."

"Yeah, right," I said, unsure whether my annoying brother was trying to make a point or win one.

Excited, he jumped off the top bunk onto the beanbag chair. There was a loud pop, followed by a million tiny white beads flying everywhere.

Laughing, I paused the game. "Smooth move, Ex-Lax," I told him.

"Shhhh...." Cockroach hissed, "or Ma will come in here to see what's going on."

"You don't think she heard that explosion?"

"You think she did?" he asked, his face filling with panic.

I shrugged. "We'll see. Either way, if I were you, I'd start cleaning up."

He surveyed the room to discover that the blast had covered nearly everything with the tiny white beads. "I don't know how I'll be able to clean all of this." He looked at me. "Can you help me, Herbie? My . . . my butt still hurts bad."

"Oh, God no." I said, laughing harder. "And you'd better get a move on, airhead. Ma sees this room like this and you're dead meat." I returned to the Atari game, happy to keep it on single player mode.

• • •

Pop returned home from work and announced, "I'm dog tired, but I need to go to Skinny's tonight and help him put his new entertainment center together."

"You're gonna help him, all right," Ma said under her breath. "Except he's not gonna lift a finger."

Pop ignored the comment.

"I was going to make English muffin pizzas for supper," she said.

Pop looked at us. "Who wants to tag along with me?"

I don't know, I thought, *I love English muffin pizzas, especially when Ma lets us add our own toppings.*

Ma reached for her favorite son—Cockroach—and pulled her

pet in for a tight embrace. "Wally and Herbie, go help your father," she said, making the decision for us, "Alphonse and I will stay back."

That's fine with me, I thought, imagining our crazy uncle sneaking us sweets. Just the thought of it made my skin tingle, like I'd broken out of a detox facility and was heading straight for the dirty streets to get my overdue fix. *To hell with the English muffin pizzas.*

Ma got up to make us PBJ sandwiches, wrapping them in aluminum foil.

"I don't want that crap," Pop told her. "I'll grab something at Skinny's."

Wally and I were already unwrapping our supper before we hit the front door.

"Wally," Cockroach whispered at the door, "while you're gone, can I play with your electronic football game?"

Wally smirked. "Aren't you the same guy who wouldn't give me a piece of bubble gum when I asked for it?"

"Yeah, but . . ."

"I don't think so, you stingy dork," he said, "and if I find out you've used it . . ."

"I won't," Cockroach said.

Wally stared at him.

"I won't," he repeated.

Damn, I thought, *this definitely isn't a Brady Bunch household.* Although my brothers and I created a tough environment for each other, I thought, *At least we tell it the way it is.* I grinned. *No one has to walk on eggshells around here.*

We arrived at Uncle Skinny's in record time. Even I could have driven the route blindfolded. There were still a few Christmas decorations in his apartment that hadn't been taken down yet. The once-green pine tree was now brown, standing dangerously close to the iron radiator. *I'm surprised Uncle Skinny has survived his own laziness*, I thought.

Pop shook his brother's hand before they jumped right in on their usual banter. "Hey, I don't know if I told you, but I just had a colonoscopy done in a van off of Route 195," Pop joked. "Although there was no co-pay, I did learn that I have a duct tape allergy."

He and Uncle Skinny laughed.

I wanted to join them, but I had no idea what they were talking about.

Wally laughed too.

I studied my brother's face, deciding, *He has no idea, either.*

"I loved a ginger midget once," Uncle Skinny said, looking at us and trying to keep a straight face, "but she was a dirty woman."

Pop laughed.

Our comical uncle had an incredibly casual relationship with the truth, so there was never any telling when he was being serious—or honest. "You were once in love with a midget?" I asked him.

"In his younger days," Pop interjected, "your uncle would have loved anything that moved."

Uncle Skinny turned to me and Wally. "When you boys finally get a girlfriend, make sure she takes good care of you." He smiled. "The thing about love is . . . if you don't feed the dog, then it's bound to get into the trash."

What? I thought, confused.

Pop laughed again. "Don't listen to him," Pop said, talking to me and Wally like we were men. It felt good. "These days, your Uncle Skinny's like a dog chasing a fire truck. If he ever caught the opposite sex, he wouldn't have any idea what to do with it."

"Oh, I'd know what to do with it, all right," Skinny said, his eyes going wide.

I wish I knew what the hell they were talking about, I thought.

As they took all of the entertainment center's parts and hardware out of the long cardboard box, they started in on Aunt Phyllis, making me even happier that I'd tagged along. Although our vile aunt gave us a paddleball every Easter and a box of ribbon candy every Christmas, the rest of the year she gave us nothing but headaches.

"Phyllis is something, that's for sure," Uncle Skinny said. "It's no wonder Bert high-tailed it out of there as soon as he had the chance."

"What ever happened to Uncle Bert?" Wally asked.

"He went out for a pack of cigarettes one afternoon and never returned," Uncle Skinny explained.

"And I'm sure he was running at a full sprint when he left," Pop teased.

"I know I would have been," my uncle said.

"You could probably smell the smoke coming off the back of his wing tips," Pop added.

"According to Ma," Wally said, getting in on the gossip, "Bert was a jackass and Aunt Phyllis is better off without him."

"Sure," Pop agreed, chuckling. "Phyllis is your mother's sister. What else would she say?"

Uncle Skinny nodded like a grinning puppet.

Ma defends her sister the same way you defend your brother, I told Pop in my head. I looked over at Wally. *I get it,* I thought, nodding.

While Pop worked on assembling the monstrous entertainment center, Uncle Skinny announced, "While you're working, Walt, why don't I run out and grab us some Coney Island hot dogs?" He looked at me and Wally. "You boys want any?"

We both nodded.

"They already ate," Pop told him, "they're all set."

Uncle Skinny looked back at us. "How many do you want?" he asked, as though Pop had never uttered a word.

I raised two fingers. Wally raised four.

He nodded and then looked at Pop, quickly doing the math on his fingers. "It's buy five and get one free, so I'll get us a dozen." He grinned at me and Wally. "You boys might have to eat the extras."

We're here to help any way we can, I thought.

"With the works?" Uncle Skinny asked, on the brink of laughter.

Remaining silent, and trying not to aggravate our father, we nodded once more.

While Pop complained and cursed with each screw turned, I watched in awe as the giant steel and wooden tower began to take shape.

"Uncle Skinny must be really rich," I commented to my brother.

"I wouldn't say that," Pop claimed, his face grimacing from turning the screwdriver, "he just doesn't have any kids to bleed him dry."

Wally and I looked at each other. The old man wasn't smiling. *Well, okay then.*

We could smell Uncle Skinny before we saw him; the distinct aroma of Coney Island hot dogs made my mouth water. I turned to my brother. *Wally looks happier than I've seen him all week*, I thought.

As soon as our uncle entered the room, Pop took a break from working and we began to eat.

"Eat 'em slow, so you don't choke," Pop told us.

"These are so delicious," I said, trying to regulate my bites.

Wally, on the other hand, was inhaling the belly bombers like a full-grown blue whale sifting through krill.

"I love hot dogs," I said.

Wally nodded "Especially when they're on a hot dog bun and not some folded slice of bread like Ma serves 'em."

I chuckled, thinking, *It's probably for the plastic bags that go inside our winter boots.*

Pop's head snapped toward us. "Watch how you talk about you mother," he hissed. "She takes good care of you boys and I won't stand for you disrespecting her."

"We're not disrespecting her, Pop," Wally said, speaking for the both of us.

"You'd better not be," he said, still glaring down at us.

"We're not," I quietly confirmed. "We wouldn't."

It took a few more hours before Pop finished assembling Uncle Skinny's newest toy. "If I'd remembered my damn tool box in the shed," he said, "this would have gone much quicker."

"No matter," Uncle Skinny said, "I'm obliged for the help." He and Pop shook hands again.

It's cool that they're still so close, I thought. *I wonder if me, Wally and Cockroach will be that close when we're old?*

"So you won this thing at work, huh?" Pop asked our uncle.

"I did," he said, nodding. "As far as I know, they just signed a contract with the company that makes them." He stood there, admiring the new furniture and smiling. "I've never won a damn thing in my life. I still can't believe it."

"You didn't buy it?" I asked, my tone betraying as much disappointment as surprise.

Uncle Skinny shook his head. "Are you kidding? I don't have a pot to piss in or a window to throw it out of." He looked at me and Wally. "I hate to break it to you boys, but your family has nothing . . ." He smiled. ". . . which is a great place to start because when you think about it, you have nothing to lose." He added a wink. "So go out into the world and chase it down."

We looked at our father.

"Chase it down hard," Pop echoed with a nod.

We returned home late and exhausted. Ma was in bed and Cockroach was already out cold.

I quickly changed into the previous night's pajamas and slid under my heavy blanket, rubbing my feet together like a cricket until I warmed the cold sheets.

What the heck, I thought, and called out, "By the power of Greyskull."

There was silence.

Wally's already snoring, I thought. *I guess all of that weight training's finally caught up with him.*

I then thought about our uncle's unexpected advice. *Nothing to lose*, I repeated in my head, *so go out into the world and chase it down.* I think I may have smiled—maybe not—before reality slowed to a creep and the entire world turned into a tiny pinpoint of light. Suddenly, even that disappeared and the world went black.

CHAPTER 8

THURSDAY

Along with even more tension in the house, a thunderstorm rolled in and shook me from my sleep. I got up for a drink of watered-down Tang when a bolt of lightning made me notice that the shed doors were open and swinging in the heavy winds. I stepped into the living room. The couch was empty. *Where's Clarence?* I wondered. *Pop's new friend is probably sitting out there alone in the darkness. Should I leave him be?* I wondered, before grabbing my jacket.

Soaked from the short walk, I stepped into the shed to hear Clarence whimpering.

"Clarence?" I asked, my eyes squinting in the darkness. "Why don't you come back into the house. There's no . . ."

"I'm tho grateful for your father welcoming me into your home," Clarence interrupted, a great pain betrayed in his moist words. "I wath hoping thomeone would offer. I've been thtarving for tho long now."

I started to nod when the odd comment caused the hairs on my arms to stand up straight. Just then, another bolt of lightening lit up the sky.

Clarence was holding a carving knife inches from my face. His tongue lapped a stream of drool from his quivering lips.

As reality registered, I swallowed hard. "But Reggie?"

Clarence grinned straight into the frightened eyes of his mid-night snack. "Reggie who?"

I felt my knees buckle and nearly fainted.

"Come on, Herbie," he whispered, "where'th that thenthe of humor?" Clarence spit out, and then lunged for me.

I tried to run, but my legs wouldn't budge. They felt restrained, like they were wrapped in a bedsheet.

As the blade sliced into my face, I thought about my mother's warning of welcoming strangers into our home and the heated argument that followed between her and Pop. A piercing sting instantly gave way to pain I'd never imagined possible. I let out a blood-curdling scream, but no one could have ever heard it. Torrential downpours and deafening claps of thunder helped to drown out my excruciating pain.

As the madman chewed off my ear, I struggled to remain conscious. *Pop was so stupid to make friends with this animal,* I thought, trying to scream again. But I couldn't. Clarence had already made his way to my throat.

"Don't worry, my friend," the hideous monster whispered. "Wally will be joining you thoon. Maybe even tonight?" Between chews, he chuckled. "And who knowth, before I've had my fill, I might even enjoy a Cockroach for dethert."

The screeching winds picked up, slamming the shed doors closed. Everything went black.

• • •

I awoke in the darkness, feeling like an elephant was sitting on my chest. I couldn't breathe. I couldn't move. I couldn't think.

Run, I heard. It was a small voice in the back of my head. *Run!* I heard again, eventually recognizing that it was my own voice. But I was paralyzed, still stuck between 602 State Road and the gates of hell. Unable to move, I looked down the length of my body to discover that my legs were restrained by the covers and that I'd just emerged from the recurring nightmare.

What the hell? I thought, violently kicking the covers off my legs. Trying to slow my breathing, I was finally able to jump out of bed.

I can't take this anymore, I thought. *I need to make it stop.* I continued to take in long deep breaths. *At least I've proven Aunt Phyllis wrong,* I thought. *When you die in a dream, you don't actually die in real life.*

While my brothers slept peacefully, I paced the bedroom floor.

Lucky bastards, I thought before looking out the window. *Try to focus on something else,* I told myself once again.

Our neighbor across the street, Ronnie, was already out shoveling his driveway. It took my eyes a few moments to find her, but I also noticed his young daughter, Kallie. She was laying in the yard beside her dad, flapping her tiny arms and legs, doing her best to create a snow angel.

I wonder what my angel's doing right now? Donna's probably still sleeping . . . which is what I should be doing. As I felt a smile pull at the corners of my mouth, I allowed my mind to go back to where it all started with my future wife.

• • •

The school cafeteria was not where most guys on the prowl for a girlfriend would consider a target-rich environment. But it was the pool I swam in. *Well, at least I've dipped my toe in a couple of times.*

It was an ordinary Thursday. I had two Sloppy Joe sandwiches—my favorite—sitting on the tan plastic tray in front of me. Before digging in like a cave man, I glanced up to see Donna Torres looking at me. My heart skipped. *Oh wow*, I thought, swallowing hard. My breathing became shallow and my forehead suddenly felt sweaty. *Is she really smiling at me?* I wondered, looking behind me to find that there was no one there. I pushed my tray away from me, waiting to eat. *Please look over here again, Donna,* I thought. *Please . . .* She did, several more times, and each time Donna and I made eye contact, we both smiled. My entire body buzzed from adrenaline. *I'm in love*, I thought, realizing that I'd just jumped into the deep end of the pool—*at least as deep as Middle School can get.* I stood and grabbed my tray, preparing to dump the uneaten food into the gray trash barrel. Donna looked at me one more time, smiling even wider. *Oh my God . . .* I gasped, forgetting to take in air. *If only I had the guts to walk over there and talk to her.*

In the days and weeks that followed, I couldn't think about anything but Donna. We were in the era of the big hair bands and power ballads, so it was the perfect time to fall in love. I daydreamed about Donna and constantly listened to music, some tunes I would have never suffered through. While Tina Turner asked, "What's love got to do with it?" Foreigner sang, "I want to know what love is." Even Stevie Wonder, "Just called to say I love you." Anything with the word love in it had me hooked. My yellow Walkman quickly became my prized possession.

I can't wait to take Donna roller skating, I thought, picturing the Doubles light coming on as she took my hand. *And our parents won't be anywhere near the rink. She'll smell like Luvs Baby's Soft and I'll sneak some of Wally's Drakkar Noir or High Karate cologne.*

I usually imagined squeezing ten people into my car at the drive-in movie theatre at five bucks a carload, but now I only wanted to take Donna alone. *And I don't care how much it costs me*, I thought.

A wave of things I wanted to do with her flooded my mind. *We can . . .*

• • •

"Herbie!"

"Wha . . . what?" I stuttered, trying to emerge from my latest daydream.

"Why do I always have to scream before you answer me?" Ma asked.

"I must have been daydreaming," I admitted. *Ma's right.* I was a daydreamer, preferring those happy fantasies over the nightmares I could never control in my broken sleep.

"You're always daydreaming," she said. "Listen, I need you to run to the store for me to pick up a couple of things."

And your cigarettes and candy bars are so much more important than my daydreams, I thought, snickering.

"Did you just snicker at me?" she asked.

"No."

"I thought I heard a snicker," she said.

I shook my head. "What do you need from the store, Ma?" I asked her, redirecting the conversation.

"Go get me money from my pocketbook," she said, "I need to make a payment to Old Man Sedgeband."

Wow, I thought. This was an honor. My brothers and I were

156156

156

taught at very young ages to never look into a woman's purse or a man's wallet, that it was a terrible betrayal of privacy. We never betrayed this lesson.

As I dove into her giant leather sack, I began pushing things around to find the wallet I was looking for and complete my coveted mission. There was always a pack of Juicy Fruit or Teaberry chewing gum, which puzzled me because Ma never chewed gum. There was some loose change at the bottom of the deep pouch; a half-pack of cigarettes, two broken lighters, a gold tube of lipstick, an empty book of matches, a copy of Soap Opera Digest; and envelopes held together by a thick rubber band. *Bills,* I figured.

Alas, I reached her bulging wallet, stuffed with more coupons than cash. The real money—the folding money—was concealed in an empty Crisco can on the top shelf in the pantry cupboard. Everyone knew this secret "just in case something happened" to my parents—*as if sixty-five bucks is going to set me and my brothers for life.*

I ran the wallet over to my mother.

"Good boy," she said, "now go to the store for me. We need a gallon of milk, a gallon of orange juice, a loaf of bread . . . and grab me two packs of cigarettes—Carlton 100's, the red pack." She thought for a moment. "You know what, make it three packs." She handed me a twenty-dollar bill. "This should put a dent in our tab."

"It should," I said, having no clue.

"And throw in two packs of Mallow Cups," she added, trying to quiet her terrible sweet tooth.

As usual, I gave her my finest smile. "Can I get something, too, Ma?"

She nodded. "Just one thing, Herbie," she said, "and keep it under fifty cents. We're not . . ."

". . . made of money," I said, finishing the famous sentence for her. "I know, Ma. I know."

Ignoring Old Man Sedgeband and Oscar, I headed straight toward the foggy-glassed coolers at the back of the store. Sedgeband's scruffy mutt, Pluto, was stretched out in front of the dairy cooler. I grabbed his collar and gave it a tug. It was the only way to get the big oaf to move. "Come on, boy," I told him, "I want to get out of here as soon as possible."

Though he clearly hated to be bothered, Pluto complied.

I placed the milk, bread, orange juice and Mallow Cups onto the counter, before gawking into the candy case. Scanning past the candy bracelets and the multi-colored candy buttons on rolls of wax paper, my eyes landed on the box of Fortune Bubble. Even though the flavor of this cheap gum only lasted a minute or so, I loved the taste, as well as the fortunes concealed within the long orange wrappers.

Sedgeband cleared his throat, signaling that it was decision time.

"Give me ten sticks of Fortune Bubble and a box of candy cigarettes," I said, intending the latter to be paid to Cockroach as hush money. He was up to two packs a week now—a terrible habit for a kid his age. *Screw it,* I thought, grabbing a pack of cream-filled chocolate Ho Hos and throwing them onto the pile. *I'll stash these for later,* I thought. "And give me three packs of Carlton 100s," I told Sedgeband, like they were for me. "Put it all on my mother's tab."

The creepy soul looked down at me through his thick goggles. "You be sure to tell your mother that her tab's behind and if she doesn't make a . . ."

"Oh yeah," I blurted, interrupting him. Reaching into my front pocket, I grabbed the twenty-dollar bill and slapped it onto the counter. "This oughta take care of it."

Sedgeband grabbed his green spiral notebook, penciled in the new items and tallied everything. Looking up from the book, he shook his head. "Tell her that the tab sits at eight dollars and forty cents now."

"Okay, I'll let her know," I promised, though I never did tell her. It was in Cockroach's and my best interest that the math remained hazy.

After throwing the wrinkled twenty into his monstrosity of a cash register, Sedgeband bagged the goods and then waved his hand, dismissing me from his store like a king discharging a peasant.

It's gonna be a real shame when you die, old man, I thought, leaving the dim cave, *a terrible shame.*

• • •

Cockroach was struggling to get ready and it didn't take me long before I was sick of waiting on him. "I'll meet you downstairs," I told him.

"Wait for me, Herbie," he pleaded.

"I'll wait for you outside," I told him. "I'm not going to sweat to death because you still can't figure out how to dress yourself."

As I descended the hallway stairs, I decided that I couldn't take being outside anymore, none of us could. *I'm going to hang out in the cellar today.*

On my way, I spotted my buddy Vic standing on the side of my house, smoking a cigarette. "What the hell do you think you're doing?" I asked him in a strained hiss.

He grinned proudly. "You want a drag?"

"No," I immediately answered; I'd witnessed those cancer sticks turn my mother into an addicted fiend. "I'm good."

Although Vic prided himself on smoking cigarettes at twelve years old, he only smoked when he could steal them from his brother, Manny. *What a dummy*, I was thinking when I realized the knucklehead was standing beside the two silver propane tanks—essentially bombs—strapped to the side of my house.

Every time my mother flicked her cigarette butt near the tanks, I thought I was going to have a heart attack. *Now Vic's going to do it?* I grabbed his arm and dragged him out of the shadows. "You wanna smoke, then be my guest," I told him, "but you're not going to blow up my house when you do."

"Relax," he said, taking another drag, "your parents don't even own this house."

A wad of bile rose into my throat, threatening to choke me—and making me want to choke him. "I wouldn't talk crap about someone else's parents, if I were you," I snapped back. "Your parents are gonna make you quit school when you turn sixteen, so you can go to work full-time and they can cash in on another one of their kids."

He blew smoke out his nose, trying to act cool. "When I get married," he said, quickly defending his mother and father, "my folks are gonna buy all of my furniture."

I laughed in his face. "That furniture had better be made of gold, numb nuts," I told him, "because it's your money that's paying for it."

As much as I loved Vic, I also disliked him. It was a strange relationship that I could never seem to reconcile. "You probably shouldn't hang out here today," I told him. "If Wally catches you smokin' . . ."

"If Wally ever lays a hand on me again, I'm tellin' Manny," he said, "and he'll . . ."

"Beat it, Chachi," I told him, cutting him off, "before I'm the one who buries your head in the snow this time."

Pulling the cigarette out of his mouth to study my face, he took a small step forward.

I leaned in closer to him. "You need to step off, Vic," I barked.

He stared at me, clearly weighing his options.

"Beat it," I repeated at a full screech, "before I rearrange those yellow teeth for you."

Vic placed the butt between his teeth and walked past me, the smell of his cigarette smoke lingering behind.

What a jackass, I thought. He was a few yards away when I called out after him. "Hey Vic . . ."

He turned around. "What?" he yelled back.

"Don't eat any yellow snow. It's not lemon Slushy, you know."

He threw me the bird.

Right back at ya, jackass, I thought, returning the one-finger salute.

I headed down into the cellar to hear Blue Oyster Cult's *Don't Fear the Reaper* playing in the background. *This place is so disgusting,* I thought. Even when we swept the floor, the dust and dirt was comparable to an erupting volcano, leaving behind a cloud of ash and debris. The cracked concrete floor was always covered in dirt. *Whether we try to clean it or not, this place will always be filthy.*

There were two rooms in the back with slatted wooden doors, just like the door to get into the cellar. These were in much better shape because they hadn't weathered the elements all these years. One of the rooms stored our bikes and some sports equipment. The other was Pop's workshop, which he never used. A long fluorescent light hung over an old tool bench, but as far as I knew the light had never worked. In the shadows, you could make out Pop's oil change equipment, as well as spark plugs and some tools he used to work on the station wagon.

Cockroach has a point, I thought. The cellar was an eerie place and, if you went down there alone, it never felt like you were actually alone. However, it was also the perfect place to play hide and seek in the winter and conceal Playboy books as we got older. *Even though we brought down a boom box and threw up some posters, this place is still a dump. But it's private*, I reminded myself. *Ma and Pop never come down here—especially Ma.*

I heard the cellar door slam shut and turned around to find Cockroach standing in the doorway, refusing to take another step. "Herbie?" he called out, his voice high-pitched from fear.

"I'm over here," I called back.

He hurried over to me. "You said you were gonna wait for me outside, but when I got out there, you . . ."

"You took too long," I explained.

"But what if I didn't . . ."

"You found me, didn't you?" I asked in a tone that didn't warrant an answer.

While he shook his head, I headed over to Wally's weight pit, expecting to see him doing reps on the bench. Instead, I discovered that my older brother had packed an old Army duffel bag with rags, and then hung it from one of the exposed beans. *Wally made his own punching bag,* I thought, and watched as he was doing a job on it—leaving his knuckles red and raw.

"What are you doing?" I asked him.

"What does it . . ." He grunted, continuing to throw haymakers at the bag. ". . . does it look like I'm doing?"

"Training for a fight," I said.

He stopped for a moment and looked at me. "Yeah, with you."

Yeah, right, I thought, knowing better.

He returned to the lumpy bag. "I just keep picturing your ugly face and . . ." He began pounding the drab green bag again, folding it in half with every straight right he threw.

"If you want to take me on, you'd better bring some people," I joked.

"You must have lost your mind, Peaches and Herb," he said, poking fun at my name.

"Not quite, Captain and Tennille."

"What?"

My mind raced for a better comeback. "You heard me, Wally Cleaver," I said.

"That's better," he said, laughing. Suddenly, his eyes turned serious and he did his best to impersonate Rocky Balboa.

I turned to Cockroach. "Wanna race?" I asked him.

He looked down at his boots. "I guess so, but . . ."

"Not outside," I told him, laughing, "and not on foot."

His brow creased in confusion.

"Follow me, Mighty Mouse," I told him.

"Sticks and stones may break . . ." he began.

I raised my clenched fist, halting him. "Go ahead and finish it, and I will break your bones."

"Yeah, he will," Wally sad, laughing.

Cockroach shut his mouth.

While Wally trained for the Thriller in Manila match and Cockroach watched me from the sidelines, I cleared enough space around the furnace—pushing everything to the outside walls—to create a circle track that was wide enough to race two Big Wheels, side-by-side. "It's not Seekonk Speedway," I told Cockroach, "but it'll do."

"I don't know if this is such a great idea, Herbie," he said, already enacting his escape plan.

"But it's the best idea I could come up with, Alphonse," I told him. "We can't go upstairs for a while and I'm not going outside to turn into a puddin' pop."

"But . . ."

"No more buts, man! It's time to grow a pair and stop being such a chicken shit." I smirked at him, hoping to challenge his pride.

"I'm not a . . ." He shook his head. "We'll see who's a chicken shit," he mumbled, heading for his neon green race machine.

Well, all right then . . .

As we sat in our plastic roadsters, lined up at an inviable starting line, Cockroach reminded me, "This is dangerous, Herbie. And besides, my butt still hurts from . . ."

I nodded my helmet-free head. "Life's dangerous, lollipop, so this is the perfect training."

His face reddened at the "lollipop" reference. Our father used it so often that it had become a trigger for all three of us.

I smiled at him. "Do you want me to give you a head start?"

Sitting low in his Green Machine, Cockroach considered the advantage—his eyes still unsure.

"On your mark," I yelled, "get set . . ."

Excited, he turned his head straight and sucked in a lung full of musty air.

Laughing, I yelled, "Go!"

As he took off ahead of me, Cockroach's legs began pumping like two well-oiled pistons. His lime-green race rocket had a suicide handle on the side, allowing him to drift into the corners. He was already cranking down hard on that handle.

That 'a boy, I thought, pedaling even harder. Within seconds, I was creeping up on his back bumper. "I'm comin' to get ya!" I screamed at the back of his head.

Squealing in delight, he pedaled faster, fueled by the same adrenaline rush that I felt.

For the next few hours, while Cinderella, Skid Row and Billy Squire took their turns wailing in the background, Cockroach and I risked life and limb, racing for nothing more than bragging rights and the privilege to stay warm.

A few times, he stopped to squirm in his seat, complaining about the growing pain in his backside. "It's getting worse," he reported.

"Suck it up, buttercup," I told him.

Occasionally, we were reminded that Wally was still with us in the cellar—either by his primal grunts, or from him swapping out the cassettes. It didn't matter. My little brother and I were swept away in our own world, recklessly competing until we either smashed into something or one another.

Each time Cockroach flipped his Green Machine and began to cry, I reminded him, "This is still safer than freezing outside, Alphonse. Now get back on your horse, cowboy."

And he did—spitting dirt and blood out of his mouth. I watched as his fear was replaced by anger, inspiring him to remount his steed—brow creased and teeth clenched—and do everything in his power to beat me to some invisible finish line.

That 'a boy, Alphonse, I repeated, hearing Pop's voice in my sweaty head. *Chase it down hard, little brother.*

• • •

By the time we got upstairs to eat supper, Pop was home from work and Ma had already prepared two full boxes of Cheeseburger Helper. Besides appreciating the big white hand on the box, I enjoyed the thick cheesy pasta meal. *I hate Tuna Helper,* I thought. *It makes me almost as sick as split-pea soup, but I love Cheeseburger Helper.*

"Did you have fun today?" Ma asked me, as I took my seat at the table.

"I've never had more fun," I told her, sarcastically.

Her nose wrinkled. "Dragon breath, when's the last time you brushed your teeth?" she asked, clearly repulsed.

"Not really sure," I answered, honestly. "Do you think maybe I need a tic tac?"

"More like a good Ajax scrubbing." She scanned the table. "All of you, go brush your teeth—now!"

We started for the bathroom.

"And if I find out you're not brushing your teeth every day from now on, you're going to be punished."

"Already punished," Wally muttered at the bathroom sink, "so we're all set there."

We each washed our hands before reclaiming our seats at the kitchen table.

"We played in the cellar today," Cockroach reported out of the blue, making me and Wally nearly snap our necks to scowl at him.

What the hell, bro? I thought.

"Oh God," Ma said. "You guys know the realtors are downstairs working during the day." She shook her worried head. "We'll be lucky if we don't get thrown out on our ears this week."

Grinning, Pop buttered a few slices of sandwich bread with his filthy hands.

"What were you guys doing down there all that time?" Ma asked Cockroach.

"Racing Big Wheels," Cockroach said.

So dumb, I thought.

"Oh God . . ." Ma repeated.

Wally and I looked at him and shook our heads.

"Besides making all that noise down there, don't you think that's dangerous?" she asked, filling his plate first. "What if you crashed into the furnace or something?"

He shrugged. "Herbie said it was okay, Ma."

Although she looked at me with disappointed eyes, she continued to talk to Cockroach. "So would you jump off a bridge if someone else did, Alphonse?"

"I might," Wally blurted, jumping into the fray, "but it depends on which bridge we're talking about, Ma."

I stifled a giggle.

"You'd better not, Wally," Cockroach said, "that's dangerous."

"No shit, Sherlock," I blurted, unable to hold my tongue any longer.

"Watch your mouth," Pop told me.

"It's true, Wally," Cockroach said, ignoring me, "you could get really hurt."

"No duh," Wally replied.

In the midst of a full eye roll, Cockroach scrunched up his face.

"Be careful," Ma said, "or your face is going to stay that way." It was as though our mother had been issued a thick book of clichés at the hospital when Wally was born. Early on, we actually believed her—but not so much anymore.

I looked to make sure Ma was distracted while dishing out our supper. "Do you want to know what else is true?" I whispered to my little brother.

"What?"

"Later tonight, when we're alone," I whispered, "I'm going to give you an Indian sunburn until it bleeds."

"Ma!" he shrieked, like a cringe-worthy steam whistle.

My mother took a break from slopping out the pasta to glare at me. "You touch him, Herbie, and you'll pay for it," she warned. "Do you understand me?"

I nodded. Cockroach grinned at me.

When my mother looked away to fill her own plate, I punched my fist into my open palm. *Just wait*, I mouthed to my little brother.

The little bastard's grin disappeared.

After a full gorging, we watched TV in the living room.

"This dude's no poser," Wally said, referring to David Hasselhoff from Knight Rider.

"He's the bomb, for real," I said.

Wally nodded. "Bad to the bone," he agreed. "Definitely legit."

"Big time," Cockroach said.

"I bet he's either a head banger or a burnout in real life, though," Wally predicted.

"No doy," I said.

"Bite me, Dexter," he fired back.

"Geez, Wally," Cockroach said, "don't have a cow."

Pop looked at Ma from his recliner. "What the hell are they talking about?" he asked. "It's like they speak a different language."

"I'm sure we were the same way when we were their age," Ma said.

"In a pig's ass, we were," Pop huffed.

Sure, I thought, *we're the ones that talk funny.*

Wally stood. "I'm bouncing," he said.

I followed him out of the room, leaving our baffled father to watch one of his and Ma's favorite shows—Hill Street Blues.

While Wally hurried off to the bathroom, I headed for our bedroom. For a short while, I lay alone on my bed, which was a rare treat. Privacy was a fantasy in our house, especially in our bedroom. *I can never be alone.* Most of the time, it was probably for the better, as we were pack animals. *But every once in a while, it's nice to have some alone time*, I thought.

With my hands tucked behind my head, I engaged in my all-time favorite pastime—I daydreamed. *I can't wait to get older and do what the high school kids do*, I thought. *Beach parties in the dunes of Horseneck Beach; rock concerts at the Providence Civic Center; owning a muscle car—a Chevy Camaro, Pontiac Firebird or one of those black and gold Trans Ams with tee tops—to do "burners." Drag racing the quarter mile and cruising the Avenue in Fall River, hooking up with friends in some parking lot to listen to loud music until we get kicked out by the cops—and then move on to another lot.* I sighed heavily, thinking about Donna. *Maybe I'll get a Chevy van instead, with its interior* carpeted from floor to ceiling, and a mattress taking up most of the back. I'd finally reached the age when I was thinking about more exciting things than pony rides.

I can't wait to buy Donna a hope chest, whatever that is, I thought. *According to Ma, that's how you know it's serious.*

As quickly as the daydreaming began, it was over—interrupted by my two brothers.

"Time to get my Atari fix," Wally announced, firing up the system.

As we begrudgingly took turns playing Indy 500 and racing each other on a circle track, Cockroach said, "I'm sorry, Herbie. I didn't think I was saying anything wrong to Ma. It's not like I wanted to get you into trouble."

"Sure, you didn't," Wally commented.

I paused the heated race and looked at my little brother. "I wouldn't want to rob a bank with you, Alphonse," I told him, "that's for sure."

"Why would I ever rob a bank?" he asked. "That's just wrong."

Wally started laughing. "Just kick his ass, Herbie, and get it over with," he said. "It'll be easier."

Cockroach looked at me, his eyes wide.

I clicked the game back to play. "Just think before you start running your mouth from now on," I told him, continuing the close race. "Nobody likes a rat, Cockroach."

"The Celtics are playing tonight, I think," Wally commented, changing the subject. "Too bad they suck this year."

"Suck this year? You must be stoned," I blurted, pausing the game again. "Okay, then tell me, what team's better?"

"The Lakers, hands down," he answered, confidently. "They played the Celts last week and won 111 to 109." He snickered. "I'm telling you, bro, Magic's so much better than Bird."

"You must be completely high!" I repeated.

"Oh really, then put your money where your mouth is," he said, challenging me.

"You know I don't have any money," I reminded him.

"Listen, I'm telling you right now, the Celtics are gonna get shit-stomped by the Lakers in the championship series this year and that's if the Celts even make it to the big show."

"And I'm still saying that you must have smoked some bad reefer," I told him.

Cockroach laughed.

Wally nodded. "Okay, how's this—whoever loses has to do the other guy's laundry for a month." He smiled. "Soiled Underoos and all."

"It's a bet," I told him, shaking his large mitt, "the Celts are taking it all."

An hour or so later, Cockroach shut off the light and scrambled up into his bunk.

I need to pick one that Wally can't refuse, I thought. It suddenly came to me. "Surely, you can't be serious?" I called out into the darkness.

Wally cleared his throat.

I waited.

"I am serious," Wally replied, "and don't call me Shirley."

We laughed.

Both my brothers were out cold when I got up and tiptoed into the kitchen to get a drink, making sure that the fridge door was closed and the light off before I dared take a sip from the orange Tupperware pitcher.

"Sure Walter, but why do I always have to be the bad guy?" Ma said in mid-conversation from the living room.

I froze in place to listen in.

"If we don't take half of Wally's paper route money and save it for him," she said, "he'll spend it all and won't have . . ."

"Then just tell him that," Pop said, interrupting her.

"Don't you think that's something we should explain to him together?"

The recliner creaked loudly, announcing that Pop was leaving it. "Fine," the old man said, "whatever. I'm going to bed. I have work in the morning."

I pulled the fridge door open and placed the pitcher back onto the top shelf—without making a peep. *The years of sneaking around in the dark are finally paying off,* I thought.

"Of course you do, Walter," Ma said, "and I'll be looking forward to another day at the spa tomorrow."

Grinning at my mother's sarcasm, I sneaked back behind the plastic accordion door.

I thought she was shaking Wally down for money, I thought. *I can't wait to tell him in the morning.* Once again, I was excited about the possibility of getting my own paper route.

CHAPTER 9

FRIDAY

By the end of the week, Cockroach's backside was infected—two purple and yellow-colored half-moons of teeth marks, causing a terrible, oozing mess.

"You bit him, Wally?" Ma asked, pretending to be shocked. "What are we, raising animals?" Her face was the perfect mix of disgust and rage. "How would you like it if I bit you?"

Cockroach grinned, while I did everything I could to hold back a laugh. *I wish she'd do it*, I thought, *I'd love to see her sink those chompers into Wally.*

"The poor little guy's going to need a tetanus shot," she said, surveying the multi-colored wound.

"A shot?" Cockroach squealed, panicked. "Please, Ma, no shot! It . . . it'll get better on its own."

This time, Wally grinned.

"No, it won't, sweetheart," Ma said, before turning to Wally. "And you . . . well, we'll see what your father has to say about you hurting your brother when he gets home."

"Sorry, Ma," Wally muttered.

"Oh, you're not sorry yet," she said through gritted teeth, "but I can guarantee you will be."

Sighing heavily, Wally dropped his gaze.

Wow, I thought, *Wally's not having a great week. Well, I guess there is one upside . . . we're definitely stuck inside now.* I looked at my older brother and nodded my gratitude. *He might have actually saved our lives.* I then looked over at our mother. *Poor Ma*, I thought, *she might have to miss her soap operas.* I gave it a bit more thought. *Nah, I doubt it.*

My mother was beside herself. Her face remained beet red until our father got home. *I don't think I've ever seen her like this*, I realized.

I could hear Pop's heavy footsteps climbing the hallway stairs. *Oh shit*, I thought, knowing that Big Walt could be heavy handed, *Wally's in for it now.* My brother was about to face a man who was probably sick with worry and ready to show his concern through physical discipline. My own body tensed up from fear. *Pop had to leave work early to take Cockroach to the hospital and I doubt he's going to be happy about that, either.*

The front door swung open, the big man stepping into the kitchen. "Let me see how bad it is," he said right away, his voice even and calm.

Pop doesn't seem nearly as upset as I figured he'd be, I thought. *He must hate his job.*

Ma spun Cockroach around and pulled down his pants to reveal the half-moon of teeth marks.

Shaking his head, Pop looked at Wally and then at Ma. "One of us must have dropped him on his head when he was young, or maybe he took a swan dive from that old steel high chair when we weren't looking?"

No one laughed but me.

He looked back at Wally. "I'll deal with you as soon as we get back from the hospital," he said.

My body instinctively locked up again.

"Hospital?" my little brother gasped.

Pop looked back at Cockroach's scrawny backside. "We need to feed this kid more," he told Ma, commenting on my baby brother's lack of weight. "Maybe I should get him checked for scurvy or rickets while we're there," he said, shaking his head.

"Why do I have to go to the hospital?" Cockroach whined.

Ma pulled up his pants. "Go get your coat on," she told him, "you need to go to the emergency room before the infection gets any worse."

"Please, Ma," Cockroach begged, "I don't want a shot." He began to cry.

"I know, sweetheart," she said, "just go get your coat on. You and Daddy can talk about it on the way."

Pop shot Ma a look that didn't imply gratitude.

She turned to Wally. "You just wait," she whispered, "I swear to God, you're going to pay for this."

Whoa . . . Even I got scared at that one.

"Let's go, Alphonse," Pop said, giving Wally the side eye as he carried Cockroach out the front door to face another one of his many fears.

As soon as the door clicked shut, I heard Pop say. "It could have been worse, Alphonse. At least he didn't bite your snapper."

It took all I had not to laugh.

Ma turned to Wally and absolutely lost her mind. "You're grounded, Wally! Do you hear me?" she screamed, inches from his stone face. "You'll be lucky if you ever see the light of day again."

That might be a good thing for him, I thought.

"In all my days, I've never . . ." She stopped to catch her breath.

"You do realize that Jesus is always watching you, right?"

What? I thought. "He's watching all of us, Ma," I quipped, feeling bad enough for my brother to share some of the heat.

In one fluid motion, she removed her slipper and took an aggressive step toward me. Although she stopped herself, her face could not conceal her desire to strike me.

Do it, Ma, I willed her in my head.

Her kind and gentle eyes were now hard and angry. She glared at me before looking over at Wally, clearly trying to decide whether she was going to attack either of us—or both.

"He's always watching," Wally whispered.

Choking back a laugh, I made a beeline to our bedroom. Before I'd reached the accordion door, I heard the bottom of Ma's Dr. Scholl slap bare skin. *Better you than me, brother,* I thought.

I lay in my bunk, trying to pick up where I'd left off the day before. With my fingers interlaced behind my head, I allowed my mind to drift away and daydream about the future. Although my brothers and I were yet to attend a rock concert, we always wore concert T-shirts. Personally, I couldn't wait to stand in the long line at the Civic Center to get my twelve-dollar ticket to see my favorite rock bands. *Journey, Def Leppard, The Cars, Joan Jett, Rush, Foreigner and Loverboy—and especially Aerosmith.* Although I always got stoked watching the awesome videos on MTV, I imagined that there was nothing better than live music. *I can't wait to party hardy!*

Once I got to high school, I planned on wearing Colorado hiking boots with the red laces every day. For a while, I even considered wearing suspenders, but eventually decided against it. *That's a tough look to pull off.* Either way, I figured I'd be working by then and able to shop for my own clothes at Chess King or the Liss Department Store.

I'd heard rumors of the crazy keg parties at the beach or in the woods and the bonfires that took place on the banks of the river. *Can't wait for all of that*, I thought.

There was a loud fart, startling me from my thoughts.

"Excuse me," Wally said, just as the rancid smell made its way to my side of the room.

"Damn, Wally," I yelled, "you need to go see a doctor or something."

Ma threw open the plastic accordian door and stepped into the room to see what the yelling was all about. "Oh my God," she said, gagging, "it reeks like a locker room in here." She hurried over to the window, unlocked it and threw it open—allowing a blast of Arctic air into the foul space. She didn't care that it was the dead of winter. "And it stays open until this dump airs out."

When she left, I slid under my blankets, pulling them up to my chin. "Thanks a lot," I told Wally, waiting to see my own breath.

"No problem," he said, farting again.

An hour later, the window was closed and my stomach was rumbling for some attention. I grabbed the pack of Ho Ho's that I'd stashed in the top drawer of my bureau, excited to jam them into my gob. As I headed out of the room to eat them in private, I caught my side reflection in the bureau mirror. *I need to lose some weight*, I thought, cringing, *I really do. Donna would definitely like me more if I was skinnier.* I stared at my chubby physique. *Like me more?* I snickered. *Maybe she'd like me—period.*

I spun in front of the mirror, unhappy with everything I saw.

You fat bastard, I told myself, disgusted at the start of jowls and a double chin.

I looked down at the chocolate, gooey treat. *Screw it!* I decided, opening the plastic wrapper with my back to Wally. *I'll start watching what I eat right after this last snack.*

After finishing the sweet treat—and just starting in on the guilt—I decided to work on my letter to Donna.

I grabbed a piece of paper and a pen, and took a seat on my bunk. Crushing on a girl—*the girl*—inspired an equal amount of butterfly-inducing fantasies and soul-crushing doubts. The cycle of insanity see-sawed between confidence and fear. *Just write the letter and don't stop until you've finished*, I told myself. *Other than that, you'll never get it done. Besides, if you don't like how it comes out, Donna never has to see it.* I took a few breaths, preparing to jump into the rip current.

"You still haven't finished that love letter, have you?" Wally asked from his bed, flipping through a Motor Trend Magazine. He never looked up.

"What are you talking about?"

"What do you think, Herbie . . . we're all stupid?"

"You really want me to answer that?"

He smiled, his eyes still on the magazine's glossy pages.

"So what's the 411 on this girl?" he asked. "You're really into her, aren't you?" This time, he dropped the magazine to look at me.

I had a decision to make. *Should I confide in him and risk being made fun of, or should I just keep it myself?*

"You like her a lot, don't you?" he prodded.

To hell with it, I thought. "I do."

"Would you kiss her?" he asked.

"Of course."

"Even when she's screaming for you to stop?"

I knew it, I thought. *When am I ever going to learn?* "You're such a buffoon," I told him.

"Am I?"

"You are."

"But I'm not the one thinking about kissing some girl against her will."

"I would never . . ." I stopped.

"I bet she's butt ugly," he said.

"And I think you've been looking in the mirror for too long," I countered.

"The love boat," he sang out of tune, "exciting and new . . ."

I completely ignored him.

"Take a chance," he sang, "we're expecting you . . ."

I remained stone-faced.

Laughing, he returned to his shiny magazine, making me even angrier. Though it didn't make sense, I envied Wally for the magazines he bought with his paper route money. While Ma liked the Star magazine, claiming, "It's the National Enquirer that's a gossip rag," Wally was into Motor Trend and Popular Mechanics. I always wished I could grab a copy of Tiger Beat magazine at the market's checkout. Besides knowing that Ma's answer would be, "No, we don't have the money," I also knew that I'd face some harsh ridicule from my brothers when they saw me reading it. Instead, I was left to imagine what the wall inside my bunk bed would look like plastered with posters of Kristi McNichol and Elisabeth Shue, the Karate Kid's girlfriend. *But comic books, Popular Mechanics and Motor Trend are acceptable*, I thought, unable to reconcile it.

Continuing to ignore Wally, I decided to return to the letter. It took me a few minutes to get started again.

Dear Donna, I've been trying to write you this letter for a while now. Although it's not easy telling you how I feel about you, I know I'll regret it for a long time if I don't. I took another deep breath, willing myself to keep going. *I like you, Donna. Actually, I really like you and I was hoping that you'd consider going out with me. I think we'd be great together. I hope you feel the same way. Herbie.*

Dropping the thick pen from my sweaty hand, I carefully lifted the letter to give it a thorough read. *Every word of it is the truth,* I thought, *and it's exactly how I feel.* I read it again. *Man, I wish I had the balls to give this to her.* But I knew I wouldn't. *I can't.* As I started to crumple it up, I stopped. *Just read it again later,* I told myself. *You don't need to decide right now.*

I got up to do some foraging for food, which I suspected wouldn't be there. There was nothing but cans of creamed corn and creamed spinach in Ma's cupboard. *I wonder if that's what happens to vegetables after they've gone bad?*

I heard someone cough behind me, making me jump. I turned to find Ma sitting at the kitchen table, smoking a cigarette. "What's going on with you lately, Herbie?" she asked. "You've been walking around more dazed than usual." She grinned. "It's a girl, isn't it?"

I opened my mouth to explain but stopped myself. *You'd never understand, Ma,* I thought, deciding to just go with a drink. I opened the fridge to find a dozen eggs, a tub of butter and two Tupperware pitchers with the plungers on top—one of Tang, *the same orange beverage the astronauts drink,* and the other one half-filled with cherry-flavored Kool-Aid.

As though she was reading my mind, Ma asked, "Do you honestly think I haven't been through everything you're going through or will go through?" She nodded. "You're not the first to feel your heart flutter, you know." She took a drag on her cigarette. "When I first met your father . . ."

I sighed heavily, cutting off the details. *Sure Ma*, I thought, grabbing the Kool-Aid and then a plastic cup, *but that was in the olden days. Things are different now. You'd never understand.*

She shook her head, still grinning at me. "I guess you're right," she said in a gentle tone, "I guess we each have to suffer things for ourselves to understand." Finishing her raspy chuckle, she poked out the cigarette. "Herbie, you just wait until you have kids and you have to sit back and watch them struggle when they don't need to."

After filling a stained plastic tumbler, purchased at one of my mother's annual Tupperware parties, I returned her smile. *I'm sure Donna and I will figure it out, Ma,* I thought.

"Why don't you do something valuable with all of this free time you have?" she suggested, sliding another cigarette out of the red pack.

"Like what?"

"I don't know," she said, getting up from the table, "maybe read a book for once?" She lit the new cigarette from the stovetop's blue flames.

Another one of Ma's lighters died, I thought before remembering, *I do have a reading assignment that's due when we get back from vacation.*

I took a sip of Kool-Aid and started back for my bedroom. "Fine," I said, surrendering, "I'll read a book."

"Where do you think you're going with that drink?" she asked. "I told you, no more food or drinks in your room."

Since that rule had been implemented, my brothers and I considered it more of a suggestion than a mandate. According to Ma, "The way you guys eat and can't find your mouths, you'll end up attracting rats." This empty threat cost Cockroach more than a few nights' loss of sleep.

"But Ma," I objected, "it's not me that makes a mess. I . . ."

She shook her head. "I bought you guys a rug a couple months ago and it's already destroyed."

She's right, I thought. There was no way to tell the original color of the area rug that took up the center of our bedroom. *I can't even count the number of drinks we've spilled on it.* With a nod, I downed the rest of the Kool-Aid and threw the plastic tumbler into the sink, where it bounced a few times before landing upright. "Swish!"

The frozen wind rapped on our bedroom windows, threatening to break in at any moment, while I read the book, *To Kill A Mockingbird* by Harper Lee—which I would have never done under normal circumstances. To my surprise, I really enjoyed picturing Scout's adventure in my mind. I also loved the character, Addicus Finch. *He's a good man like Pop,* I decided, *even though they're total opposites in a lot of ways.*

Turning page after page, I finally stopped to take a break and maybe grab a snack. According to the kitchen clock, several hours had already passed. *There's no way,* I thought, stepping into the living room to confirm it. *It's true.* Both clocks matched. *Wow,* I thought, *I must have really gotten lost in that story.* Although I hated to admit it to myself, I thought, *Maybe I do actually enjoy reading?*

I returned to the kitchen and opened the fridge again. There were several empty containers; everyone but Ma was too lazy to throw them out, causing her to scream with each new discovery. *No left-overs*, I thought, not surprised. My brothers and I ate like we were cattle, so it was rare for anything to be spared from our gorging. Besides a container of French pork spread and a bottle of Pop's hot sauce on the top shelf, there was a few cans of Tab and Fresca. These were Ma's and Ma's alone. Each of us had our drinks and everyone was expected to stay in their own lane, with milk being the common beverage for all. Halfway down the fridge, there was a special drawer for Pop's beer, Miller High Life. No one dared to crack open that drawer.

"We're not eating until your father and Alphonse get home," Ma called out from behind me, startling me for the second time that afternoon. "We'll have supper together."

"What are we having?" I asked.

"I told your dad to pick up a bucket of fried chicken on his way home," she said.

Awesome! I love fried chicken, I thought, riding a wave of excitement all the way back to my bunk bed.

Hours later, Pop finally returned home—enraged at Wally. "We sat in that God-awful waiting room for hours, while they took patient after patient before calling for Alphonse." He slammed the bucket of chicken onto the kitchen table.

"There must have been worse cases," Ma said, searching the cupboard for paper plates.

"Not to me, there weren't," Pop said, looking at Wally. "Time I'll never get back, thanks to you, Dracula." He looked back at our mother. "He's punished, right?"

She nodded. "He's in the house until he goes back to school—and no TV."

"Who's going to do my paper route?" Wally asked, risking a backhand.

"You are, smart ass!" Pop barked. "And if I were you, I wouldn't make another peep tonight . . . unless you want to wear my boot in your ass."

Wally nodded that he understood. I did, too—involuntarily.

Wally's gonna take forever to finish his paper route the rest of the week, I thought, considering how I'd approach his dilemma, if it were me.

We all sat to eat—in silence.

Cockroach retired to the top bunk, exhausted from his long day at the hospital and whatever medications they'd put him on. It didn't take long before he was sleeping, his hand hanging off the side of the bed. *I've never seen that before,* I thought. With all of his fears, he usually kept each of his limbs tucked in like a skittish hedgehog.

He's completely wiped out, I thought.

Wally cleared his throat to get my attention. "Have you ever heard about that thing where you put someone's hand in warm water and they piss themselves?" he asked.

"That can't be real," I said.

He grinned. "There's only one way to find out."

I thought about it. "You're in enough trouble, aren't you?"

His grin widened. "I was just hoping to watch."

Trying not to giggle, I sneaked into the kitchen. Most of Ma's Tupperware containers didn't have lids that fit, which she blamed on us. Fortunately, she was able to replace her stock with Cool Whip and margarine containers. *There was a time when Ma was obsessed with Tupperware*, I remembered. "Most quality products are made out of plastic now," she claimed. "Ice cube trays, dinner plates—pretty much everything." Fortunately, that fad quickly wore off.

I filled an empty Cool Whip bowl with warm water and tip-toed back to my bedroom. Ever so gingerly, I placed Cockroach's hand—which was still dangling over the side of the bed—into the water.

"This'll never work," I whispered to Wally.

"Give it time," he whispered back, laying on his side with his head resting on his right arm.

Cockroach stirred a few times until he started to moan—and that's when I saw it, a dark wet circle expanding outward from his crotch.

He's peeing himself, I thought, trying not to laugh.

Cockroach kept moaning, while the circle grew larger until it reached his bedding.

Standing to get a better look, Wally started laughing.

Oh shit, I thought, *it does work.* And then it dawned on me. *This wasn't the smartest idea*, I realized, scolding myself. *He sleeps right above me.*

Launched into a fit of hysterics, Wally didn't have the same concerns.

I sneaked out of the room, dumped the water and put the bowl back under the sink where I'd found it.

As I returned to the bedroom, I thought, *That was so bad, doing that to Cockroach.* My mind scrambled to find the positive. *At least he won't get in trouble for wetting the bed. He went to the hospital today and that's a get-out-of-jail-free card for the next few weeks.*

A half hour later, Wally lay in his bed playing with his Mattel handheld electronic football game, each red dot he moved on the screen beeping loudly.

That thing's so annoying, I thought when Ma stomped into the room, marched straight to Wally's bed, ripped the game out of his hands and left the room—not a word spoken between them.

"Now that's messed up," Wally mumbled, still laying on his back.

"Maybe she just wanted to take a turn?" I joked.

"Whatever, Sigmund the Sea Monster."

A few seconds passed when Ma stepped back into the room. "Since you have plenty of time to kill, Wally, why don't you get dressed and do some laundry for the family?"

"Are you kidding me?" he asked.

"Consider it just another part of your punishment," she told him, smirking.

"And there's more where that came from," Pop added, sticking his head into the room to get in on the fun.

At least I'll have clean towels for my bath later, I thought, heading into the living room to see what the rest of the family was up to.

Bundled up in his winter gear, Wally lifted the overflowing laundry basket and grinned all the way out the front door. "I'll be down there until everything's washed and dried," he yelled toward the living room.

"What's that?" Ma asked, taking a break from her conversation with Memere on the phone. "I want you right back . . ."

The front door slammed closed.

Ma and Pop exchanged a look, both shaking their heads.

They're both too tired and lazy to go after him, I thought. *Well played, brother.*

"That was Wally," Ma explained, returning to her phone call. "Wait until I tell you what he did to Alphonse." She shook her head. "You won't believe it, Ma."

I looked at Pop, who'd returned to cutting his toenails in the recliner. The distinct *kathunk* of his 8-track jumped to the next song. The old man never flinched.

How does that not bother him? I wondered. *The other song didn't even finish yet.* I shook my head. *Pop really needs to get with the times and switch to cassettes.*

My father snipped another toenail, sending it flying. "Incoming!" he called out.

That's so disgusting, I thought, hustling back to my bedroom. When the old man trimmed his toenails, you either wore safety goggles or you left the room—anything else was lunacy. The loss of eyesight was a very real risk. *And no one wants to stumble around like Mr. Magoo,* I thought.

I spent the next hour or so in my bunk, daydreaming. *I can't wait for summer,* I thought, my mind travelling a few years back.

• • •

I could still picture it: The whole family piled into Pop's wood-paneled Chevy station wagon with no exhaust, a cold beer resting between our father's legs. Ma sat in the passenger seat, sucking on one of her cancer sticks, with the three of us sitting in the back. No one wore seat belts. The steel buckles had been intentionally tucked into the bench seat because when the sun beat down on them for more than a few minutes, our skin could get branded for life.

The power window in the rear of the wagon never worked. Even still, my brothers and I thought that the rumble seat was awesome. Pop would clean out the back of the rolling tank—removing the spare tire, lug wrench, an old tool box, the bushel basket and half-inflated inner tube used for gathering quahogs in the summer—so we could sit back there. I couldn't think of anything more thrilling than facing oncoming traffic that sped only inches from our legs, our future mobility protected by a rusted steel bumper.

"When we get to the Drive-In, I want you guys to duck down on the floor and pull that blanket over you."

"Why, Pop?" we called from the back.

"Some guy at work said he thinks they're charging by the head now and not the car load."

"Are you serious?" Ma asked.

There was silence.

He must have nodded, I thought, jumping over the seat and grabbing for the tattered blanket.

My brothers followed me, preparing to hide.

"And you want the boys to hide like refugees, so we can sneak them in?" The disgust in Ma's voice was palpable.

"How the hell do you think I'm getting my beer in, Emma?" he asked.

As Pop turned right and drove down the lane to the drive-in's guard shack, we wedged ourselves onto the back seat's floor, yanking the moldy blanket over our heads.

"This is awesome," I whispered, before holding my breath.

The station wagon squeaked to a stop.

"Good evening to you," Pop said, in answer to someone we couldn't hear. "Hey, you charging by the head or the car load now?"

There was some mumbling, sounding a lot like Charlie's Brown's teacher.

"Okay, the coast is clear," Pop yelled to us, "you boys can come out now."

All three of us emerged from the blanket and looked out the back window to see the drive-in attendant staring at us in shock.

Pop handed over the money. "But you still went up another dollar this year, didn't you?"

"Not my call, buddy," the guy said, handing Pop a ticket to place on the wagon's filthy dashboard.

"It's somebody's call," Pop said, unwilling to let it go. "My name's Tucker, not sucker."

"All right, Walt, can we go see the movie now?" Ma said. "I didn't even want to come see Indiana Jones and the Temple of Doom. You're the one who . . ."

"You're gonna love it, hon," Pop teased.

"That's what you said when you dragged me to see Porky's."

He laughed. "Well, I didn't know what that movie was about . . . but you liked The Warriors, right?"

"No," she said, "*you* liked The Warriors. I hate movies with violence in them. You know that."

"Let 'er go," he said, laughing harder. It was Pop's signature saying; while the Italians had "Forget about it," the old man had "Let 'er go."

Ma shook her head.

"Tonight will be different, my angel," he said. "You watch, this'll be just like our first date."

Gag me with a spoon and make me barf, I thought.

Ma looked over the front seat at us and smirked. "Sure it will, Walt."

As Pop eased the wagon forward, we made faces at the guy in the booth—until he made one back, making us giggle.

I loved going to the drive-in movie theatre. We got in our pajamas and, besides the popcorn that Ma brought in brown paper bags from home, she also packed cans of soda pop in the cooler. *The old man's beer is stashed somewhere,* I knew, though no one asked.

Pop parked the car toward the middle of the theatre grounds and hung the silver speaker onto his window.

"I hope we don't get eaten alive by mosquitoes again this year," Ma complained.

"It's part of the experience," Pop told her.

Slamming the car doors behind us, my brothers and I took off running toward the swing set in front of the massive movie screen.

There won't be any playing on the swings when I'm old enough to take Donna to the drive-in, I thought, sprinting for an empty swing. *If things go right, we won't even be watching the movie.*

I loved the summers when we were young and allowed my mind to stay there for a while longer.

Sometimes, on the weekends, it was a real treat for my brothers and me to ride in the back of our Uncle Skinny's pickup truck to make a dump run. We'd barrel down the highway, exceeding the speed limit. Each time one of us stood up to peek his head over the roof of the cab, Uncle Skinny would yell at us from the split-glass window, "What are you nuts? Sit the hell down!"

Although I was young, I remember wondering, *You're speeding down the highway with kids in the back of your truck and you think we're the crazy ones?* No matter, I loved riding in the bed of that old Ford, driving under the overpasses and yelling out our names to hear the echoes.

When we'd been "really good" and Pop was in a generous mood, he treated us to a Saturday night at Seekonk Speedway to watch the local stock cars battle it out on the concrete oval. To save money, I remember him filling two coat sleeves with beer, tying off the cuffs with thick brown twine. As we watched him prepare, he shot us a wink. "The trick is to make sure it's heavy twine."

As we approached the track's ticket booth, Pop turned to me. "When they ask, you're seven years old."

"But I'm ten, Pop."

"Not today," he said, shaking his head, "today, you're seven."

"But . . ."

He glared down at me. "If they ask you how old you are, Herbie, you're seven. End of story."

Once we made it through the first obstacle, we headed to the security gate. With fold-out chairs in hand, Pop carried his small Igloo cooler filled with ice and two cans of soda. Tucked under his other arm was his heavy flannel jacket—much too warm for the season—both sleeves stuffed with full beers.

The police officer at the gate searched the red cooler.

"Do you want a soda?" Pop asked the cop. "I need to make some room."

I can't believe it, I thought.

"No thanks," the cop said before smiling at me and my brothers. "You boys have a good time tonight, okay?"

"Oh, we will," Pop said, returning the smile.

Two steps into the track, I thought, *Pop's got some real big ones.*

• • •

When Wally returned from the dungeon, disturbing my peace, I decided, *I should take that bath before we start watching TV.*

Stained linoleum covered the bathroom floor, the area around the lion claw tub tainted extra yellow from the gallons and gallons of water that had been spilled. Stripping naked, I filled the tub with warm water.

"Don't stay in there all night," Ma yelled through the locked door. "Your poor brother had an accident and needs to get cleaned up."

Poor Cockroach, I repeated in my head, trying not to giggle. In our house, bath time was like cleaning up after an aggressive mud-wrestling match. It always sucked being the last person to bathe. *Good thing I jumped in first.*

For the next half hour, I worked that bar of Ivory soap down to the nub, taking my sweet time before getting dried and dressed. Unsure whether I'd remembered to brush my teeth in the morning, I decided, *I might as well do it now while I'm here.* The Crest toothpaste's cap was nearly welded to the bathroom vanity. *Friggin' Wally!*

Preparing to leave the bathroom and face my mother's scowl, I spotted a cardboard tube where a roll of toilet paper had once hung, promising some screamed vulgarities from the next person to take a seat on the throne. I shrugged, deciding, *I'm sure Ma will replace it.*

While Ma prepared Cockroach's bath, I decided, *I want my MTV.* It was such a rare gift to have the living room's old Zenith console all to myself. I watched music videos until VJ Martha Quinn swept me away in some beautiful trance. Genesis and David Bowie led to Billy Joel and The Police, who—along with Michael Jackson— were topping the Billboard charts in 1984. It seemed insane to follow one of Madonna's videos with a Bruce Springsteen jam, but that's how it played out. *I love it!*

"That's enough," Ma said, shattering my trance. "You've been watching these stupid videos for an hour already."

"They're not stupid, Ma," I said, insulted she would even suggest such a thing. "An hour?" I repeated, surprised.

"Yes, an hour," she said. "See, you're already frying your brain with this stupid channel."

It's not stupid! I repeated in my hazy mind.

After getting nice and clean, Cockroach and I stayed true to our normal Friday night routine—watching the Dukes of Hazzard, while munching on hand-cut French fries from greasy brown paper bags.

"Do you know how many single socks there are again?" Ma asked, folding the laundry that Wally had washed and dried. "It's like the dryer eats them, or something."

Cockroach and I shrugged.

Wally was stuck in our bedroom—his new jail cell—which I believed only helped to fuel his growing rage.

Bang . . . bang . . . bang . . .

I could hear the distinct sound of a pinkie rubber ball hitting our bedroom wall, over-and-over. *Wally's bouncing it against the wall, playing catch with himself,* I surmised.

"Stop," Pop yelled from his recliner.

There was another bounce.

"Wally, stop bouncing the ball against the wall," our father yelled louder, making himself crystal clear to most of the neighborhood.

There was silence, followed by another bounce.

The squeaky sound of the recliner's footrest coming down was the most terrifying sound ever. Usually, it meant the old man was pissed off and he was coming for one of us.

Suddenly, there was silence—from everyone except Boss Hogg on the TV—until we heard the ratcheted sound of the recliner's footrest going back up.

Wally was quiet for the rest of the night. I walked past our bedroom once to use the bathroom. My brother was doing sets of push-ups and sit-ups; he'd been reduced to a prison workout. *Give it a rest*, I told him in my head. *Owen's a foot taller than you and there isn't a damn thing you can do this week to change that.*

Are those Toll House cookies I smell? I wondered. *Can't be. Ma wouldn't . . .*

It was true. Obviously trying to get Wally back for his terrible behavior, Ma had made fresh-baked chocolate chip cookies, the wafting aromas sure to torment my older brother. *Oh, he's really being punished now*, I thought. Unfortunately, so was I. *That smell is torture.*

"Go ahead," Ma told me and Cockroach, extending the plate of warm cookies toward us, "help yourselves." She looked toward our bedroom and yelled, "But animals don't get cookies."

"They'd rather eat butts," Cockroach commented. He looked at me and grinned.

I shook my head, putting on my best disappointed face.

His smile instantly vanished.

Ma held the plate of gooey treats under my nose.

I shouldn't, I told myself, *I have to lose weight. Donna doesn't want a chubby boyfriend.*

Ma pushed the plate closer.

But this is a rare occasion, I thought.

The heavenly scent was overwhelming.

To hell with it, I thought, feeding my face, *I'll start tomorrow. Yeah, that's what I'll do. I'll just starve myself all day tomorrow to make up for it.*

The first bite rolled my eyes to the back of my head. *Damn Ma,* I thought, *you've got a real dark side, messing with Wally like this.*

As I lay in bed, wondering if Wally was sleeping, Cockroach checked the bedroom closet and shut off the light. *I doubt he's asleep,* I thought. "Andale . . . andale . . ." I called out in my best Speedy Gonzalez accent.

There was silence.

Wally's probably sore at us for eating the cookies without him, I decided. *But he's the one who went all cannibal on Cockroach's rear end.* I snickered.

The silence droned on.

"Arriba . . . arriba . . ." Cockroach called back.

Better late than never, I thought. "Night, Alphonse."

"Night, Herbie."

My thoughts—both detailed and vivid—alternated between Daisy Duke and Donna Torres until I fell asleep.

CHAPTER 10

SATURDAY

"When you find him, lock him in his room until I get home," Pop barked, "and I don't care if you have to nail his windows shut. Make sure he doesn't move, okay?" Pop's volume increased with each word. There was a pause, returning his voice back to normal, "Okay, I gotta go for now. I'll be home by six o'clock. Just make sure Herbie knows that I'm not happy with him."

I swallowed hard.

The next thing I knew I was sneaking out my second-floor window and shimmying down the icy drainpipe until I hit the ground. *Freedom,* I thought, smiling to myself. And that's when I saw the white van screech to a stop in front of the house, with Clarence jumping out of the driver's seat and sprinting straight toward me.

But the shed . . . I thought, *this . . . this already ended in the shed.*

Clarence was only a few yards away now, still coming for me.

Run, I told my rubbery legs, but they wouldn't budge. *Run!* I screamed in my head. Still, I stood paralyzed.

"Here'th my thpecial friend," Clarence said, grabbing me by the arms and dragging me toward the van. "Time to play!"

I tried to scream—I swear I did—but I never made a peep. *Oh God,* I thought, my mind buzzing from the terror that consumed me. *I'm so dead . . . again.*

Clarence threw me into the back of the van, where he bound my hands and feet with duct tape. He smiled at me, his teeth glistening like tiny knives. "Let'th go for a ride," he said, giggling.

As the back door slammed shut and the world went dark, I fought off the urge to vomit—realizing I might drown if I did.

Wake up, I screamed to myself, somehow aware that I was stuck inside another twisted nightmare. *Wake up, Herbie!*

It was early afternoon, Thanksgiving. Pop was drinking a Miller High Life in his recliner, talking on the telephone—the long green cord stretched to its max.

"The food's ready," Ma yelled.

"Okay Skinny," Pop said, "I gotta go." He hung up the phone, checked the football score on the Zenith and then stretched out once before heading for the bathroom. On the way, he called out, "Let's go, boys. It's time to eat."

Wally and Cockroach sprinted for the table.

"Whoa," Pop grunted, "slow down. Where's Herbie?" He raised an eyebrow. "You know your mother," he said. "If we're not all seated when she serves Tom Turkey, there'll be hell to pay."

Wally shrugged. "I thought he was watching the game with you, Pop?"

"Me too," Cockroach echoed.

Pop shook his head. "I've been on the phone, talking to your uncle for almost an hour. Herbie hasn't been with me." He froze in mid-step. "Go outside, Wally, and see if he's out there." As my husky brother ran off, Pop complained, "Son-of-a . . . , your brother's gonna test my patience yet."

Cockroach nodded in agreement.

Wally rushed back into the house, shaking his head. "He's not out there, Pop."

From the open kitchen window, Pop's beckoning traveled the abandoned street. "Herbie . . . Herbie?" Only the moaning wind responded. Agitated, he grabbed his boots and slid the first one on when the telephone rang. "Hello," he snapped, answering the annoyance.

"Happy Holidayth!" Clarence said, "I jutht wanted to let you know that . . ."

Pop's angry face filled with blood. "You sick bastard. How did you get this number?" Before Clarence could respond, Pop went off. "Listen to me good, now," he screamed, "If you ever call this house again, I swear I'll . . ."

I didn't know Pop and Clarence had a falling out! I thought, confused over the time and context of their conversation.

"No, you lithten to me!" Clarence spat back. "I called to tell you that your luck'th run out and that there'th thomeone here that agreeth with me."

"Pop?" It was my voice, sounding small and broken.

Oh God! Panic filled every cell in my trembling body.

"Herbie?" Pop squeaked before gasping for air.

"Herbie doethn't think I'm a freak or a piethe of garbage," Clarence said, returning to the call. "He likthe me. Herbie really likthe me." There was a sick chuckle followed by a dial tone.

Pop went straight to his knees, a cold sweat squeezing the phone from his hand.

The crash had Ma running. "What is it?" she asked.

"Oh God . . ." Pop cried.

"What?" Ma screamed.

"Herbie must have snuck off again and . . . and that freak in the white panel van . . . Clarence . . ." He stopped.

"What?" Ma screamed. "What about Clarence?"

"He has Herbie," Pop cried.

Ma's ear-piercing shrill turned my blood to ice water.

• • •

I awoke, holding my breath.

"Let's go," Pop said, his face inches from mine. "I need your help."

Wha . . . what? I thought, completely confused and trying to breathe.

"We're in for some pretty bad weather, Herbie," he said, while I struggled to process what was happening, "and I want to make sure your grandparents have everything they need to get through the storm."

I lay there for a strange moment, still trying to reconcile Clarence's demented world from reality.

"Let's go. Get a move on," my father said, before heading for the accordion door.

As he left, I noticed he was wearing a colored pocket t-shirt, which he only wore when he needed to be presentable. With Clarence's voice still causing goosebumps up and down my body, I slid out of my bunk. Shaking my head, I tried desperately to clear the cobwebs.

Just let it go, I repeated in my head. *Just let it go. It was only another bad dream.*

A blueberry Pop Tart and a half later, I was dressed in layers and hustling off to Pop's old wagon, ready to jump in and help him do some Good Samaritan work. *No cartoons today, I guess. Rocky and Bullwinkle will have to wait another week.* I shrugged. *And old Elmer Fudd will have to hunt wabbits all by himself.*

Climbing into the car, I thought, *I may be wrong, but it doesn't feel as cold out today.*

Pop's beat-up station wagon was a rolling dumpster, with plastic six-pack holders poking out from under the front seat.

After finishing my breakfast, I dropped the Pop Tart wrapper, watching it float to the floor.

"What do you think this is," Pop yelled, "a trash can?"

Ummm, yeah . . .

"Have some respect for other people's things," he said.

Really?

We travelled for a few miles in silence.

"Pop, do you think we'll ever get nuked by the Russians?" I asked him.

He shook his head. "I don't," he said, shrugging. "If someone's stupid enough to launch a nuke, then both sides lose, right?"

I nodded. *Makes sense*, I thought, feeling a little better.

"Where the hell's this coming from, anyway?" he asked.

"My history teacher talks a lot about the possibility of it happening."

He shook his head again. "Maybe your history teacher should concentrate on teaching the past and not trying to predict the future." He looked at me. "It's not something you need to worry about, Herbie. If it ever happened, God forbid, we probably wouldn't even realize it until it was too late." He grinned. "Let 'er go."

I considered my father's logic, quickly realizing that it made me feel worse. I scrambled to shift my thinking. *Wally's gonna be stuck in the house until we go back to school,* I thought, feeling jealous. *Basically, he's been rewarded.*

"What's going on with Wally?" Pop asked, as if reading my mind. "He's always down in that cellar and . . ."

Oh that, I thought. "He goes down there to lift weights," I told him, being honest.

"Every day?"

"Yup." I thought about it, realizing that this might be my only opportunity to help my big brother. Even though he could be a tool, I'd felt bad for him the entire week. *If it had been me who'd been threatened, Wally would have gone to war for me,* I realized, *and not been half as tortured as being challenged himself.* My brother's protective instincts would have overpowered his fear. I just knew it. *In some crazy way, it's too bad it wasn't me that Owen targeted.*

Pop continued looking at me.

"He's having problems with a bigger kid on the bus," I blurted.

Pop's forehead wrinkled in surprise.

I told my father about the entire bus incident, being overly-dramatic in the hopes of saving Wally. "You had to be there, Pop. You really did. It was terrible." I shook my head. "And this dude Owen's no wannabe. He's the real deal," I said. "Wally's shitting bricks and I don't blame him."

"Watch your mouth, Herbie," he said.

Really? I thought. *You walk around here, swearing all the time, and I should watch my mouth?* "What are you going to do, Pop?" I asked.

"Nothing," he said. "It's for Wally to take care of. He's getting older and he needs to learn to stand up for himself." He nodded, confidently. "Your brother needs to be a man."

"So you're not going to talk to him about it?" I asked, shocked.

He shook his head. "I'm here if Wally needs to talk, Herbie. He knows that."

"But the guy who threatened Wally is a lot bigger than him, Pop," I told him, as a last ditch effort. "A lot bigger."

To my surprise, Pop smirked. "Your grandfather used to say that God never put the heart of a lion into an elephant. I have no doubt that your brother's going to step up and meet this challenge." His smirk turned into a full-blown smile. "Just wait and see."

We drove in silence again for a while. "He's been really quiet all week," I said.

Pop nodded. "That's because he's up in his head about it." He took a deep breath and sighed. "Don't worry so much, Herbie. Things'll work out." He winked at me. "They always do."

Sure, Pop, I thought, *unless I don't realize there's something to worry about until it's too late.*

The radio man labeled the day, "Blustery." I wasn't really sure what the word meant, but I did know that it was pretty cold outside and that the winds were kicking up as much snow as what was being dumped on us from above. *I don't know how Pop can see anything out that windshield*, I thought. It was a screen of white, much like TV static when the rabbit's ears used to act up. Still, Pop's large hands remained locked on the steering wheel, keeping the station wagon steady and moving straight ahead.

"This ol' girl's getting harder to control than your mother," he joked.

I didn't know whether to laugh or be more worried.

"As long as we make it to the package store for beer and scratch tickets before they close," he said.

Of course, I thought.

Pop slowed even more, causing me to look out my window. It seemed every time I rode in the back of Pop's station wagon, I was looking out one window or another, paying attention. The old man had a habit of stopping in the driving rain or Arctic cold to help folks in need. He'd change tires or give people a ride to the next filling station for a can of gas. He even picked up hitchhikers when my brothers and I weren't in the car—most of the time, anyway.

I squinted to focus, realizing, *There's definitely something—or someone—on the side of the road.* At first, I couldn't make it out. Slowing to a crawl, Pop and I peered through the puddled window. A pang of fear ripped through my body. *It's a silhouette,* I realized, my brain finally deciphering the message sent from my wide eyes, *the shape of a man . . . a very large man.* His thumb was extended and a glare of desperation covered his big face. *Oh God, please don't stop,* I thought, a different storm suddenly swirling inside me.

But I knew Pop, and I knew what he'd do. On any other night, there would have been nothing for him to think about, no dilemma to solve. Given that I was in the car, my father would have just passed the stranger by, hoping that another person would stop and pick the hitchhiker up. *But this isn't any other night,* I realized. *We haven't seen another car in over a half hour.* Although I knew the choice Pop would make, I hoped it wasn't a life-or-death decision.

The station wagon slowed even more, making me shudder at the horrible possibilities.

As we came to a stop, Pop half-turned to address me in the back seat. "I have no choice, Herbie," he said. "If we don't help this man, he'll die in this weather, for sure."

I nodded and, with a paralyzing fear, waited for the passenger side door to open. Several endless seconds later, it did. Every hair on my body stood on end.

The large shadow we saw on the side of the road had done this man no justice. He stuck his head in first. *Oh my God, he's enormous*, I thought, my breathing also coming to a momentary stop. The stranger was actually forced to cram various parts of his body into the car until, an eternity later, the whole of him was in. My hands began to tremble at the sight of his giant paws. *They're bleeding*, I realized.

As the passenger door slammed shut, I nearly jumped out of my gooseflesh. Almost in slow motion, the giant turned his head toward Pop and grinned sheepishly. He was missing a tooth. "I can't thank you enough . . ." he moaned, pausing when he noticed Pop was staring at his hands. "Yeah, the blood . . . sorry about that," he slurred, "I must have put my hands through the windshield when my car slid off the road. It's still sitting in a ditch back there." He shrugged. "I tried to get it out, but I couldn't budge it." The man spoke as if he'd been drugged.

I was mortified, thinking, *I never saw any stranded car.*

"I appreciate it," he repeated into Pop's giant pupils. "Mighty decent of you to stop."

I could almost hear the faint echo of my cautious mother and nearly burst into tears. *I can't believe Pop's gotten us into this.* And then I realized, *We're still parked in the breakdown lane.*

The stranger turned his massive head and nodded toward me. I nodded back, hoping I wouldn't vomit on the back seat. *My nightmare's coming true*, I thought, *and this guy makes Clarence look like a joke.*

Waiting for Pop to pull back onto the road, I contemplated the chances of me and him abandoning the station wagon and successfully fleeing on foot. But those thoughts were quickly interrupted by an angry grunt. *Oh God . . .* It took all the courage I had left to look over the front seat again.

The monster was running his paws across a billboard forehead. He was covered in blood, some of it trickling down his eyebrows and into his face. With one hand, he tried to cup the oozing crimson; the other hand stayed exactly where it had been since he'd gotten into the car—wrapped around his heaving abdomen. "If you can get me into Fall River to . . . to a hospital, " he stammered, grimacing, "I'd . . . I'd be grateful."

Pop didn't question the request. He stomped on the gas, kicking out the wagon's back end and nearly hurling the car into the guardrail.

While my father concentrated on the driving, the stranger went silent. I knew right away, *This is a very different experience from when we picked up that old geezer who'd run out of gas.*

From the beginning of our journey together, my mind painted a thousand and one terrifying nightmares: *The hitchhiker's a serial killer who didn't have time to clean up; the giant's an escaped felon from Southeastern Correctional Center only a few towns over in Bridgewater. Maybe he's even a drug dealer who's being hunted by the police that shot him?* As I considered the chances of him killing us both, my hands shook violently. When my mind had finally exhausted every brutal possibility that was sure to lead to our demise, only one thought remained: *Pop's so stupid!*

The ogre didn't speak a word. It seemed peculiar so, with the sneakiness of Cockroach, I slowly glanced over the front seat to steal a peek at our executioner. *The giant's fast asleep.* I leaned in for a better look. *He's out cold.* The voice in my head continued to get louder. *Get out now!* But part of me also understood why Pop had stopped to help. *The man's in serious trouble and needs our help.* While my heart and mind battled it out, Pop turned on the interior light.

"Holy shit," he muttered.

I looked over the seat and, instinctively, the gruesome sight made my trembling hand go to my mouth. I didn't want to scream, nor did I want to vomit on the titan.

"He's not sleeping," Pop told me in a low voice. "He's lost so much blood that he's . . ." My father turned off the light and stomped on the gas once more. "Charlton Memorial Hospital's four miles away," he reported.

Murderer, escapee or drug dealer, I thought, *we definitely can't leave another human being for dead.*

Hyperventilating through the remaining miles of the dangerous trek, I fought off the panic that threatened to consume me and had nearly succeeded when Pop pulled into the front of the hospital. My father laid on the horn until he grabbed the attention of the annoyed security guard. "Let's go," Pop yelled.

With one glance into the car, the guard knew enough to call for backup. The rest seemed to transpire in slow motion.

While I watched on in horror, hospital personnel forcefully extracted the bleeding stranger from the interior of the station wagon, leaving a massive pool of blood in his place. When they were done, the entire interior was a gory mess. I looked over at Pop's clothes and saw that he was also painted in the deep crimson. "Sweet Jesus," I whispered, following my father and the speeding gurney into the hospital.

Doctors and nurses swarmed the man and worked with a frightening urgency until wheeling him through a set of swinging doors. One nurse even announced a "Code Red" over the emergency room intercom. There was no time wasted.

Frozen in a fog of shock, Pop and I were quickly blind-sided by one of the intake nurses. "I'll need some information on your friend," the nurse said.

Pop shrugged.

Friend? I thought. *For all we know, this guy's a homicidal maniac.* The idea of the giant being labeled a friend sent even more anxiety through my overworked system.

"Oh no," Pop replied, shaken from his own daze, "that poor guy's a stranger we picked up on the side of the highway." With a steady voice, he explained how we'd found the scary dude on Route 88. The nurse jotted down every detail.

"What a night, Pop," I muttered, taking a seat beside him in the waiting room. I tried to calm my nerves. It was no use.

"Yeah, it's been something," he said.

Within minutes, a frantic woman burst through the doors and approached the intake nurse. "I'm Rose Cowen, Brad's wife. I got here as soon as I could!"

I watched her. *The monster's name is Brad,* I pondered, *and he has a wife named Rose. I didn't picture this in the nightmare.*

Breaking my train of thought, Rose said, "You're saying that the priest has administered last rites to my husband?"

"Yes," the nurse replied, "Father Martin arrived no more than five minutes ago." They talked in hushed tones for a few minutes before the nurse pointed to me and Pop.

Unnerved, Rose Cowen provided pages of common insurance

information, all the while glancing between the nurse and the doors to the E.R. I couldn't take my eyes off the poor woman. *She's more of a wreck than me.* Once done, the frazzled woman hurried for the seat beside me and Pop and attempted a formal introduction. It didn't work. Her tears would not allow it. "Thank you," she eventually managed between sobs. "Thank you so much for stopping to help my husband. He's a good man and we have a little girl at home who . . ." She started bawling.

With a single nod, Pop began rubbing the trembling woman's back. "Everything's gonna be okay," he said, trying to comfort her. "Your husband's in good hands now."

Rose Cowen's body convulsed at his every word.

In a time that seemed suspended from reality, one of the doctors dressed in blue scrubs approached. "Mrs. Cowen?" he inquired. His face looked professional but kind.

Rose stood on wobbly legs.

"Your husband had some internal bleeding and he's lost a lot of blood, but I'm happy to report that he's going to make it." He nodded. "I was present when a very talented surgeon performed the initial procedure. Once we stopped the bleeding, I felt it was important that you know." A smile broke through. "Your husband's going to be fine."

Rose collapsed back into her chair, her sorrowful weeping turning to relief and joy.

"If he'd arrived here five minutes later, he probably would have died from his injuries," the doctor concluded. "Your husband's an incredibly lucky man." With that, the paper-covered shoes scratched the floor back behind the swinging doors.

Rose composed herself enough to look straight into Pop's eyes.

This time, there were no stuttered words of gratitude. Instead, she hugged him for a long while.

"I told ya," Pop muttered into her shoulder.

Pop looks like he might melt in Mrs. Cowen's arms, I thought. And that's when she let go of him and latched onto me for the warmest embrace I'd ever felt.

When she and I broke apart, Pop looked at me and winked.

For the first time since the nightmare began, I wished I could be alone—where I could finally cry and let it all out. *Pop and I are safe now*, I told myself, *we're safe*.

As we walked out of the hospital, Pop looked at me. "You okay?" he asked, his coat covered in dry blood.

I nodded.

"Did you shit your britches?"

I shook my head. "Came close, I think, but no."

Laughing, he patted me on the back. "That 'a boy. Let 'er go."

I thought for a few moments before deciding to ask. "You weren't afraid at all, Pop?"

He stopped on the sidewalk and turned to face me. "It got a little hairy there for a while, that's for sure." He shrugged. "But can you imagine if we let our fear stop us from helping that poor man?"

"He would have died," I thought aloud.

Pop nodded. "That's right, and a little piece of us would've died with him." He took a deep breath and exhaled. "That's what cowardice does, Herbie," he said, "it kills away pieces of us until there ain't any of the good left." He placed his hand on my shoulder again and smiled. "And I'd rather have you whole."

I nodded, grateful for the tough lesson.

"Now let's go see to your grandparents," he said, starting toward the car again.

You've got to be shittin' me, Pop?

"And remind me to stop at the package store for some beer and scratch tickets." He looked up at a dark gray sky that continued to dump snow on us. "I'm thinking it'll be a few days before I'll be able to get my hands on either."

I'll remind you, I told the hero in my head. "Can I get something, too, Pop," I asked him, "Maybe even a candy bar?" Somewhere along the way, I'd become a shameless beggar.

He looked at me. "Whatever you want, son," he said, grinning. "I'd say you earned it."

"Thanks Pop!"

Although he'd never put it into words, my father's motto on life was simple: "It's not about me." He never did anything for himself, always thinking of others first.

It's what I admire most about him, I realized.

CHAPTER 11

SUNDAY

Flipping through the TV channels. I reached Mister Rogers' neighborhood and stopped. Although I was well past the age to visit Sesame Street, Romper Room and Mr. Rogers' perfect neighborhood, or spend any real quality time with Captain Kangaroo, I wasn't too old to miss my childhood babysitters.

"Change it," Wally called out. "I think the Munsters are on channel 38."

"I love the Munsters," Cockroach said.

"Relax, Eddy Munster," I told Wally, "I'm just . . ."

". . . about to shut the TV off, so you can all go outside and play," Ma said, stepping into the room just in time to finish my sentence.

We all looked at her.

I'm gonna miss Casey Kasam's top 40 countdown again, I thought, *because we're being forced to go outside again.* I shook my angry head.

After our usual breakfast of simple sugars, we began piling on the thick layers.

It didn't take long before Ma snapped. "For God's sake, you guys should be old enough to get yourselves ready for school or to go play outside," she barked. Me and Wally had been dressing ourselves for years now, so she was only talking to Cockroach. But in our house, everything was "you guys." It was our parents' best attempt at either being fair or else not having to repeat instructions.

Ma grabbed two bread bags, the heel of the bread still in one of them. "Empty the bags and then put them on," she told Cockroach.

"Pita bread bags might be better to avoid yeast infections," Pop joked.

Although I had no idea what he was talking about, I still laughed. I then pictured a couple of squirrels watching my little brother from a safe distance, waiting for the bread bags to blow open and help feed their family.

Cockroach sat on the floor, trying to dress himself for the harsh cold.

Although the bread bags were supposed to go over the socks and inside the boots, Alphonse had paid the same attention on how to get ready as any other task that had been performed for him; he hadn't paid any. Left to his own devices, this promised to be comical. I lingered around to watch.

Cockroach put on his socks, then his boots and then he slid the bread bags over his boots.

What a dope, I thought, shaking my head. Ma was no longer paying any attention to him, so I wondered, *Should I tell him?* I chuckled. *Nah, let's see what happens.*

"Have fun, boys," she said, with her back to us.

As we started to leave the apartment, Wally asked, "What about church, Ma? I thought we were going back to church this week?"

She turned back, her eyes as sincere as the week before. "We need to start getting up earlier," she said, nodding. "We'll go next week."

"Sure, Ma," Wally said, drawing a bad look from her.

"Do you want to spend another day in the house?" she asked, challenging him.

Although he continued to look at her, he remained silent.

"Get out of the house," she said, "I'll deal with you later."

"Sure, Ma," he repeated.

We reached the outside stairs to find that the gray sky was dumping so much snow that I could barely see ten feet in front of me. *It's a whiteout,* I thought, unable to remember the last time I'd felt so excited. I slapped Wally's muscular arm and pointed toward our little brother's feet.

He shook his head. "He put the plastic bags *over* his boots?" he whispered, clearly amused.

I nodded. "This ought to be something," I whispered back.

Clueless, Cockroach looked back at us and smiled—before taking off for the open yard at a sprint. I couldn't believe it. *He's running in the fresh, slippery snow.* Instantly, my heart and mind faced off in a tug of war. *I should stop him,* I knew, but the idea of putting a halt to a sure laugh wasn't the easiest thing to do. *I mean, what's the worst that can happen?*

I looked to my side to see Wally watching with his mouth hung open. I then looked ahead to see my little brother a few steps away from a terrible wipe-out. "Stop Cockroach," I instinctively screamed out, "you're gonna . . ."

But I'd waited too long. *Oh no . . .*

Cockroach slid for a couple of yards until his feet flew into the air and he was completely upside down. What I thought was going to be hysterical proved to be anything but. Even with the horrific scene being blurred by the blinding snow, I realized, *He's hurt.* The truth of it stole my breath away.

"Oh no," Wally repeated aloud, starting into his own trot and matching me step-for-step.

When we reached the scene of the crime, we expected to hear Cockroach's usual cries and screams. He was silent.

Oh God, I thought, my heart pounding out of my chest. The snow beneath his head was stained red. *He's bleeding.* I pushed my baby brother's shoulder, checking for signs of life.

Cockroach suddenly gasped for air, sounding a lot like a dog's squeak toy. Three breaths later, he was screaming his bloody head off.

Thank God!

Wally bent down, scooped him up and rushed back toward the house. "You're gonna be okay, big guy," he huffed, trying to comfort Cockroach en-route. "You're gonna be fine."

Snatching up Cockroach's blood-soaked hat from the ground, I hustled after them.

As soon as the apartment door flew open, our mother took one look at Cockroach and began her own screaming. "Oh, my Lord! Alphonse!"

Cockroach wailed in pain.

Pop came running into the room. "What happened?"

"Alphonse was running in the yard and slipped," Wally reported, setting our little brother down onto one of the kitchen chairs.

"And he split his head," I added.

Cockroach continued to cry.

Hyperventilating, Ma took off toward the bathroom for a warm face cloth. "Walter," she gasped, looking to our father for help.

"I'll take him to the emergency room," Pop said, hurrying for his boots. "I've become a regular," he added under his breath.

Ma quickly returned with the cloth. She went to her knees in front of Cockroach and gently placed the cloth on his head. While the white facecloth turned pink, she glanced down and spotted the bread bags on Cockroach's boots. "No wonder you . . ." She stopped in mid-sentence, looking up at me and Wally, her eyes were filled with contempt.

Wally and I simultaneously shook our heads.

"We never noticed," Wally said in a stoic tone, nearly convincing me.

"Sure you didn't," she said, returning her attention to Cockroach.

"You gotta be shittin' me," Pop complained, throwing on his heavy barn coat. "This'll be Alphonse's second visit to the E.R. in a week." He shook his head. "My third."

"I went three times last year too, Pop," I quickly reminded him, "when Wally liked splittin' my head open."

"Those were accidents," Wally chimed in, "all three of them."

"Animals," my mother said, looking up from her knees at my father, "we're raising animals."

Pop shook his head. "Let 'er go, Emma, they're boys, just boys."

The old man scooped Cockroach into his arms and hurried for the door. "We'll be back after he gets a few stitches."

"Stitches?" Cockroach repeated, shrieking like a possessed banshee.

"Enough," Pop roared, "you need to be a big boy now!"

Cockroach's shrills were reduced to sorrowful whines.

Ugh, I thought, feeling awful for a whole lot of reasons.

When the front door closed behind Pop and his petrified patient,

Ma turned back to us. Her eyes were fiery slits.

"It wasn't our fault," I lied, confirming Wally's claim. "We never noticed the plastic bags, Ma. I swear it."

Her eyes remained locked onto mine for a few dreadful moments. When she finally looked away, I began breathing again. *We were so stupid*, I thought, feeling ashamed that we'd let my little brother get hurt. *I just hope he's okay.*

Ma left the kitchen.

She doesn't even want to be in the same room as me and Wally, I thought. *Well, at least we won't be visiting Memere's house this week. I don't think I could take the pea soup leftovers.* Any other time, I would have been thrilled about this, but I couldn't feel good about anything.

In the privacy of our bedroom, I grabbed the Magic 8 ball and turned it over. *Good, it's not broken*, I thought.

I shook it a few times. *Please tell me that Cockroach will be okay*, I said with my eyes closed. As if in prayer, I turned the ball and peered into the small window.

Yes, it read.

Oh, thank God, I thought, feeling an instant sense of relief.

I took a few deep breaths and started shaking the ball again, like I was preparing to drink a Yoohoo. "Come on now," I said, "what about me and Donna? Will we be together?"

I flipped the ball to gaze into the purple fluid.

The triangle read, *Better not tell you now.*

I shook it again and flipped it.

Ask again later.

"You've got to be kidding me!"

I shook harder and flipped it.

Signs point to yes.

My breathing picked up. I shook it one last time to be sure.

It is decidedly so, the plastic fortuneteller predicted.

Filled with joy, my body flooded with adrenaline. *Yes,* I thought, *I knew it!* I couldn't stop smiling. *I just knew it.*

I spent the next few hours lying in my bunk, my thoughts alternating between Cockroach and Donna. Whenever I started feeling sad about my baby brother, I'd listen to another Bryan Adams song and focus on my future bride.

Pop and Cockroach finally returned home from the hospital and the terrible storm. We all hurried into the kitchen to greet them.

Besides a ride to the E.R. in Pop's makeshift ambulance—the horn undoubtedly blowing the entire way—Cockroach received five stitches where his forehead met his hairline.

"He was very brave," Pop told Ma, placing the little guy into her arms. "He's gonna be fine."

"Thank God," she said, looking at Cockroach. "I've been worried sick about you, Alphonse."

"I'm okay, Ma," he mumbled, like a hero returning home from war. He then looked at me and Wally.

"That's gonna make a mean-looking scar," Wally told him, grinning. "The girls are gonna love it."

"Very handsome," I agreed, unwilling to reveal the fear that I'd felt for him all afternoon.

Although Cockroach nodded, he knew the entire act was intended for our parents. He might have been young but he was experienced enough to know that the worst was yet to come—having to endure the hours of ridicule from Wally and me. "I don't care if you guys laugh at me," he said, "it doesn't bother me anymore."

"We're not going to laugh at you," Wally said.

Good for you, Cockroach, I thought, nodding. My baby brother's thin skin was finally being replaced by scar tissue.

My brothers and I went to our bedroom, where my thoughts quickly returned to Donna.

It was Sunday—the day before returning to school—and I had my best outfit planned for the first day back: Parachute pants and a Led Zeppelin concert shirt with three quarter length sleeves—*baseball style*. Although I hadn't yet attended a concert, the more mature look was guaranteed to give the message I was shooting for. My dilemma with the outfit was that it was sure to clash with my favorite piece—a dark maroon leather jacket. A major decision still loomed over me.

I'd researched the cafeteria menu to see my options for lunch that day. I preferred to buy lunch at school, as most lunch boxes—metal or plastic—smelled like old bologna to me, no matter what Ma packed in them.

Although American Chop Suey was one of my few favorite dishes at school, I quickly decided, *It's out. The way I eat, I'll be wearing half of it on my shirt and I can't risk that*, I thought. *This is going to be a big day—maybe the biggest ever—and I need everything to be just right.* I thought about it. *Nope, I'll be in the a la crate line, grabbing a plain chicken sandwich . . . which was probably flying over Horseneck Beach a few hours earlier, searching for its own lunch.* The chicken and cheese quesadilla—a high-end Pop Tart—was delicious, but it also threatened leakage. *I love it,* I thought, *but I just can't take the chance.*

I grabbed the letter to Donna, hidden in my sock and underwear drawer, that I'd been working on all week. Ensuring that Wally and Cockroach weren't watching, I folded it up and headed to the bathroom. *It's the only room in the house where I can get any privacy*, I thought, *although there's still no guarantee.*

I sat on the toilet, unfolded the paper and read, *Dear Donna, I've been trying to write you this letter for a while now. Although it's not easy telling you how I feel about you, I know I'll regret it for a long time if I don't.* I took another deep breath, willing myself to keep going. *I like you, Donna. Actually, I really like you and I was hoping that you'd consider going out with me. I think we'd be great together. I hope you feel the same.* Signed, *Herbie.* I folded up the letter and slid it into my back pocket.

My breathing suddenly became shallow and my heart began to race. *What the hell are you doing to yourself?* I thought. *Why are you putting yourself through this torture?* I tried to slow my breathing. *Is she even worth it?*

Pacing the floor, I pictured Donna's brown eyes and angelic smile. She was an incredible mix of cute and sexy, all in one package—like Cheryl Tiegs and Stevie Nicks rolled up into one amazing beauty. If I concentrated hard enough, I could smell her perfume. *Hell yeah, she's worth it*, I decided, my heart thumping hard in my ears.

I left the bathroom and returned to my bedroom—and my daydreaming.

"Mars to Herbie? Come in, Herbie."

I emerged from my thoughts. "Sorry," I said, grinning, "I was just . . ."

". . . in your own world," my mother said, finishing my sentence.

She shook her head. "You're always in your own world, Herbie."

I maintained my smile, but never responded.

"It must be a nice place in your world," she added, "because you spend enough time there."

"It's better than here," I muttered under my breath.

"What's that?" she asked.

"Nothing, Ma. What do you need?"

She raised one eyebrow like she was preparing to scold me. Instead, the eyebrow relaxed. She wagged her finger at me, gesturing that I follow her into the kitchen.

I did.

"I need you to run to the store for me," she said, turning to face me. "We have to stock up on a few things just in case this storm lasts longer than they predict." She thought about it. "Bring your brother to help."

"Which brother?" I asked.

"The bully."

"Ummm . . . okay," I said, considering the irony of Wally's world right now.

"Milk, bread and cigarettes?" I asked, trying to beat her to the chase.

She nodded. "Yes, two gallons of milk, three loaves of bread, a four-pack of toilet paper and get me six packs of Carlton 100's, the red pack." She sighed heavily. "After Alphonse's accident, my nerves are completely shot."

"Can I . . . ."

"Yes, Herbie, you can get yourself something. But remember, no candy." She shook her head. "I swear you're going to land us in the poor house yet."

I started to throw on the layers of winter outerwear. *Sure Ma,* I thought, forcing myself not to snicker.

"And get me a pack of those marshmallow snowballs," she said.

"Old Man Sedgeband never has them in stock," I reminded her.

"Suzie Q's, then," she said. "I need something sweet."

No kidding.

"Get your brother to help you," she reminded me.

I shook my head. "I can handle it." When it came to store runs, I preferred going alone. When one of us scored a soda, the other would maul him and chug it down within seconds. Whether we liked it or not, my brothers and I shared everything—even cold sores.

"Are you sure?" she asked.

"It's my job, Ma. It's what I do."

The snow was heavier and deeper than I'd expected. At certain points, where the snow drifted high, my knees nearly slapped my chest. *Maybe I should have brought Wally with me?* I thought, trudging on toward R&S Variety. It took me twice as long as usual before I reached the front door. *Hopefully, they're open.*

I grabbed the front door handle and gave it a tug. It cracked open. *Of course Old Man Sedgeband is open for business,* I thought, *if there's any chance at making more money . . .* For a few seconds, I wrestled the wind before I was able to duck into the place.

The store was empty; even Oscar was nowhere to be found. *Wow,* I thought, *I don't think I've ever been in this cave without seeing Oscar sitting beside the old codger.* As my eyes struggled to adjust to the darkness, I looked to see Sedgeband staring at me through his Coke-bottle glasses. *Just make it quick,* I told myself, picking up the pace.

After grabbing everything on my mother's list, I thought, *Maybe*

Ma's right? Maybe I won't be able to get to the store for a few days. I bent down to stare into the glass case. *Maybe I should get some of those flying saucers?* The multi-colored Satellite Wafers were filled with tiny candy balls. *Nah*, I decided, *they taste like the Holy Eucharist we get at church . . . whenever we actually go.* I considered a box of Chiclets or pack of a Fruit Stripe gum. *Nah*, I decided, *and the Hubba Bubba bubble gum tape is way too expensive.* The bottle caps were definitely appealing. *Nope*, I thought, finally going with a cherry Melody whistle pop, a bottle of Mellow Yellow, two packs of Pop Rocks, a pack of Indian pumpkin seeds—*the red pack*, I thought, chuckling—and a sleeve of multi-colored Necco wafers. I hated the taste of the chalk discs, but Cockroach loved them. *They'll come in handy to barter with little Scrooge during the storm.*

The zombie behind the glass counter tallied up the total in his green, spiral notebook.

"Can you please double-bag everything, Mr. Sedgeband?" I asked him, grabbing all my loot and stuffing it into my coat pockets. "The storm's pretty bad out there and, if the bag breaks, I'll be in pretty big . . ."

"Ugh," the old man sighed, cutting me off. "Maybe I should start charging for the damn bags now," he said, before reluctantly doing as I asked.

"Thanks," I said, steeling myself for the hard journey home.

The walk back seemed even more challenging. *The roads are empty*, I realized. *There's not a single car on the road.* I was halfway home, my shoulder muscles burning from lugging the heavy bag, when a town plow rambled by, throwing a white rolling wave onto the side of the road. *That's a lot of snow*, I thought, waving to him. He laid on the air horn, returning the gesture. *A lot of snow,* I repeated in my head, whistling.

When I got home, I found the rest of the family hovered around Pop's short-wave radio—even though every other electronic device in the house was available. *It's a sign,* I thought.. *We're not going to school tomorrow.* I hurried to peel the cold wet clothes off of me. *There's no way.*

Happy Heck, the radio host on WSAR, was listing the school closings. "Fall River has no school tomorrow. Neither does Somerset, Swansea, Westport . . ."

My brothers and I cheered. "Yes!"

"There's no school for Dighton, Rehoboth, Berkley . . ." You could almost hear the laughter in Happy Heck's voice.

From my mother's face, she obviously detected the same. *But Ma's not laughing,* I noted. *She looks like she's ready to cry.*

Usually, Happy Heck announced Foster-Gloucester and a handful of other schools as being closed for the day. *But not this time.* His list went on for nearly five minutes.

When he repeated the list and read off our town again, my brothers and I cheered just as loudly.

"Dear God in heaven," Ma mumbled under her breath, looking even closer to tears.

I felt torn. *I won't be able to see Donna tomorrow, but this also gives me more time to get ready for the big day.* I nodded. "I'm psyched," I announced, "I have gym on Mondays and I hate gym."

"Who's Jim?" Pop asked.

"Just some guy I smashed in dodge ball," I joked.

Pop grinned. "That'a boy," he said, before opening the fridge and chugging from a full gallon of milk, making me wish I didn't have to drink from that same jug.

"Herbie, where's the toilet paper?" Ma asked.

My heart dropped. *Crap!* I thought.

"Well?" she asked.

"Sorry Ma, I must have forgotten," I admitted, shrugging. "They're not on the usual list."

She sighed heavily.

"I can go back," I quickly volunteered, realizing that I'd caved in too soon.

She considered the offer. "Nah, we still have a full pack in the hall closet," she said, "and if we run out, we'll just use tissues."

Ewww . . .

For the remainder of the afternoon, Pop—a man possessed—went straight to work like he was preparing for the Apocalypse. "We're going to be stuck in this house for days," he said. "Who knows when we'll get back to school or work."

"Oh God," Ma blurted.

"I've stockpiled candles and batteries for the radio and flashlights in case there's a power outage," he said, ignoring our mother. "The next thing we need to do is fill the bathtub with water."

"To take baths?" Cockroach asked.

He shook his head. "If you guys need a bath, then go wash your dirty asses now."

We looked at each other before shaking our heads. "We're good," Wally reported for all of us.

"We need the tub full so we have water to flush the toilet," Pop explained.

I started laughing, thinking he was joking.

He wasn't. He turned to Wally. "Go down to the cellar and bring up both Igloo coolers."

"Why?" my brother asked.

"In case the fridge goes down," he said. "Now get a move on, son. Who knows when we'll need them."

"Where are we going to get the ice for the coolers?" Cockroach asked.

Pop looked out the window and then over at Ma. "We might need to get him some extra help at school," he said, and it didn't appear that he was kidding.

Once I was done laughing, I felt a strong surge of excitement pulsate through me. *This storm is freakin' awesome,* I thought, almost giddy over our current situation. *We're all gonna be stuck in this house for days!*

"Maybe we will need more toilet paper?" Ma commented.

I quickly slithered off to my bedroom.

When we finally settled in for the night—Cockroach completing his perimeter check for any unwelcome monsters—we lay in silence, the wind rapping away on our drafty windows.

"I am not an animal," I called out, trying my best to sound like the Elephant Man.

The bunk bed shifted and I could picture Cockroach pulling the covers over his head.

"I am a human being," Wally replied, doing a much better impression than mine.

Wally's probably relieved that there's no school in the morning, I thought. *But wouldn't it be better to just get it over with?*

CHAPTER 12

MONDAY—
UNTIL ALL TIME IS LOST

As predicted on the radio, the snowstorm quickly turned into a full-blown whiteout. Even Pop was home stuck with the rest of us—settled into his corduroy slippers and a bathrobe that was a half foot too short. *I'm not sure if Ma's happy about it,* I thought, *or just pretending to be.* For me, however, this was beyond huge. Pop never stayed home—not ever. I was so excited about this that I felt giddy.

We listened to the constant weather reports on the old man's short-wave radio, which added to the excitement. Although it was late in the season, the weatherman labeled the storm, "A Nor'easter unlike anything we've seen since '78."

That's all Pop needed to hear. "If it's anything like the Blizzard of '78, then we're really in for it," he said.

"That was a bad one, Pop?" I asked, vaguely remembering.

His eyes grew distant for a moment. "The worst one in my lifetime."

My body filled with equal amounts of fear and excitement. *I hope we get slammed with snow and can't leave this house for a long time,* I thought. . . . *none of us.*

While we ate breakfast, Ma announced, "I need one of you to go down to the cellar to get my clam boil pan."

"We're having a clam boil?" Cockroach asked, hopefully.

She shook her head. "I'm going to make American Chop Suey, and a lot of it, because it'll keep for a few days." Essentially, this meant she was going to make a couple pounds of elbows swimming in a diluted jar of Ragu sauce, a dish that would have made Chef Boyardee, himself, green with envy.

Wally's eyes lit up. It was one of his favorite dishes, amongst many.

That's great news, I thought, *a vat of American chop suey*. I loved it, too, when I could sneak a few shakes of salt onto my plate. There were no spices in Ma's kitchen, except salt and pepper which she refused to put out on the table.

"I'll go," Wally volunteered, grabbing his coat.

"Fine," she said, "but I need it right now."

"Okay," he said.

"I mean it, Wally," Ma said, "I know you love it down there, for whatever reason, but I want you right back up here with the pan."

"Sorry I offered," Wally muttered under his breath.

"You know what," she said, stopping him, "wait a minute." She hurried out of the room, returning with a full basket of towels. "While you're down there, why don't you throw in a load of laundry."

"Are you . . ." Wally began to complain.

"After you start the wash, I want you right back up here with the pan," she said, cutting him off.

Shaking his head, Wally headed out the front door, slamming it behind him.

Ma looked at Pop. "If he keeps it up," she said, "you're going to have to set that boy straight."

Pop nodded. "It's coming," he said, tightening the belt on his terrycloth robe.

Oh, that's not good, I thought.

Early in the storm, Wally and I shoveled snow, creating paths to the cellar door and the mailbox—which made no sense, as all my parents ever did was complain about every envelope pulled from the rusty, dented box. "Bills, that's all we ever get is bills. Never any good news." But here I was, feeling the slow burn in my back as I worked my crooked old shovel, struggling to keep those original paths clear.

We got back into the house to find two steaming mugs of hot cocoa waiting for us.

"Thanks, Ma!" I yelled.

"You're welcome," she said, stepping into the kitchen.

"No marshmallows?" Wally asked.

"Is it a holiday?" Ma asked in response.

I was taking my first sip when the kitchen telephone rang, immediately followed by an eerie silence. There was such madness in our house, a constant symphony of yelling, but when the telephone rang it was as if we were all in on some unspoken secret. Like the little angels we weren't, each one of us put on our sweet voice. But as soon as that rotary phone was hung back on the kitchen wall, the cease fire was lifted and we were back at it—like mercenaries paid to kill each other.

Ma answered and talked for a few minutes. "Boys, come say hi to your Memere," she yelled out, extending the kitchen phone for one of us to take. Our house telephone, mounted on the kitchen wall, was a rotary phone with a long, spiraled cord, allowing Ma to walk freely from one ashtray to the next around the apartment.

I grabbed the drab green receiver first. "How are you doing, Memere?" I asked. "Do you and Pepere have everything you need to ride out the storm?"

"I most certainly do," she said, "thanks to you and your father."

I smiled, feeling good that I'd been able to help my grandparents, while also getting a glimpse of why Pop helped anyone he could—any time he could.

Cockroach took the phone from me. "Hi Memere."

I stepped up to the kitchen window to see the thick sheet of white covering everything. Even the picnic bench—that hosted the family's famous barbecues in the summer—was now nothing more than an unrecognizable lump under the massive blanket. There was a labyrinth of deep paths—to the mailbox and Pop's car—created by hours of child labor. *Ugh . . .* These tiny roadways appeared to be mere scratches from our second-floor window.

Each time the crystallized window steamed up, I wiped away the dew, mesmerized by the Currie and Ives scene before me.

The neighborhood had essentially disappeared in the whiteout. Nothing existed now except shapes; whatever had been buried was left to either memory or imagination.

Cockroach joined me at the window to stare at the giant willow tree in our front yard, its weighted branches bending beyond belief from the glistening ice and heavy snow. Although it was clearly struggling against the storm, it looked so beautiful.

"That tree's badass," I whispered.

A branch from a nearby oak snapped, breaking off from the thick ice clinging to it. It sounded like the crack of thunder, making Cockroach jump.

"That's it for me," he said, heading for the safety of our bedroom.

But I remained at the window, watching with respect as the mighty willow stood strong.

Pop stepped up behind me. "It's like they say." He shrugged. "If you can't bend, you'll break."

A few hours passed—with Ma cooking the entire time—when Pop suggested, "Maybe we should get some take-out from Oriental Pearl before it gets too . . ."

"Are you kidding me?" she snapped. "I've been cooking all day and you want to get take-out?"

"It's not like the pan of pasta will go to waste," he said.

"It's not just the pasta," she said, cutting him off. "There's meat loaf, fried chicken, franks and beans . . ."

My stomach flopped at the last suggestion. My mother was referring to hot dogs and baked beans that she also served with canned brown bread. *And bread should not come in a can*, I thought. *I'd rather choke down a bowl of Alpo.*

"You know we'll eat all of it." Pop looked at us and smiled. "We have three machines to fuel."

We all nodded.

"There's no way Oriental Pearl is open anyway," Ma said, bending like the willow tree and inspiring hope in all of us.

"They're always open," Pop claimed, "I don't think those people ever close." According to him, "Long after the postal service throws in the towel, the Chinese are still open for business."

Ma called the Oriental Pearl and, sure enough, they picked up on the first ring. She placed the regular order. "A large order of chow mein, large order of fried rice, large order of chop suey, two orders of chicken fingers with extra duck sauce, two orders of beef terryaki and an order of egg rolls."

Smiling, Pop turned to me and Wally. "Go and pick it up together," he said, reaching for his back pocket for his worn wallet.

"I thought I was grounded?" Wally asked.

"If I hear that from you again, you're going to be stuck in this house until you're married," Pop said, his bottom lip starting to curl over his teeth.

"I doubt Wally's ever going to get married, Pop," I commented, trying to defuse the tense exchange. "I mean, who will have him?"

"Get going, the both of you," my father said, trying not to smile.

"Speak for yourself, Sherman," Wally said to me as we started for the door.

Whatever, Mr. Peabody, I thought.

Me and Wally trekked through the deep snow like two heavy-breathing South Pole explorers, prepared to plant our flag in the land of egg rolls and chop suey.

"This weather's nuts," Wally said, pulling the wool scarf up over his nose.

"It's awesome," I replied, high-stepping through the snowdrifts. "You wouldn't rather be out here than stuck in the house?" I asked him over the wind.

"Of I course I would," he yelled back.

"Then why complain when they send you out to run an errand?"

He stopped and looked at me. "Herbie, you don't get it yet, do you?"

"Get what?"

"If you let Ma and Pop know you enjoy something, then they'll put an end to it. If you bitch and moan, then they think they're doing a good job parenting." He shrugged. "Think about it." He started marching forward again.

As we trudged through the snow, I did think about it and it didn't take me long to realize he was right. *Thank you, Hong Kong Phooey . . . oh wise one*, I thought in my best Chinese accent. *Grasshopper sees now.*

When we returned home, I hurried to strip off my clothes and tear into our mouth-watering feast. "It's so bad out there," I responded, "I can't believe that place is still open."

Pop shrugged. "Don't ever mess with the Wongs," he said, ripping into a stick of beef teriyaki, "or you might get the Wong number."

"Nice, Walt," Ma said.

"What?" he asked. "What did I say wrong this time?"

"Don't you think you've screwed up these boys enough?" she asked. "Just keep your prejudices to yourself, Archie Bunker."

Archie Bunker, I repeated in my head, nearly choking on a chicken finger.

Pop's mouth hung open. "I'm not prejudice of the Chinese," he vowed. "I love those people."

By late afternoon, my brothers and I were already getting bored and decided to do some trading— baseball cards, cassettes— anything we owned. Like those who had once traveled the Silk Road, we were natural traders. We bartered for record albums, baseball cards, posters, whacky packy and garbage pail stickers—you name it—negotiating the best deals possible.

"There's no way I'm trading you Yaz for Fred Lynn," Cockroach said like an experienced merchant of the Arabian Desert.

"But it's Lynn's rookie card and he was rookie of the year," I justified.

"Then throw in Carlton Fisk too," he said, smirking.

"Not even! There's no way I'm givin' up Pudge, Alf."

"Did you just call me Alf?" he asked.

"Did I stutter?" I replied. "You're the one who's acting like some goofy alien puppet, not me."

And on it went—hours of haggling and bartering with very few items ever exchanging hands. All the while, Cockroach sat back wearing a smirk and waiting to pounce. Although he was the youngest, Wally and I both knew that, by the end of the day, he was the one who would walk away victorious. It didn't matter that he was still in elementary school. He had the shrewd instincts of a snake oil salesman. *I'm pretty sure that when Cockroach grows up, he isn't going to make a decent living,* I thought, *he's going to make an indecent living.*

Without warning, Ma stomped into the room, dumping a laundry basket of assorted socks onto our bedroom floor. "Here," she said, "why don't we see if you guys can find a single pair. I'm done trying." She left the room.

My brothers and I exchanged a few awkward glances, before Wally started laughing.

Shifting from cards to cassettes, we were at the end of our bartering when I traded Cockroach Pat Benatar for Foreigner. "But only if you throw in your Meat Loaf tape," I told him.

He reluctantly agreed.

An hour later, Cockroach was placing all of his cassettes—in alphabetical order—into his brown pleather case, the Meat Loaf tape included; he was clearly reneging on our deal.

"You gave me that Meat Loaf tape and now you're taking it back?" I screamed. "You're such an Indian giver."

"I am not. I said you could borrow it, not keep it," he fibbed.

"Indian giver!"

I seethed for a few minutes. I couldn't help it, and I couldn't let it go. "You know what?" I asked him.

"No. What?" Cockroach said.

"You're a queer."

"I know you are, but what am I?" he said.

My fists instinctively clenched. I hated when he started in on that foolishness; it triggered a strong desire in me to strangle him. "Go ahead and say it again," I challenged him, "and I'll beat you down right here."

"You're the queer," he said, getting back on track.

I nodded, preferring this exchange. "You're a queer," I mumbled.

There was silence.

"Queer," Cockroach said under his breath.

"Queer-boy," I echoed a little louder.

This moronic exchange went on for a solid half hour, until I left the room to sneak back two drinks and some snacks.

"Here you go, flamer," I told my little brother, handing him his Kool-Aid.

"Thanks, flamer," he repeated, kicking off round two.

Having to shovel during the storm was deemed part of Wally's punishment, but as he and I shoveled the same paths—side-by-side, over-and-over—I had to think, *I guess I'm punished too?*

It was an insane process. No sooner were we dry and warm when it was time to don our winter gear and head back out for another exhausting round of snow removal.

The giant drifts made it hard to lift the snow and throw it over my head. I was sweaty, but if I stopped to take a breather, I started freezing—inspiring me to get the work done as quickly as possible. The whole time, I kept thinking, *I hope Pop's warm and dry in his recliner. I'd hate for him to get a chill and catch a cold.* Wally and I labored and sweat like coal miners at the start of a double shift, only to go through the same torment a few hours later.

Each time the giant town plows made a pass by our house, they buried us in—wiping away all the work we'd completed at the base of the driveway, the snow piled high again and crusted in ice. *Asshole . . . asshole . . . asshole,* I repeated in my head until it became my mantra. *The plow driver must love seeing us suffer,* I thought. During one pass, the smiling driver in the giant orange truck beeped at us. I was so pissed that I gave him the middle finger, which may have had a much greater impact if I wasn't wearing mittens. *Asshole . . . asshole . . . asshole!*

During a quick breather, I stood there and took it all in. It was like the world was standing still, the silence unlike anything I'd ever known. *It's so quiet out here,* I thought, my laboring heart pounding in my ears. There were no cars traveling the busy road we lived on, only the occasional town truck with its scraping plow. *Asshole . . . asshole . . . asshole!*

We returned to our heated apartment to discover a stack of grilled cheese sandwiches waiting for us at the table, along with steaming bowls of Campbell's tomato soup to dunk them in.

In record time, we stripped off our winter layers and skin-tight boots. Wally even kicked off his bread bags. I sat to eat, still wearing them. *They waited for us to eat*, I realized. *I can't believe it.*

"Soup by itself isn't a meal," Pop said, being the first to dunk his gooey sandwich.

"I agree," I said, "even pea soup."

He looked at me. "You need to let that go, Herbie."

Nodding, I wiped my sweaty brow with my sleeve. "Just as soon as Memere stops making it and torturing me."

He laughed.

Ma didn't find it funny. "Your Memere's split pea soup is the best. You just don't know what tastes good."

"Yeah okay, Ma," I said, suddenly realizing that I'd said it aloud.

Instantly, her gentle eyes became dark. "The next time we go there to eat, I'm going to pry your mouth open and pour the soup down your . . ."

Wally started laughing, halting her.

She glared at him.

"I'd really love to see that," he told her.

"Keep runnin' your mouth and you'll do more than see it," Pop hissed, defending his frazzled wife. "I'll pry your mouth open, myself."

The table went silent, everyone focused on their meal.

That still wouldn't be fair, I thought, taking my first bite. *Wally likes pea soup.*

That night, hiding behind our plastic accordion door, Wally found two bottle rockets left over from the previous July. We'd gotten into deep trouble for launching them from our second-floor bedroom window into traffic. "What do you think?" my brother asked me.

Cockroach pulled the covers over his head, wanting nothing to do with the asinine conspiracy.

Even though we understood that the consequences would be pretty harsh if we got caught, Wally and I looked at each other and shrugged.

"If we get busted . . ." I began to weigh out.

"To hell with it," Wally said, the temptation too good to pass up, "let's light 'em up."

"Let me go find one of Ma's lighters," I whispered.

Wally nodded. "That'll work." He winked at me. "And if we get caught, we'll just blame Alphonse."

"I don't think so," came a voice from beneath Cockroach's bedspread. "They'd never believe you liars, anyway."

Wally and I both laughed, before I quietly slipped out of the room to complete my foolish mission.

. . .

The next morning, I palmed a full bowl of Fruity Pebbles and stared out the kitchen window. *Having to clear the heavy snow off of Pop's car seems even more ridiculous from up here*, I thought. The road in front of our house was completely snowed in. *There's no way Pop's going anywhere.* Besides, Happy Heck's distinct radio voice had called for a travel ban an hour before. *And I can't remember the last time a town plow has come by our house either.* I thought about it. *Not to mention, there hasn't been a car on the road for days.*

Still, the old man insisted that his car be brushed off and the tires free from snow. "Just in case there's an emergency and we need to get to the hospital."

I thought about that too. *There better not be an emergency or else someone's dying,* I realized, worried for Cockroach.

Pop stepped up beside me to survey the same winter wonderland from the kitchen window. "You mark my words, we're going to lose power any minute," he announced loud enough for anyone willing to listen.

"Really, Pop?" I asked.

He nodded. "I'm surprised we still have lights on in this house." He looked down at my cereal bowl. "Don't drink all the melk, Herbie."

"Milk?" I asked, hoping to correct him.

He nodded. "Yeah, melk."

Leaving the window, I finished my breakfast and grabbed one of the extra blankets from the hall closet. After tossing it onto my bed, I reached for one of the Atari controllers. "Let's play Space Invaders while we still can," I told Cockroach.

"I'm in," he said, taking a seat beside me. "I hope you're ready to lose, Herbie the Love Bug."

"What?"

"From the movie," he quickly explained.

"Yeah, I'm gonna lose," I said, shrugging. "There's a first time for everything, I guess." I looked at him and grinned. "Now let's play, you little Muppet."

The power suddenly went out.

"Told ya," Pop yelled; he was like a walking Farmer's Almanac.

"Don't waste the toilet paper," Ma told us. "Thanks to Herbie, we have to ration it."

Ignoring her, we immediately pulled out the board games—

Trouble and Life—and began playing them by candlelight right away. It was our first power outage. We were virgins.

"Why can't we play the battleship game?" Cockroach asked.

"Because the batteries are dead," Wally reminded him.

Cockroach thought about it. His eyes lit up. "Pop, can we . . ."

"We're not wasting fresh batteries on a stupid game," Pop told him. "We have no idea how long the power will be out and your mother's gonna need a working flashlight to see my pretty face."

Wally and I both laughed, while Cockroach chose to sulk.

Wally leaned into him. "Looks like Pop just sunk your battleship," he teased in a whisper.

"Whatever, scrotum breath," the scrawny kid retorted before getting up and storming out of the room, his shadow dancing across the candle-lit wall.

Wally looked at me in shock.

I shrugged. "You can't get him for lying."

Wally punched my arm.

"Ouch" I blurted, before catching myself from whining. *The Mangler's weightlifting is paying off,* I thought, rubbing my upper arm. It felt like I'd just been struck by a Louisville Slugger.

There were definitely some upsides to the power being out and our family being caged up together. Ma began cooking whatever was left in the fridge. "We need to eat everything before it goes bad," she announced.

I was kind of surprised we didn't applaud.

Ma balled up some raw hamburger and popped it into her mouth.

So gross, I thought, though I had no problem chomping on an uncooked hot dog. And cookie dough was a thing in our house long before it became "a thing."

As Ma finished making Manwich sandwiches, or sloppy joes, and served us each two, I thought, *The record at school for these is four.* Although I was pretty confident I could destroy that record, I wasn't sure I wanted to. *Being a food hog probably isn't the Middle School legacy I want to leave behind.* At home, we didn't enjoy sloppy joes on hamburger buns like the hair-netted cafeteria ladies served. Ma slopped the seasoned meat onto sliced white bread with the same amount of care, only she saved the plastic bag. *But they're still so good,* I thought, digging right in and dropping some of the greasy meat onto my torn Rolling Stones t-shirt.

For the first time in our short lives, my brothers and I weren't only allowed to gorge, we were expected to eat everything: Shake and Bake chicken, homemade meatloaf, franks and beans—everything. *No brown bread for me, thanks.*

"Nothing can go back into the fridge." Ma confirmed, though she was equally clear that, "The freezer door had better stay closed!"

We stayed away from the fridge's top handle like it was made of kryptonite.

"I should probably check in on your grandparents," Ma said, grabbing for the kitchen phone. She looked at the receiver, sadly announcing, "That's it. The phone's dead too."

I wondered what the word *too* referred to, but I never asked. *At least we don't have to block calls now,* I thought, which simply meant taking the phone off the hook. *Even though Ma hates when we do that, in case Memere or Aunt Phyllis needs something.* I smiled. *And one or the other always needs something.*

I was heading back to my bedroom when it dawned on me.

We're really alone now, completely cut off from the outside world. As exciting as that seemed, it was also a little scary. *Wally and I should probably leave Cockroach alone for now, just in case.*

Cockroach lay in his top bunk, flipping through the same old disc in his View Master, while I lay beneath him playing my hand-held Waterful Ring Toss game. Every time I squeezed the white button on the bottom, the small rings would shoot upward through the water, floating down toward their targets.

"This is already getting old," I complained aloud.

"You can say that again," Cockroach agreed, clicking to the next picture.

"This is already getting old," I repeated.

"You're such a comedian, Herbie," he said.

"I'm funnier than you are," I said. "I know that."

"Funnier looking," he mumbled.

The initial excitement of being isolated from the outside world had already worn off, turning into cabin fever. Everyone was getting on everyone else's nerves. Amongst other things, the relentless storm was prolonging Wally's torment.

Hoping to break up the monotony, Ma announced, "Take a seat at the table, boys. I think it's time we pass out the cereal box prizes."

"Yes!" Cockroach and I squealed in celebration, hurrying to claim the kitchen chair closest to our mother.

Wally moped behind us, pretending he was too old for our bi-annual awards ceremony.

Ma looked at him. "You're being punished, Wally," she reminded him, "so consider yourself lucky to even take part in this."

"If you want me to leave, Ma, then I . . ."

"Take a seat!" she yelled, much louder than normal. "Enough with the drama already."

Every time we devoured a box of cold cereal—and we ate truckloads of the corn-based filler—we had to place the prize into a large Danish cookie tin sitting on top of the fridge. "I don't want you fighting over those stupid toys," Ma told us. So to avoid that, she would sit us down a couple times a year, write the numbers one to ten on scraps of paper and then throw them into one of the same paper bags she used for her hand-cut French fries. Drawing a number out of the bag, she always started with Cockroach, "Pick a number from one to ten, Alphonse." He'd guess—usually wrong—and then it was my turn. If I didn't guess the right number, it was Wally's turn. Whoever guessed right could pick the prize he wanted. Then the remaining two would play until we each won. The game would then start over.

Within the first three rounds, Cockroach scored a yo-yo, a balsam wood airplane—some assembly required—and a pack of chewing gum. I grabbed the only candy bar in the treasure tin, making Ma cringe but still hold her tongue. I also claimed a puzzle. On my third pick, for whatever reason I froze and couldn't make a decision.

"Let's go, Herbie!" Cockroach yelled.

"Just pick already," Wally groaned, "it's all junk, anyway."

My mother stared him down again.

I scanned the pile of prizes—back-and-forth, back-and-forth.

"Come on, Herbie," Ma said, "it's not like you're on a shopping spree at K-Mart."

I snatched up the tiny action figure; it wasn't because I particularly wanted it. I simply succumbed to peer pressure.

"Your turn, Wally," Ma told him.

Without any excitement or even thought, Wally grabbed all of the trading cards in silver cellophane.

He's going to use them to barter with me and Cockroach later, I thought. *Very smart.*

The entire process was civil and polite, confirming to me just how clever our mother was. Although we pretended like we didn't care, we did. And if we'd claimed the plastic toys in any other manner, we would have ended up killing each other.

"See, boys," Ma said, "you actually can get along for more than an hour without making each other bleed."

Wally grinned. "But the hour's up, Ma."

I nodded in agreement. "It's time to trade."

In her undeniable wisdom, our mother got up from the table and left the area.

The heated round of swaps began, taking hours of yelling and even tears before it was over. Even with all of Wally's trading cards, in the end Cockroach owned those too—emerging the clear victor.

"You should get into the stock market," I told my little brother, as we left the table.

"Or organized crime," Wally said.

Cockroach thought about it and shrugged. "Whichever pays better, I guess."

Hours dragged into days until time became cruel.

We ate banana sandwiches on buttered toast, which I actually enjoyed.

"It's a great source of potassium," Ma claimed.

So it's cheap, then, I thought.

We also devoured giant cans of Snow's clam chowder. The

coagulated gel slapping into the saucepan on the gas stove made my skin crawl, but Pop loved the thick soup. "It reminds me of warmer days," he said.

Between meals, my brothers and I played checkers and a card game called Crazy 8s, until Ma asked me, "Do you want to learn a real card game?"

I nodded. "What game?"

"Gin Rummy," she said in her sweet voice, confusing me.

I nodded more vigorously, following her into the kitchen. *I wish Ma would wear her mood ring*, I thought. *It would definitely make life a lot easier around here.*

We sat alone at the table, playing cards by candlelight. "So, who's this girl you're pining over?" she finally asked me after teaching me the rules of the game.

"I'm not pining over anyone," I said, pretending to study my cards, "whatever *pining* means."

"We both know that's not true, Herbie. I'm sure whoever she . . ."

"Her name's Donna," I surrendered, paying close attention to how my mother shuffled the cards, "I . . . I . . ."

"Really like her," she said, finishing the sentence for me.

I nodded.

"Does she know?"

I shrugged.

"You haven't told her?"

"It's not as easy as it . . ." I stopped, sorry I was sharing my feelings with someone who could never understand.

"Oh, but it is easy, Herbie," she said, grinning, "and you're never going to know how she feels until you find the courage to be honest with her first."

"Okay, Ma," I said, trying to put an end to the conversation.

"It may be the best thing you've ever done, Herbie."

I lost another hand. "And if it isn't, Ma?" I asked. "What if she doesn't feel the same way about me?" I decided to try my hand at shuffling the cards.

"At least you'll have no regrets," she said, watching me play 52-card pick-up all by myself.

I nodded from my knees, thinking, *I hate it when she's right.*

"I'm going to bed," she said, bending down to kiss my forehead.

"But it's so early," I told her.

She shrugged. "Doesn't matter to me," she said. "I lost all track of time days ago." She placed her hand on my shoulder. "All I know is that I'm tired and I'm going to bed. Goodnight."

"'Night, Ma."

No sooner did my mother walk out when Wally walked in. "Wanna play football?" he asked.

I laughed. "It's a little cold outside, but . . ."

"Table football," he said, already folding up a piece of white-lined paper into a tight triangle. "Unless you want me to make you a paper fortune teller?" he asked, grinning.

"A chatter box?" I said, referring to the paper flower that girls folded up in school, writing names, colors and numbers on it— claiming that they could predict who you'd marry and how many kids you'd have.

"That's right, a cootie catcher."

"Nah, I don't think so," I told him, thinking, *I have my Magic 8 ball for that.*

He took a seat across from me at the kitchen table, holding up the paper triangle. "So do you wanna play?"

Although the Washington Redskins and San Francisco 49ers were dominating the NFL, we were still New England Patriots fans—no matter how bad they were.

"Of course," I said, and it began—each of us trying to flick the football through the uprights represented by our opponent's extended thumbs.

"You looking forward to going back to school?" I asked him, kicking off my investigation the same way Detective Columbo might.

"Not really," he said, "but being penned up in this house is getting old, that's for sure."

"No doubt," I agreed, aiming the football at his pimpled forehead.

"You?" he asked.

"I am and I'm not," I said, missing my shot.

He nodded, taking his turn.

"Remember two summers ago, when Rodney stole my bicycle from the yard?" I asked, ducking my head to avoid catching the football's pointed tip in the eye.

"Yeah."

"Pop found out and put me in the car. We were driving down Route 6 when we spotted Rodney riding my bike toward Lincoln Park. Pop turned to me and said, 'If I lay a finger on this kid, I'll be sent to jail.' He looked me right in the eye. 'But one of us has to take him down, right?'"

Wally laughed. "That's Pop, all right."

"I'd never been so scared in my life," I admitted.

"For having to fight Rodney or dealing with Pop if you didn't?" he asked.

"Both," I said, scoring three points.

He nodded. "I get it."

"So, Pop pulls up in front of the kid, cutting him off. I jump out of the passenger seat and tackle him, knocking him off the bike. All I remember is punching him as hard and as fast as I could, hoping Pop would break it up."

"But he didn't," Wally said, helping to recount the story.

I shook my head. "Nope, he didn't. He just picked up the bike and put it into the back of the station wagon, while Rodney and I wailed away on each other."

"Gnarly," Wally said, grinning.

"I was never so scared in my whole life," I repeated, studying his face. "Don't you think that was pretty messed up that Pop made me fight that kid?"

Wally half-shrugged. "I don't know," he said, gritting his teeth for the next shot at me, "it might have been more messed up if he didn't."

Wow, I thought, catching the pointed football right off the cheek and feeling its sharp sting.

Wally chuckled in celebration.

As I rubbed my face, I realized I'd finally gotten some insight into my big brother's psyche.

"I hate fighting," I told him.

"Everyone hates fighting, Herbie," he said, "but it sure as hell beats feeling like a friggin' coward."

And there it is, I thought.

We played folded triangle football by candlelight at that table, talking and laughing. There was no concept of time. Although neither one of us would have ever admitted it, it was a night we'd never forget—*at least I never would.*

CHAPTER 13

The storm began to subside. The power was restored and the roads were cleared enough for Pop to return to work—whistling all the way. *I've never seen him so happy*, I thought.

My brothers and I, however, were still exiled to the Island of Misfit Toys.

Another day passed—maybe three, I couldn't tell anymore—since the fateful night me and Pop had met the bleeding giant, Brad Cowen. The newspaper reported the accident, indicating that Mr. Cowen had been returning home from work when he lost control of his vehicle and rolled it into a ditch on Route 88. *The man's recovering well*, they concluded.

Although Pop took great joy in the fact, for whatever reason, our chance meeting had proven so traumatic for me that I couldn't shake Brad Cowen from my thoughts—and most of those thoughts were anything but pleasant.

I have Brad Cowen to keep me company during the day and at night, I thought. *How psyched am I?*

Once Pop had cleaned out the station wagon with bleach and the telephone had stopped ringing off the hook—with family and friends either criticizing or applauding his decision to stop and help—I thought, *I wish life would just go back to normal.* My vivid and disturbing thoughts, however, would not allow it—*even at night now. Well, at least Brad Cowen's chased away old Clarence . . . for the time being anyway.*

The tossing and turning continued on until one icy morning. The doorbell rang and, as an answer to my prayers, closure waited to be greeted.

I swung open the door and nearly fainted. It was the giant. He was standing there, with one tooth missing from his mysterious smile. In one of his massive hands, he held a case of beer; in the other, the hand of a tiny girl. Instinctively, I turned to look for my parents. Although Pop was at work, Ma was home and quickly entered the kitchen. Reluctantly, I told the mismatched pair, "Come on in." It was silly, I knew, but I couldn't help myself from trembling inside.

"Name's Brad Cowen," he said, introducing himself, "is your dad home?"

I shook my head. "He's still at work, but he should be home soon." Right away, I felt my stomach twist, thinking, *I might have just made a big mistake.*

The titan slid his hand from the girl's and offered it to me. "I don't remember if we've formally met, but I heard you were there that night with your dad . . . that you helped save me." His face was gentle and I was surprised to discover that his handshake mirrored the same.

"Yeah, I was there," I forced through my dry throat.

"Can I offer you something to drink, Mr. Cowen?" my mother asked over my shoulder.

Although the question sounded odd to me, I couldn't imagine her saying anything else.

"No, thank you." Shrugging, he looked back down at me. "I

hope we're not intruding, but my daughter's been haunting me to bring her by here. And if I'm being honest, I wanted to meet you and your dad too." For a moment, it appeared that the man was blushing. He quickly gestured for the little girl to stand before him. "Go ahead, Amber," he whispered, following it up with a wink for me and my mother.

The small child was as nervous as I was. "My daddy says that you and your dad are heroes," she said, her tiny voice cracking, "and that you saved his life. So, I made this for you." She handed me a length of blue ribbon. Confused, I accepted it and was equally surprised to discover that something heavy hung from it. I lifted it and the homemade gift made my eyes swell with tears. *It's a medal,* I realized; it was a priceless award made by the hands of a five-year old angel. Instinctively, I gave Amber a hug, surprising myself as much as her.

Pop came home from work and was greeted with the same enthusiasm from Brad and his young daughter.

"It's the least we could do, my friend," he told Brad, shaking his massive bandaged hand. "You were in tough shape that day. There's no way me and Herbie were gonna leave you like that on the side of the road."

"You saved my life," Brad said, holding on to Pop's hand.

"Well, I don't . . ." Pop started.

"You saved my life," Brad repeated, cutting him off, "and I'll never forget it."

"And neither will I," little Amber said, bringing tears to my eyes again.

With a final hug, Brad and Amber left the apartment.

Over a less-than-fancy dinner of Tuna Helper, making me gag and forcing me to hide most of it in a handful of paper napkins, I proudly wore the hero's medal around my neck. I was happy to finally meet the monster who'd been haunting my dreams. My perception of the man had been totally incorrect and, after getting to know him, I now felt fifty pounds lighter. *There's no reason to fear him*, I decided, feeling even more weight lifted from my shoulders. The apprehension was suddenly replaced by pride. *I may not be a hero*, I thought, *but I was definitely there to support one.*

Although Ma offered the praise deserving of any true hero, she also told my stubborn father, "No more hitchhikers!" Her eyes were glistening with tears. "Your lives mean more to me than anyone else's." She shook her head. "With the way the world has changed, it just isn't worth taking the chance, Walter."

I'm not sure I agree, I thought, surprising myself once more.

Pop simply nodded. "You're right, hon," he said, "you're right." He then looked at me and winked; it was the same wink he'd given me in the station wagon that unforgettable day.

I couldn't wipe the smile from my face.

As I quietly lay in bed that night, I realized that I'd faced one of my greatest fears—only to discover that, as usual, my imagination was much more brutal than reality. *Do you hear that, Clarence?* I thought. *You're gonna have to go bother someone else from now on.* I closed my eyes, smiling all the way to slumber land. Somehow, I knew in my heart that the insane-looking pedophile driving the white van no longer had the power to torment me.

• • •

At the tail end of that awesome—and awful—blizzard, Ma stormed into our bedroom. "What on earth is this I found, Alphonse?" she barked, making us all think she'd gotten the name wrong.

"What, Ma?" he squeaked.

In one hand, she held a single piece of paper; in the other, Cockroach's cheesy Transformers backpack. "What is this?" she asked.

"What?" he asked again, his voice a full octave higher.

Someone's in deep shit, I thought.

"Stop playing stupid," she said.

"He's not playing," Wally commented from his side of the room.

Ignoring my older brother, she said, "Alphonse, not only did your teacher send home a progress report, letting me know that you're in trouble for talking too much in class . . ."

"Oh yeah, I forgot to give that to you," he said, scrambling to establish his defense.

She stared at him. "Then you must have also forgotten that you signed my name to it."

"Cockroach forged a progress report?" Wally asked, jumping to his feet to see the tampered document.

Oh, this is too good to be true, I thought, hurrying to my mother's side to see the signature for myself.

"I'm . . . I'm sorry, Ma . . ." the tattletale whined.

"Save it for your father. Just wait until he gets home and sees this one."

As Cockroach started to cry, Wally and I studied the document.

Other than one or two letters, it looks just like Ma's signature, I thought. *Definitely good enough to get by any teacher.* I looked at my mother. Her eyes were as wild as her hair; she was clearly at the end of her rope. *I would have never guessed that Ma's precious pet would be the final straw to break her back*, I thought.

Even though the crime was as plain as the white on Farrah Faw-cett's teeth, I still couldn't believe it. *Maybe a life of crime is the path for Cockroach?* I thought, trying not to laugh—until I saw Wally's satisfied grin. I burst out laughing. *Good for you, Cockroach*, I thought, *there's hope for you yet.*

In a huff, Ma rushed out of the room. "Your father can deal with this," she muttered. "I'm so done with all of you."

So much for that get-out-of-jail-free card, I thought.

Cockroach continued to weep.

"Oh, save it," Wally told him, "she's gone." He patted our little brother's back. "Honestly, that was solid, bro."

He looked up at both of us, a grin creeping into his handsome face.

I smiled back at him. "Yeah, great job on Ma's signature, brother. I'm sure I'll be needing your talents before the school year's out."

"That makes two of us," Wally said.

"I just hope Pop doesn't come down too hard on me," he whispered.

"I wouldn't worry about that," I told him.

"I'm with Herbie on that one," Wally said. "Besides, no one could ever punish you more than you punish yourself, Alphonse."

Although the TV was back up and running, we hovered around the radio and watched as life returned to Ma's sorrowful eyes. Happy Heck, our once-favorite radio host on WSAR, was listing the school openings for the morning. "Fall River has school tomorrow, as does Somerset, Swansea, Westport . . ."

My brothers and I looked at each other and shook our heads.

It felt so confusing. *Although we're sick of staying home, it's still better than going to school . . . I think.*

"There will be school in Dighton, Rehoboth, Berkley . . ." This time, you could hear the mercy in Happy Heck's voice, as he offered us the perfect ying and yang life lesson.

From my mother's face, I could tell she was beyond grateful. *She looks like she wants to dance,* I thought.

"Thank you, God," Ma mumbled, "thank you so much."

Happy Heck's announcements went on for another ten minutes, while our mother sat at that kitchen table, hypnotized—her smile threatening to swallow up her entire face.

When Happy Heck repeated the list and read off our town again, my brothers and I headed to our bedroom to beat back our dismay. The last thing I heard was Ma singing her own original jingle. "School tomorrow, baby . . . school, school tomorrow, baby . . ."

Not cool, Ma, I thought. *Not cool at all.*

My brothers and I were now the ones ready to cry.

Pouting on my bed, I considered the week ahead, reaching down deep to recognize the positives. *Well, school picture day is coming up,* I thought. *At least we get to keep the new plastic comb.* I dug deeper. *And right after school pictures, the school nurse usually checks everyone for head lice.* This was always an interesting and interactive game. *But we don't get to keep the wooden tongue depressor for that one.* The last thing I ever wanted to hear from the nurse was, "Is your mom or dad home, Herbie?"

I looked across the room to see Wally lying on his bed. *For the most part, he's been quiet all week,* I decided. My brother had obviously paid a heavy price all vacation long, being tortured by the anticipation of a terrible fight and the inevitable beating.

Wally could be an animal and, when the vacation week started, there was a big part of me that had hoped he'd get his ass kicked by Owen on the bus. *I hope he gets his because no one deserves it more,* I'd thought. But as we neared the eleventh hour, I was silently praying that he wouldn't get touched. *After all, the donkey is my brother.*

Getting ready for bed, I peered into the bathroom mirror and spotted a bright red blemish on the side of my nose. *Holy Rudolph!* As I leaned in closer, my heart rate picked up. *No,* I screamed in my head, *not now!* It was the start of a pimple, an award winner that threatened to cover the entire side of my face. Given my unfortunate experience with these monsters, I knew that this one was due to appear in its full glory right around the time I stepped into first period class. *No,* I thought again, *of all the times!* I shook my head. *I just can't catch a break.* I grabbed the letter to Donna from my pocket and quickly skimmed it over. *Well, I can't give it to her now, that's for sure,* I decided, *at least not until Mount Vesuvius erupts.* I looked in the mirror again to study my new nemesis. *Damn you, zit!*

As I stepped out of the mirror, I decided to wear the same outfit I'd planned all along. *Just because I can't give Donna the letter,* I thought, *that doesn't mean I can't look my best for her.* I faced the mirror one last time and shrugged. *Maybe this will give me some more time to lose a few pounds?*

Before turning in for the night, I saw Wally finish a final set of push-ups. Then, to my surprise, I watched as he dropped to his knees and clasped his hands together. *It's the first time I've ever seen my brother pray*, I thought, the weight of his demoralizing situation suddenly rocking me to my core.

• • •

I really need to lose some weight, I thought, gazing into a circus mirror—my physique as distorted as my slumbering thoughts.

"Why are you always daydreaming?" Ma asked, startling me.

"Wha . . . what?" I asked, stepping out of the mirror.

"Herbie, your Aunt Phyllis is waiting for her kiss," she said. "Don't be rude."

I lost my breath. Even the suggestion of that cold snail sliding down my cheek made me break out into a cold sweat. "Please Ma, I don't . . ."

"Please, nothing," my mother barked. "She's your aunt and she wants her kiss right now!"

Swallowing hard, I turned to face my aunt's bristled moustache. *Oh God*, I thought, *please . . .*

"Kiss me, Herbie," Aunt Phyllis said, the caterpillar sitting above her top lip stretching around the sides of her rancid mouth.

Leaning in, I felt ready to vomit. *This is so unfair. I don't deserve this*, I thought. *Why am I being punished when Wally's the one who deserves . . .*

• • •

Awakening in a familiar cold sweat, I could still picture my aunt's puckered lips inching closer toward me. My entire body shuddered. I sat up straight to catch my breath. *It was only a dream*, I told myself.

You're okay now. I tried to shake my aunt's image out of my head. *Maybe Clarence wasn't so bad after all?* I thought. *At least he only exists in my imagination.*

Morning had come much too quickly, reminding me and my brothers that reality had returned.

Ma pushed the Cream of Wheat like she was working on commission for the company. I politely declined as usual, opting for a bowl or three of Frosted Flakes. Within minutes, the cold milk turned to sugary water, making me smile. *Ahhhh, mother's milk . . .*

Sitting in my kitchen chair, I contemplated all that had happened since we'd stepped off of Bus 6 the Friday before last. *What a bitchin' week*, I thought. *Absolutely outrageous!*

I dumped more Frosted Flakes into the orange Tupperware bowl.

Vacation's finally over, I thought and, as much we'd tested fate, we somehow survived the time off. Although we still had a few weeks ahead of us before we could emerge from the long New England hibernation, I thought, *At least we're almost there.*

I headed for the bathroom to brush my teeth when I discovered the door locked. I was about to step away when I heard someone retching. I leaned in to listen. *It's Wally*, I realized, *and he's puking up his guts.* I knocked on the door. "You okay, bro?" I asked.

There was silence.

"Wally, are you . . ."

"I'm fine," he yelled. "Go away." He retched once more. *Damn, brother.*

We'd just finished dressing for school—with Wally avoiding all eye contact—when Ma announced, "I need to take a picture of the three of you." This was our mother's way to commemorate the complete joy she felt for her three angels returning to school.

She's smiling again, I noticed.

Rather than grabbing her Kodak camera, Ma went with the Polaroid. The film was very expensive, so she took them sparingly. *But this is clearly a special occasion for her,* I thought—an event that she didn't want to wait to have developed—*instant gratification.*

"Okay, scooch together," she said, "and smile."

Each one of us groaned.

The flash went off, temporarily blinding us. *Another picture for a photo album that no one will ever look at or care about,* I thought.

Ma snatched the photo from the camera and quickly shook it back-and-forth. As the image appeared, her smile grew wider. "Back to school" she whispered, as though she were staring at a winning lottery ticket.

I looked at the plastic photo. *The three of us look like total bums,* I thought, realizing that my outfit didn't have the effect I was shooting for—*not even close.* I shrugged. *Too late to do anything about it now.* I remembered the mountain that sat on the side of my nose. *I just need to lay low for a few days.*

I couldn't wait to wear the pair of Chuck Taylors I'd gotten for Christmas. The new rubber smell reeked of money. *But I refuse to destroy them in this bad weather.* Ma had headed to Sears, "where America shopped for values," and picked up two pairs of tough skins for Cockroach; for us bigger boys, she bought new rough-housers with the thick patches sewn into the knees. Santa brought each of us a new windbreaker jacket as well. It wasn't the Members Only jacket I'd been hoping for, but I understood. *Our parents don't have the money for brand labels.*

Preparing to head out to catch the bus, Ma asked, "What about your coats and boots?"

Wally and I shook our heads in unison. "We're all set," we told her. The heavy parkas and ugly rubber boots were okay for home but, no matter how cold or stormy it was outside, we refused to wear any of it to school. *I'd rather slip and fall in high tops than be made fun of,* I thought.

She didn't argue. By her glowing smile, I knew, *She's all done arguing.*

Stepping out of the apartment, I thought about my friend Vic for the first time in days. *It'll be good to see that idiot again,* I decided.

Standing at the dreaded bus stop, several long and tense minutes passed before I turned to Wally. "Listen," I said, "I know you're . . ."

He pointed down the street, stopping me in mid-sentence. I looked past him to see that the bus had appeared on the white horizon. I took a few deep breath—a couple for me and the rest of them for Wally. *Please God,* I thought, *don't let him get hurt too bad. I know he's a pain in the ass, but . . .*

As we prepared to board the big yellow torture chamber, Wally turned to me. "I'm going to punch Owen in the face as soon as I see him," he told me, his face calm.

"Are you serious?" I asked, immediately filled with the incredible anxiety my brother had carried with him all week.

He nodded. "As hard as I can."

I studied his face. He wasn't just calm. He was confident. *Oh shit,* I thought, *it's on.* My fear for him instantly turned to excitement. *This is righteous,* I thought, *and so clutch!*

As I stepped onto the bus—back amongst the mix of jocks,

preppys and motor heads—I followed Wally, noting that the look in my brother's eyes was a familiar one. *Wally's going to pound the sand out of that bully,* I realized, and couldn't have stopped myself from smiling if I tried. *At least he won't get in trouble with Pop.*

Wally was still walking down the bus aisle when I claimed my seat beside a nerd in the front.

"Hey bitch, remember me?" Owen barked.

Before I could even turn around, I knew he was talking to Wally.

Suddenly, I could hear my heart beating hard in my ears. My breathing became quick. *Owen's not talking to me. He's talking to Wally.* But it still felt like it was me. I gagged like I was going to vomit. *What a nightmare!*

I then heard a scuffle, followed by a distinct thud—skin on skin, bone on bone.

"I . . . I think he just broke my nose," Owen screamed.

There was silence, everyone in shock.

"He broke my friggin' nose," Owen wailed, whining like one of his many victims.

Yeah, he did, I thought, smiling proudly. *Wally broke your nose,* "So who's the bitch now, bitch?" I blurted aloud.

My geeky bus mate looked at me, terrified.

The entire bus erupted in cheers, while Old Man Gifford squinted hard in his rear-view mirror—trying to get a read on what had just transpired.

The fight, the beating—whatever, I thought, *is so much easier than the mental torment leading up to it.*

Looking at my brother, I felt inspired. *Zit or no zit, I'm giving Donna the letter tomorrow,* I thought, throwing Wally a thumbs-up.

He offered me a subtle nod in response.

But you're still a tool, bro, I thought.

• • •

Although Wally got kicked off the bus for a full week, Pop hardly minded. In fact, he was proud of him. And as he'd predicted, Owen left Wally alone from then on. "Lions do not concern themselves with sheep," Pop confirmed. "Fear or no fear, you have to stand up."

Pop became very busy working overtime after that—saving money for a top-loading VCR that played bulky Beta tapes—to keep our family up with the Joneses. "If you can't pay cash for it, then you haven't earned it yet," he claimed. "You mark my words, credit cards will be the death of this country."

Later in the year, Owen threatened me once but Wally was right there to defend me—snarling. *A brother's love is a brother's love,* I realized. *Wally might beat on me and Cockroach at times, but he'd never let someone else lay a finger on us.*

PRESENT DAY

To our collective surprise, all three of us emerged from childhood alive, not one of us worse for the wear. *It's true, childhood is filled with terrors,* I thought, *but I wouldn't have traded any of those difficult lessons for the world.*

As I think back, I realize that Ma was the best, while Pop tried his best—and we wouldn't have had it any other way. No matter what they did, or how strangely they did it, they continued to prove that love never requires perfection. Walter and Emma were not helicopter parents. In fact, they were the opposite, being much more hands-off. *Pop had some bizarre methods,* I thought, *but he definitely taught us the right lessons.*

The 80s really were a magical time. We were out all day until the streetlights came on, our parents allowing us to wade into deep waters to either sink or swim. And you know what, we swam—all of us—each learning how to navigate life's strong currents and avoid the scary, jagged rocks. For those hidden obstacles we crashed into, it only happened once. We were independent, travelling on foot or by bicycle—screaming for our friends to "come out and play." If the weather was nice, being stuck in the house was considered a punishment. We fell off our bicycles and dropped out of trees, learning to get right back on the proverbial horse. With a single ball—regardless of the type—we made friends, none of us ever poking out a single eye. We didn't lock our doors. We borrowed supplies from our neighbors. When anyone bought something new in the neighbor-hood, we all went outside to check it out. There were no childproof lids on medicine bottles, and helmets were unheard of unless your last name was Knievel.

Growing up in the 80s also helped to define who we'd become. Lessons were offered on a daily basis, most of them learned by trial and error. We practiced courage. We gained wisdom. We were not protected by bubble wrap, so when a challenge arose or a difficult situation presented itself, we did not shrink or wither; we stood up and faced it—win, lose or draw. There was only one trophy to be won and we had to fight for it—and it made us better because of it. We were the opposite of entitled and, although we may not have been the greatest generation, we definitely weren't the "me" generation either. Bullies had to be stood up to and mistakes had to be answered for. Grades and money were earned through hard work. We were taught to give our word and to keep it. to think of others and be considerate—even act selflessly. We may have worn funky clothes and wild haircuts; we may have listened to some goofy synthesized music, but we were taught right from wrong—and abided. It was a time when an adult's word was taken over that of a fibbing child's. It was also a time of real discipline and punishment; there were consequences for bad decisions and we understood this going into each and every choice we made.

We were neon, break-dancing gladiators, warriors that rumbled to the shriek of a rock and roll guitar solo. *We were so lucky,* I thought.

In 1984, the Boston Celtics beat the Los Angeles Lakers in the seventh game of the NBA Finals. It was a real nail biter. Wally was a man of his word—*kind of.* He did my laundry for two weeks before tapping out, threatening to "hurt me bad" if I didn't excuse the remainder of the debt. I did.

Our family eventually moved out of our apartment at 602 State Road. It was the hardest thing I'd ever done. This didn't happen, however, before Ma announced, "Walter, I'm pregnant."

"Are you shittin' me?" Pop said, his eyes wide.

"I shit you not," she said, "and I'm praying for a girl this time."

Who can blame her? I thought.

Pop nodded. "A boy will wreck your house, for sure," he muttered under his breath, "but a girl will wreck your head."

Thrilled over the news, my brothers and I celebrated with an unnecessarily aggressive wrestling match.

Good, bad or indifferent, Uncle Skinny kept right on being Uncle Skinny, while our remaining three grandparents passed away, one right after the next. Aunt Phyllis was the next to depart the earth and her funeral was the first I ever attended. There wasn't a moist eye in the parlor, teaching me a very important lesson in life. "People remember you by how you've treated them," Pop explained out of Ma's earshot, "nothing more."

Wally went on to become a race car driver. Cockroach became a successful businessman. And I became the storyteller of the family, with plenty to tell.

• • •

Back in my sons' bedroom, I felt nothing but gratitude for all I'd experienced—the incredible joys, as well as the paralyzing fears. Although I needed to share it with both of my boys, for now, my youngest son was my only audience.

"Alex, it's important for you to understand that, throughout your life, you're going to have to face one kind of fear or another," I explained. "You just need to accept that." I smiled. "Once you've accepted that, it's just a matter of managing those fears."

"But fear or no fear, I need to stand up, right Dad?" he said, giving me his undivided attention.

I nodded. "Remember, son, fear is a monster. The more you feed that beast, the bigger it'll grow."

"I know."

Yeah, I know you do, I thought, *but you're not alone.*

I leaned in until he and I were face to face. "You come from me and from Grandpa and from Uncle Wally and Uncle Alphonse—a long line of men who've had to stand up and face their worst fears," I told him. "You're never alone, remember that."

"I know," he repeated, nodding.

"I don't want you looking for a fight—ever—but I don't want you backing down from one either."

He sucked in a deep breath, holding it for a moment.

"You are not small, Alex," I whispered, believing that it was exactly what he needed to hear. "You're a giant. Always remember that."

He grinned.

"The next time Matt comes after you, just push back, whatever that may mean."

"I will, Dad," he said.

"You make sure of it, Alex."

"I will."

"Good boy," I said, stepping out of his room.

Filled with gratitude for the many blessings of family, I grabbed my cell phone and dialed my father.

"Yellow?" the old man answered.

"Hi Pop, it's Herbie. Sorry I haven't called."

"But you just did."

"Yeah, I know. I meant that I haven't been in touch for a while."

"No worries, kid. You're raising a family. I get it. I've been there."

I'm fifty years old and he still calls me kid, I thought. "Hey, how about we get together for lunch on Tuesday? Maybe we can hang out for the afternoon?"

"Sure, that'd be super great," he said. "Let's get a game plan together."

We talked for a while, getting caught up on our lives—mine, too busy, his, simple and predictable.

"I hit a hundred bucks on a scratch ticket last week," he happily reported.

"That's great, Pop!"

"Yeah, they'll get it back from me soon enough though."

I laughed. "Is Ma around? I'd like to say hi."

"No such luck, kid," he said. "She's out shopping for baby clothes with your sisters." He chuckled. "She's really good for the economy, your mother."

I laughed, remembering well.

"How's Donna?" he asked.

"Doing good," I told him. "She's the one keeping it all together at our house."

"I get it," he said. "Your wife's the glue, just like your mother's always been." He paused for a moment. "I might have put food on the table, but your poor mother was the one who had to buy it, prepare it and serve it."

"I know," I whispered, feeling even more grateful.

He chuckled again. "Ain't no doubt in my mind that she got the shit end of the stick."

I laughed.

"How are the boys doing?" he asked.

"They're on winter break from school and all they do is fight."

He started laughing. "Of course they do. That's their job. Remember when your mother used to call you and your brothers animals?"

"I remember, Pop."

"Go easy on them," he said, "those boys are angels."

"Yeah, when they're sleeping."

"Maybe you should just sneak them a sweet?" he suggested.

This time, I laughed. "The last thing those animals need is more sugar."

We laughed together.

"Well, I should get going," I told him. "I need to call Alex's principal and have a little talk."

"Is everything okay?"

"Nothing that can't be fixed," I said, leaving it at that. "I just need Alex to know that I have his back."

"In the end, maybe that's all any of us needs to know," he said.

I suddenly thought about all my father had done for me—all that he was to me. "Thanks for everything, Pop," I said, pleased that my voice didn't crack from emotion.

There was a pause. "You don't have to thank me, Herbie. I'm always here."

"I know that," I said, and always did. "It was good talking to you."

"You too, kid. Have a nice weekend."

THE END

POP

by Steven Manchester

When I was young, I never dreamed
how hard it must have been
to teach me what you had to
and still remain my friend.
I learned by your examples
of kindness and respect;
beliefs we must stand up for
and family to protect.
Providing all I needed,
you taught me "be a man"
and though it's taken many years
I finally understand:
That true strength lives within the heart
and love is often shown
by men who seldom say the word,
but make sure that it's known.

Steven Manchester is the author of the #1 bestsellers *Twelve Months, The Rockin' Chair, Pressed Pennies* and *Gooseberry Island*; the national bestsellers, *Ashes, The Changing Season* and *Three Shoeboxes*; and the multi-award winning novels, *Goodnight Brian* and *The Thursday Night Club*. His work has appeared on NBC's Today Show, CBS's The Early Show, CNN's American Morning and BET's Nightly News. Three of Steven's short stories were selected "101 Best" for Chicken Soup for the Soul series. He is a multi-produced playwright, as well as the winner of the 2017 Los Angeles Book Festival and the 2018 New York Book Festival. When not spending time with his beautiful wife, Paula, or their four children, this Massachusetts author is promoting his works or writing. www.StevenManchester.com

facebook.com/AuthorStevenManchester

twitter.com/authorSteveM

Be sure to visit Steven's site at www.StevenManchester.com and sign up for his mailing list.

Made in the USA
Lexington, KY
28 October 2019